TOWARD
A HUMAN WORLD ORDER

TOWARD
A HUMAN WORLD ORDER

Beyond the
National Security
Straitjacket

By

Gerald and Patricia Mische

PAULIST PRESS
New York, N.Y./Ramsey, N.J.

Library of Congress
Catalog Card Number: 76-41440

ISBN: 0-8091-1977-3 (Paper)
ISBN: 0-8091-0216-1 (Cloth)

Published by Paulist Press
Editorial Office: 1865 Broadway, N.Y., N.Y. 10023
Business Office: 545 Island Road, Ramsey, N.J. 07446

Editor: Richard J. Payne
Cover Art: Sr. Miriam Thérèse   Printed and bound in the
Cover Design: Nigel Rollings   United States of America

ACKNOWLEDGMENTS

We are pleased to acknowledge the following authors and publishers
for permission to quote excerpts from their works.

Ruth Leger Sivard, *World Military and Social Expenditures (1976 and 1977
editions),* WMSE Publications, Box 1003, Leesburg, Va., 20075.

George Orwell, *Nineteen Eighty Four,* Harcourt Brace Jovanovich,
Inc. Copyright, 1949 by Harcourt Brace & Jovanovich, Inc. Reprinted by permission of Brandt & Brandt.

Elisabeth Mann Borgese, "World Communities," from the Sep-
tember/October issue of *The Center Magazine.* Reprinted from *The
Center Magazine,* a publication of the Study of Democratic Institutions, Santa Barbara, California.

Material from *Technology and Human Values* (a 1966 Occasional
Paper), reprinted with permission from *The Center Magazine,* a pub-
lication of the Center for the Study of Democratic Institutions, Santa
Barbara, California.

Contents

4. The Powerlessness of Heads of State 69

Because they are bound by priorities that are determined by the imperative of national security competition over balance of weapons, balance of payments and scarce resources, heads of state are rendered practically powerless to reorder priorities or to use humanistic, person-centered values as criteria for public policy.

5. The National Security Big Six 101

Six departments of the United States presidency are examined as instruments of national security policy. These are the Departments of Defense, State, Justice, Treasury, Commerce and Agriculture.

6. The Soviet Security State 146

A substantial justification of Soviet totalitarian rule is national security. The humanist/personalist world view of Marx was subordinated to the national security imperatives which logically dominated the Soviet State from its inception in 1917.

7. Liberation for Being 170

Third and Fourth World nations have also become National Security States and in the present world system, liberation scenarios are doomed to fail. Liberation theology and the Third World liberation movement must identify the need for liberation from the national security straitjacket.

8. Human/Religious Values Are "Subversive" 200

Two questions are examined: why human/religious values are excluded from the criteria used for determining public policy; and why movements to change values and priorities have, up to now, been largely ineffective.

9. On Conceiving a New World Order

Various conceptions and models for a more just and human world order are examined. Special focus is on the role of functional agencies in a world security system.

10. Strategies for a Just World Order
Part I: Multi-Issue Coalitions

A multi-issue coalition strategy for developing a grass-roots world order movement gets central attention.

11. Strategies for a Just World Order
Part II: Network Programming

The focus is on strategies which utilize existing issue, educational, professional and religion-related networks as actors for world order.

12. World Order and Authentic Religion

Explores the need for a *holistic* approach to the development of a new world order in which *inner growth* is correlative to *external* change in the world system. The potential relationship and substantive contribution of people of faith is considered in this holistic context.

13. The Birth of a New Era

Examines the final quarter of the 20th Century as a pregnant period of history in which humankind is straining to give birth to new stages of human development. The positive impact which a world order perspective has on immediate problem solving is outlined.

Notes

TO ANN, MONICA, NICOLE
AND
TO ALL THE EARTH'S CHILDREN

THAT ALL THE COATS
THE WORLD PROVIDES FOR THEM
MAY PROVIDE PLENTY OF GROWING SPACE.

ACKNOWLEDGMENTS

Like most people who work on a book, we had a lot of help from our friends. While they should share none of the blame for any mistakes or weaknesses in the book, they have contributed in various ways to make it possible. To our parents Ted and Rose Schmitt and Louis and Celia Mische; to Lorna and Morris Milgram; to Trina Paulus; to the Browns, Rita Fairbanks, Gina, Steve and the Flanagans; to Joe Moore, Bob Manley, Ernie Kerstein, Bob Antczak, Jack Radano, Charlie and June Guettel; to Sister Miriam Therese, Sister Agnes Bernard, the Dominican Sisters of Caldwell, Fred and Hedy Ferber, the Kleisslers, and Hugh Lally; to the Hope Community at Convent Station; to Harry Hollins, Urban Intondi, Carol Brady; to John Cardinal Wright, Jim Berna, Janis Jordan, Bill McIntire, Joe Fahey, John Mitchell, Helen Horowitz, Helen Arnold, Saul Mendlovitz, Ian Baldwin, Tom Adams, Don Clark, the Weirs, the Naughtons, Hohensteins, and to all our friends at the Inn of the Spirit; to Dick Payne and the staff at Paulist; to the staff at the Institute for World Order; to the staff of the East Orange Library; to Liz, Margot, the Grudzens, Florence, Julie; to all Global Education Associates and to many friends and advisors in Africa, India, Europe, Latin America and our North American homeland, we say a deepfelt thanks. Work on this book would not have been possible without their encouragement, support and creative suggestions.

The Coat That Got Too Small
An Introductory Parable

From *Encounters on a Strange Planet*—a book still to be written—we share with you the following:

. . . They stood there, in all sizes and shapes, not seeming to take much notice of each other's misery. There appeared to be about 150 of them but I found it hard to count, even though they barely moved. Their contorted facial expressions and the gasping and groaning sounds they made were very disconcerting to me.

More than anything else, though, the coats were what first caught and held my attention. They were much too small. Buttons and zippers were being strained to the limit and seams threatened to tear at the sides. Their bodies bulged against the overstretched fabric as if the contents had been stuffed in with tremendous effort.

When I approached one particularly pitiful-looking creature and extended my hand (as is our custom when greeting a friend or introducing ourselves to a new acquaintance), she could not lift her arm even as much as two inches. Her jacket was so constraining as to render her practically immobile. Her face was quite puffed and rather bluish and she was struggling for breath. She eventually whined an apology. "You see, I can't move my arms," she got out between gasps. I thought tears began to appear in her eyes.

"It's your coat," I said.

1

"What about my coat," she gasped again, sounding more defensive and anxious than I thought was necessary since it was only an observation and one meant to help.

"It's too tight," I said. "Maybe you should get a new one that fits you better. It looks like this one has served you in the past, but now it is more like a strait-jacket than a coat."

"What's a straitjacket?" she gasped again, her bulging eyes looking a little puzzled and still defensive.

"It is a special kind of coat used to constrain people who are losing control," I explained patiently. "It has very long sleeves and when it is put on a person, their arms are crossed against their chest and the long sleeves are tightly tied behind their backs. Then they are rendered powerless to use their hands and arms."

"That sounds terrible!" she exclaimed, and then a few tears of pain rolled down her cheeks. She had taken too deep a breath in her indignation.

"Could you tell me why everyone I see is, like you, wearing coats that are too small?" I asked, trying to keep my tone as delicate as possible, although that was rather difficult since I found the situation so amazing.

After considerable time (in which she was, no doubt, trying to get enough breath as well as gathering her thoughts) she started, between gasps, to tell me their story. They had had these coats since they were young, she said. It seemed to be the fashion. No one ever questioned it before.

"But surely, you have grown very much since then," I said incredulously, trying to constrain myself. "Have you ever looked in a mirror?"

"But what else is there?" She strained, but went on whenever she could get enough breath to say that she liked this coat. It had, after all, been hers for a very long time. "I'm used to it now. It makes me feel . . ." She searched for a long time, looking for breath and for the right word. ". . . *Secure*," she puffed out at last.

As I left that place I thought I heard a great tearing sound, but I couldn't be sure, because of the loud groaning. I wondered what would become of these strange creatures who could not dance or laugh with each other.

———

This book is about a coat that got too small.

1
A Crisis of Growth

What appears to be a breaking down of civilization may well be simply the breaking up of old forms by life itself.

Joyce Carol Oates

There can be no more meaningful journey—nor a more pragmatically necessary one—in the world today than the journey toward a more just and human world order. That journey is at once both the greatest challenge and the greatest opportunity of our times.

It is crucial that we recognize that the times are not bad. Dangerous? Yes. Threatened with the possibilities of national and global breakdown? Yes. But they are also exceedingly full of promise. The multiple crises the human community is experiencing today, which leave so many people feeling frustrated and powerless, need not be diagnosed as a cause for despair. Rather they can be analyzed as symptoms of a crisis of *growth*.

This crisis of growth is one in which the development of human institutions has not kept pace with the rapid evolution of global interdependencies. Today's growing sense of powerlessness—experienced on deeply personal as well as global levels—is related to that structural lag.

A period of crisis can be a period of imminent breakdown. But it can also be a period of imminent breakthrough. Rather than reading the signs of our times as signs of human history winding down, we can read these times as a pregnant period in which the human spirit is challenged to new heights of creative effort. Beneath all the surface evidence of upheaval and confusion, there is evidence that these times could be the advent of a positive thrust forward in human history.

The positive pregnancy of our times is evidenced in the growing consciousness of our interdependence. It is evidenced in the awareness of the fact that we have critical problems and that these problems are commonly shared. For "naming the problem" is the first step toward effective liberation. It is evidenced in growing numbers of people exploring alternatives, including world order alternatives. And it is evidenced in the increased awareness of the need for global approaches to problem solving. Where once calling for global approaches was considered a visionary ideal, now even conservative heads-of-state are calling for "global strategies."

But most of all, a positive thrust is evidenced in the rapidly growing new vision of earth and of human potential. This new vision of the earth in time and space and of the human capacities of the individual riders aboard has all the potential of a Copernican Revolution in changing the course of history. For we all live in a certain paradigm of reality. Effective change—an authentic revolution—begins in the imagination. When the limits of old, restrictive paradigms are broken by the advent of a new framework for perceiving our situation, we are liberated for new initiatives.

The new paradigm of our shared destiny and mutual dependency on one earthship and our growing awareness of the imperatives on us to find global solutions to global crises are leading us toward the formulation of a new social contract—this time a *global* social contract. The question is not so much whether there will be a new world order, but what form it will have. The nature of that contract, the underlying assumptions on which it will be based, and whether it will serve humanity for good or for ill, will depend on the quality and values of persons involved in the formulation processes. Hopefully it will be a contract capable of guaranteeing its human constituents the basic securities and empowerment so lacking today, one built on principles of social justice for the whole human community rather than the benefit of a few at the expense of the many.

This book relates to the *why*, *what* and *how* for embarking on the journey to a new world order. It suggests that this journey is not only a moral imperative; it is a question of *pragmatic self-interest*. There need be no contradiction between self-interest and the vision of a better human future. Indeed, neither can be achieved apart from the other.

The following chapters examine the integral relationship between problems at the local level and problems at the global level. Special focus is placed on the *linkages* between unmet local needs and the unregulated global forces that are devastating the domestic priorities of peoples of "developed" and "developing" nations alike. The analysis suggests that this growing sense of powerlessness has substantial roots in the lack of global structures to control these rampant global forces. Following this analysis, the final chapters will consider scenarios for an alternative system based on world order structures and then examine strategies for building upon present trends to make such institutions a reality.

POWERLESSNESS

The first step in the journey toward a more human world order is to understand the nature and the causes of the growing sense of powerlessness being experienced by people around the world. It is a powerlessness not only experienced by "the people." National leaders also stand increasingly powerless before the rampant forces within the present global arena.

Thus, although we write about a basis for hope, we begin by noting despair.

This despair builds on a sense that today the problems are too many, too big, too complex. It feeds on the feeling that the world has gotten out of hand and in the face of it all the human "I" has shriveled so small and insignificant that even to pose the question "What am I to do?" seems an absurdity.

It is not only the poor and hungry or the socially disenfranchised who suffer the symptoms of this spreading malaise. Like a deep but silent river, this sense of powerlessness flows unchecked through middle class suburbs and affluent estates as well as tense ghettos and urban slums.

Today the dread questions we try not to ask, but which persist in haunting us all, keep flowing: Where are we going? Do we want to go there? Will we survive? Do we want to? What is happening to our humanness? Does anyone care? Is there a Lord of history and love within and among us? Or is human nature somehow depraved?

In election years national incumbents around the world tell the people that everything is all right and will get even better. We hear the familiar words but in the marrow of our bones they don't seem to make any sense. We know differently. We have experienced too much, come too far, not to know anxiety.

AREAS OF POWERLESSNESS

The English word "power" derives from the late Latin "potere" and its root meaning is "to be able to." It is a verb that cannot stand alone. The types of phrases that would complete the sentence "As a citizen of _____ I have power to _____" are declining rapidly in people's estimation of their own individual capacities as citizens. The types of phrases that would complete the negative phrasing of that sentence, "As a citizen of _____ I am *not* able to _____," are increasing:

- —"Not able to ensure adequate food and housing."
- —"Not able to ensure quality education for my children."
- —"Not able to ensure clean air and water."
- —"Not able to ensure a healthy environment."
- —"Not able to ensure adequate medical care."
- —"Not able to walk the streets safely."
- —"Not able to get a good job."
- —"Not able to trust our elected officials."
- —"Not able to influence governmental policy."
- —"Not able to control technology and technological processes."

"Not able to _____ ."

"Not able to _____ ."

"Not able to _____ ."

"Not able to _____ ."

Powerlessness is felt to different degrees by different people in different areas of their lives as citizens. But it is safe to assume that almost all people today are experiencing some form of powerlessness:

Powerlessness. One has only to stand in a long unemployment line, week after week, to know what it means. Powerlessness is being trapped in dilapidated and crowded housing and having no other choice. Powerlessness is when you find yourself alone on a dimly lighted city street and the shadows lurch at you with the threat of violence.

Powerlessness. The elderly do not need a dictionary. It is when, with fading vision and arthritic limbs, you search the grocery shelves for more than an hour and when you finally go to the checkout counter with one can of the cheapest tuna fish and some beans and take out all the money you have left from your social security check, they tell you it is not enough and you wonder what you will eat today and start once more your search up and down the long rows of abundant, withheld promise.

Powerlessness. Wage earners do not need a dictionary either. It is when your wages stand still but the prices of everything—food, rent, mortgages, heat, car repairs, gasoline, clothing, taxes, education, medical and dental care, gas and electric, telephone, subway and bus fares —including the price of a newspaper to check the want ads for a better-paying job, all go up and you wonder if leaving out beer and cigarettes will really make enough difference.

Powerlessness. The black majority in South Africa, the

victims of totalitarianism and military domination, and political prisoners everywhere know the powerlessness of having no recourse beyond the government that holds them captive, that is also their judge, jury and jailer.

Powerlessness. When you cannot be sure the plane you are traveling on will not be hijacked, or the airport bombed by terrorists, or the museum you've stopped in won't be blown up

Powerlessness. Scientists and environmentalists know. You can spend years in careful research, whether about the importance of phytoplankton in the sea to earth's oxygen supply or the devastating effects of nuclear testing and supersonic travel on the protective ozone layer, or the dangers of increasing acidity in rain from industrial pollution, or the environmental threat represented in nuclear power plants and strip-mining. You can put more years into raising public consciousness and political lobbying. Then, just as you foresee some minor gains, all the hard-earned promises of legislative support can be overturned in a day by an oil embargo from abroad and an energy blitz at home or an international scramble for economic gains while dismissing environmental concerns as secondary.

Powerlessness. When you read about the growing exploitation in Brazil of the Amazon jungle which, known as the "Lungs of the World," produces 25% of the world's oxygen supply and you realize one national government alone controls it, without any accountability to the whole of humanity.

Powerlessness. Ask the hungry. The hungry everywhere

in the world know. Know even if they only stare in silent space. It bulges like their bloated bellies and despairing eyes and when they ask when there will be more food available they cannot understand the strange answer they hear, first from their own government and leaders: "It is not favorable to our balance of payments to grow more food for domestic consumption when we can grow cash crops to obtain foreign exchange from sales in the world market"; and then from the foreign governments: "It is not favorable to our balance of payments and balance of power needs to send food to your country. After all, how much can you pay? Will your government align with ours? Would you accept our military bases there?" And you learn that the wheat that is denied you is sold instead to the Soviet Union to be fed to cattle because they can afford it and because it is good for the U.S. balance of payments.

Powerlessness. When your government spends more than 50% of the national budget on defense-related expenditures and yet can not guarantee, despite all the detente handshakes, that there will be life on earth tomorrow. It is when 30 years after Hiroshima, all the demonstrations against nuclear weapons, all the documentation, all the hideous photographs of dismembered bodies and radioactive tragedies, all the appeals to reason and to heart, all the SALT negotiations, have added up not to nuclear dismantling but to a proliferation that has more than *15 tons of TNT per person* in the world stockpiled against you and your children everywhere. Powerlessness is when that proliferation is compounded further by building thousands of nuclear power plants everywhere in the world while knowledge spreads on how to transform plutonium into nuclear weapons. It is when the world can find $350 billion for military expenditures but not enough to feed the starving or overcome illiteracy. Powerlessness is when your feeble protests are pooh-poohed with the ultimate logic: "No nation can afford to disarm unilaterally and so all must arm beyond all reason to preserve the delicate balance of power and terror," and you feel the only way to cope is to accept the death sentence as if it were no more than common table salt sitting before your dinner plate.

Powerlessness. Those prophets still left among us trying to shake us from our moral inertia know what powerlessness is. Their moral arguments fall impotent beneath the patronizing pat on the head which commends them for the purity of their vision while putting them down for their great naivete. "My dear moralist, we must be logical and pragmatic about these things. This call to base decisions on the common good of all humanity may be well and good in church or at a prayer meeting, but in the real world a government must shape its foreign policy in the 'national interest.' If a government is to survive economic and military competition, it must be guided not by moral principles but by what will give it better advantage. There now, how would you like to lead the next opening of Congress in prayer?"

Powerlessness. Strangely, our heads of state know what powerlessness is too, although they may be loathe to admit it, especially not in an election year. For their most carefully developed plans for stabilizing the economy and curbing inflation, and all their most up-to-the-minute detente deliberations, are frail before the slightest wind blowing from unilateral decisions of other governments and before unregulated global monetary and economic forces. They too walk the high wire without a balancing pole.

The growing breach of faith in national leadership today is much more complex than the perennial corruption to which government leaders everywhere seem susceptible and to which we are becoming accustomed. A more serious factor in this breach of faith is our growing awareness that national leaders everywhere, whatever their ideological or political platforms, are unable to do effectively what their citizenry expects from them, i.e., to provide true military, monetary, economic, and environmental security, and to secure their capacity to obtain adequate housing, food, health care, education and safety from crime and violence at a cost they can afford.

PROBLEMS ARE NOT THE PROBLEM

It is important to keep in mind that the growing sense of despair and powerlessness is not due to the fact that there are unresolved problems. Problems and crises are not new to humanity. Human evolution is the story of growth through the struggle to overcome challenges and difficulties. The human psyche is not quick to despair but has shown amazing capacity for problem solving.

But there are several aspects in the nature of the problems challenging humanity now that contribute to a sense of hopelessness. Aside from the sheer *number* of problems, and the communications system which heightens our awareness of them even when we don't directly experience them in our own communities, critical problems today appear so *complex*. Few are isolated issues, most are *interrelated*. Thus the question of employment is not resolvable apart from issues of global inflation, trade patterns, and balance-of-payment factors. The question of poverty is not resolvable apart from the question of employment which is related to global inflation, trade patterns and balance of payments. The question of hunger is related to the question of poverty which is related to the question of employment which. . . .

This "House that Jack Built" scenario makes it difficult to clearly focus on a pressing issue and approach its resolution without undertaking first a complete diagnosis—a diagnosis capable of suggesting a cure that is both realistic and holistic.

This interrelatedness of issues causes some to speak of a "crisis of crises." It is a concept which has people building personal barricades, worried about constructing a fallback shelter when "everything comes down."

A further complicating aspect of contemporary crisis is that they are *global*. The difficulties involved in relating to a neighborhood zoning problem are formidable enough, but how does one effectively relate to deterioration of earth's life support system? We know that zoning issues may be taken by citizen committees to our city council for a ruling and effective action, but where do we go for effective action on global inflation?

In a world system still psychologically attached to the principle of absolute national sovereignty, there are no structures with adequate authority to deal effectively with the global aspects of many issues at the heart of world concern.

On top of the complexity and global scope of

many contemporary crises, we are faced with a sense of *urgency*. The sheer rate at which problems such as population and hunger and depletion of resources can be compounded seems overwhelming. Gloomy forecasts based on computer calculations which predict collapse of the world system by the year 2,020 unless we change present trends and life styles[1] have left people anxiously asking: "Do we have time?"

INCOMPLETE ANALYSIS

But perhaps the greatest reason for a loss of hope today is an incomplete analysis. Strategies for resolving a particular problem or for achieving a particular goal are successful only if they flow from an analysis that identifies *all* the causes of the problem or *all* the obstacles to that goal.

While contributing valuable insights, most analysts of contemporary problems fall short because they fail to identify a new *structural lag*. It is a lag in which new global interdependencies have surpassed the capabilities of the existing world system, a system based on an obsolete principle of unlimited sovereignty that was formulated in a past history when nations still enjoyed a relative self-sufficiency.

The present state of powerlessness experienced by citizens and national governments alike is certainly not due *only* to the lack of institutions adequate to cope with the global crises that impinge on our lives. In no way is this analysis intended to be reductionistic. In no way do we believe that systems alone are either responsible for, or the cure of, all the world's maladies. Greed, materialism, rising expectations, corruption, ignorance and apathy are not likely to disappear because they move to a building of a different design. A common ethic, or a shared concern for justice, or a widely shared philosophical or spiritual base, however elemental that may be, are essential to a viable world community. But while at least a minimal vision and values choices precede the development of social structures, it is the structuring of life which gives it form and determines whether or not and in what manner a vision becomes reality or values become operative.

Structures can only provide a framework to facilitate the achievement of goals. They do not, in themselves, comprise the goals any more than a new building is created for its own sake. Yet social and political structures are essential to the achievement of human goals. Good will, or individual moral reformation on a global scale, or a new vision of our one humanity are not sufficient *in themselves* to provide us with world security and justice.

Einstein once said that humanity needs to invent new systems to resolve the problems created by old ones. Today the multiple problems created by an obsolete system of individual nation states, each trying to ensure its survival and well-being independently or in competition against the others, confront us on every side. These multiple problems should not be read as symptoms of a failure of human nature (a theme developed in the next chapter). Rather they can be seen as symptoms of inadequacy of the existent world system in the face of new interdependencies that have exploded all around us.

Nor should these multiple and global problems be perceived as a cause for despair or for more screaming at each other in a search for demons on which to fix the blame. Rather they should be seen as symptoms challenging us to new levels of human creativity; symptoms which now, for our mutual survival and well-being, make it imperative that we create a more just and human world order—and that we do it *together*.

It is imperative that we realize that despite our seeming powerlessness, we are *not* powerless. Together humankind possesses all the inner resources and capacities, the positive energy and the necessary knowledge and global infrastructure, to create not only a future that ensures human survival and minimal needs, but one that opens history for the first time on a mass basis to the realization of higher human potential.

2

Human Development and The "Security Straitjacket"

> It is now quite clear that the actualization of the highest human potentials is possible—on a mass basis—only under 'good conditions.' Or more directly, good human beings will generally need a good society in which to grow.
>
> By Good Society I mean ultimately one species, one world.
>
> A. H. Maslow

If there is anything in the midst of today's forebodings about the future that merits some excitement, it is the recognition that out of this period of a crisis of growth may emerge those structures which, for the first time in history, may make both basic and higher human development goals possible of realization for the great majority rather than a minority of the world's people.

The temptation is strong to blame our seeming powerlessness and the destructiveness of our times on human nature. To give in to such a temptation is to despair. It is to say, "we cannot do better because we are condemned from the start." And we thereby both absolve ourselves of responsibility and atrophy our impulse to act.

In this chapter we will consider areas of human potential and how realization of that potential is vitally related to the systems or structures within which persons grow. In particular, we will look at the way the existent system of individual, competing National Security States is an obstacle to fuller human development.

For awhile in the last two decades it seemed as if biological evidence was mounting to incriminate the human species. Negative conclusions about human nature were made on the basis of the works of people such as Robert Ardrey, Konrad Lorenz and Desmond Morris.[1] Homo sapiens was traced as descended from killer apes. Our peculiarly human characteristic of organized warfare against others of the same species was linked with the territorial instincts of our animal antecedents. The implication was that our destructive wasteful behavior, our violent aggression and capacity for wanton killing were attributable primarily to our genetic coding.

But what has so often been overlooked in the human nature-nurture debate is the even more interesting evidence (from earliest cave-time existence to human interaction in contemporary times) of the human capacity and corresponding need for love, affection, esteem, knowledge, peace, justice, unity and many other values related to the quest for meaning; and that these needs and capacities, evidenced in all human groups, are as much a part of our genetic coding as is a capacity for destructive aggression.

Countering the arguments on the side of biological determinism have been a long list of biologists, ethologists, anthropologists and thinkers from other disciplines, including René Dubos, Alexander Alland, Jr., Irenaeus Eibl-Eibesfeldt, Leon Eisenberg, Leonard Berkowitz, Morton Hunt, Kenneth Boulding, Ashley Montagu and Margaret Mead, to name a few.

Even a casual observer of human relationships will usually witness more positive than negative human interaction over a given period of time. A visitor present in Guatemala when that country was ravaged by earthquakes in early 1976 was impressed by the way in which people reached out to others even when they were in need themselves. "People who had lost members of their family, food and personal possessions still gave money to help others. The people of San Lucas who escaped the worst of the earthquake, traveled to nearby villages bringing food and water, thus depleting their own reserve."[2]

In *Love and Hate*,[3] a work that deserves to get far more attention than it has in this country, ethologist Iraneus Eibl-Eibesfeldt, a former student of Konrad Lorenz, documents his studies of animal and human behavior. His conclusions bring into balance the negative theories of some biologists and behavioralists. For although in all his studies of different human groups Eibesfeldt found evidence to support biological theories of the inherent human capacity for aggression and hostility, he also found equally evident an inherent capacity for love, affection and human bonding. He found this biological potential and its correlative *need* for love manifest in all the human groups he studied without exception. It was a potential and need given expression in their relationships and responses to each other, their gestures, their greetings, their language and in the social institutions they created.

The Tasaday, a recently discovered group of cave people in the Philippine Islands,[4] are a living contradiction to the "killer ape" theory of human nature. Living in almost total isolation in the deepest reaches of a huge tropical jungle, and utilizing crudely made tools of stone to survive off wild plants, the Tasaday have developed a society highly advanced in human relationships. All members of this small cave community have an equal share in decision making. Save for childbearing, there is no sex role stereotyping. All alike participate in the gathering of food and its preparation, in the care of children and in other group tasks. In a system of equitable distribution, all food is equally shared among the group, child and adult alike receiving equal portions. The Tasaday have no words for hate or anger or war. They appear to be a society without violence.

Within the frame of monogamous marriage, there is much love and affection shown all members of the group, with individual differences accepted and affirmed. And the few strangers who have appeared suddenly among the Tasaday from the outer world have been warmly welcomed with affection, hugging, stroking, smiling and joy.

It does not matter that the Tasaday or similar human groups are exceptions in contemporary times when violence is everywhere on the increase. Though exceptional, they are not aberrations of human nature, but rather real and symbolic witness of human potential.

Nor does it matter that the Tasaday live in isolation. Indeed, as we will see shortly, it is this isolation that helps make a point central to this book. Secure from military, economic and monetary threats from external forces, the Tasaday need not subordinate other areas of human need and potential to the priorities of mobilization for group security. It is a point to bear in mind as we explore in the next chapters the rationale for a world security system.

Throughout history there have been individuals and groups, and periods of relative human advance, that have appeared as beacons of human potential and possibility. The flowering of knowledge and artistic expression and spiritual insight in all of the great civilizations during periods of relative peace, and the phenomena of such great spiritual leaders as Buddha, Abraham, Jesus, Muhammed and Gandhi in times in which the social and historical milieu was ripe for their ideas and insight, is further evidence that we are not locked in as a species. Rather, the high degree of integral development and humanization achieved by our saints, prophets and great heroes (whose qualities we have too often ascribed to suprahuman capacities and, therefore, beyond our abilities to achieve) are, in reality, evidence of our great potential as a species. Indeed, was not the central mission of these religions to open their followers to a new vision of human possibility? Jesus told his followers—"Even greater things than this can you do if you but believe."

THE ROLE OF SOCIAL CONDITIONING

But the potential for greatness is no guarantee of its achievement. The effect, for good or ill, of social structures and social conditioning on human growth cannot be overemphasized. From their studies of human groups, ethologist Eibesfeldt[5] and anthropologist Alexander Alland[6] concluded that while the genetic inheritance of human beings does include a capacity for hate and destructive aggression, it also includes a commensurate capacity for love and human bonding.

What accounts for differences between some human groups and others is environmental conditioning and the social systems of which they are members. That is, either of these capacities—for love or for hate—can be reinforced in such a way that it begets a more dominant set of values and behavior patterns than the other.

Thus, in some societies, aggression, competition, warfare and mistrust have become dominant values, sometimes owing to the legitimate imperatives of survival and sometimes to the illegitimate manipulation of the human capacity for aggression by ruling elites who capitalize on this trait as an instrument of war and genocide to serve purposes of greed, power or vengeance. The Nazi extermination of the Jews is only one case in a long history of such manipulation of the human capacity for harmful aggression.

But in other societies the capacity and need for love have been given more positive reinforcement while nonharmful ways have been devised to channel inherent aggression tendencies. Alland and Eibesfeldt both conclude that it is imperative that humankind find ways to develop, and institutions to reinforce, this human genetic propensity to bond with others, and that we learn to extend our inherent capacity to love in widening circles of love and loyalty to humanity as a whole. This conclusion is based on the supposition that it is not possible to change our nature, but it is possible to change the nature of our conditioning.

But while it is paramount that as a species we find and nurture positive alternatives to violent and destructive forms of behavior that threaten our existence today, what needs more explication in the above admonition is the relationship of social structures to such a goal. What kind of social framework is required to make such a "whole earth" identity system, and the human bonding on a global scale feasible? The present system of competing nation-states mitigates against rather than on behalf of nurturing such potential.

A HUMAN DEVELOPMENT PARADIGM
In recent times there has been a gradual trend in

psychology toward a developmental framework within which to view human behavior. The studies of Jean Piaget, Lawrence Kohlberg, Erik Erikson and Abraham Maslow all led them to parallel conclusions about developmental stages through which all people move in a process of growth or maturation.

The works of these men have provided valuable insight and direction in the fields of education and psychology. The *developmental* perspective they evolved through years of scientific research and study of individual persons and human groups displaced more deterministic theories in their fields and has led to a deeper understanding and appreciation of the human person and the human growth process. It is a perspective that has important bearing on our perception of the nature and potential of the human community as a whole.

We personally find a developmental model more useful than others (such as power or territorial models) for assessing the human condition and possible human future. For one thing, it provides a more holistic perspective, allowing for a greater range of human behavior and motivation. Secondly, without ignoring negative realities in human behavior, it provides a positive or open view of human potential.

The developmental framework of Abraham Maslow is particularly helpful as a model or paradigm to help us understand where we may now be in our historical growth as a human community.

In a change from the pattern of psychiatrists such as Sigmund Freud, who developed their theories from a study of persons who were psychologically ill, Maslow felt that he would find more solutions to aid in preventing and curing human illness on an individual and mass scale by studying people who were well and the reasons that made them well.

Maslow's subsequent studies of highly developed, self-actualized persons throughout history and in contemporary times led him to conclude that there was a growth process through which all healthy persons passed in a series of stages corresponding to human needs and potential. In his schema certain needs are *basic*. These include physical needs (such as food, water, air, etc.), safety needs, belonging, love and esteem needs. Beyond these needs, but just as intrinsic and integrally related to human potential and health, are *meta* needs (*Being* or *meaning* needs). These include the human need and capacity for knowledge, understanding, beauty, truth, goodness, wholeness, justice, peace, universal love, harmony, order, etc. (See Figure A.)

These meta or meaning needs are synonymous with the deeper spiritual values and goals of the world religions (where these words are used to describe God or Pure Being) as well as with humanist aspirations. They are integral alike to the Western theology of a *God within* and to the Eastern philosophy of integral unity with the *Great Self.* For many, self-realization is not alien or apart from, but rather synonymous with, the realization of God as the Ground of All Being in whom the human person is called to share a higher form of participation in life.

In Maslow's theory, human needs are basically hierarchical in nature. That is, the basic needs must be reasonably met before meaning, or Being, needs and potential can be realized. In this regard, the process of human growth and maturation (or the process of realizing human needs and potential) can be called a process of *Becoming* (more fully human) or a process of *Self-actualization*.

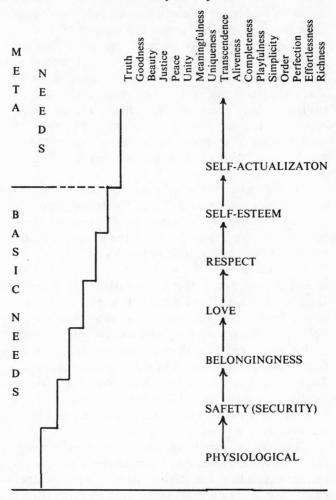

Figure A.
Abraham Maslow's Theory on the Hierarchy of Human Development

This process of Becoming more fully human, or more fully self, can be imaged as a process of growing more deeply *inward*, (i.e., more in touch with the self within) and, simultaneously, as an outward process of *transcending* self (i.e., becoming more universal in vision and identification). In other words, highly self-actualized persons are highly individualized in the development of their uniqueness as persons and by the very same process of deeper inwardness share deeper unity and harmony with all other persons and the whole of life.

The discovery and nurturing of a self-actualizing person's own inner core is the discovery and nurturing of what is central and common to all humanity. Such persons grow in consciousness of the integral connectedness of their own values, needs and activities to the life and well-being of the whole and they live their lives in deeper accord with that consciousness. Thus Jesus, Gandhi, Martin Luther King, Jr., (and many other unnamed persons past and present, in whom spiritual insight and action were integrated) strove for a peace, justice, unity and love that was *universal*, as well as deeply personal, in its philosophy and applications. Transcending culture, creed, race and other diverse loyalties, their words and lives provided symbolic and real efficacy for more than one group of people only, in one area and one time.

The natural human genetic propensity for bonding and unification, and inherent human needs and potentialities—including the higher meaning or spiritual needs—are a given organic center around which shared global consciousness and world unities can be consciously and creatively nurtured for purposes of human survival and human fulfillment.

But while there are positive trends and forces in

this direction, there are also major obstacles to fuller human development both as individual persons and as a species. Abraham Maslow writes about this human vulnerability:

> This inner nature is not strong and overpowering and unmistakable like the instincts of animals. It is weak and delicate and subtle and easily overcome by habit, cultural pressures and wrong attitudes toward it.

> Even though weak, it rarely disappears in the normal person—perhaps not even in the sick person. Even though denied, it persists underground forever pressing for actualization.[8]

In Maslow's frame, unmet needs, whether at a basic physical level, or at a deeper level of meaning and being, result in "illness." This "illness," which can be manifested physically, psychologically and/or spiritually, and which can result in negative forms of behavior, is more aptly described as a state of *deprivation* than an aberration or failure of the human person or of human nature.

Deprivation at the level of basic needs almost always *precludes actualization* of the higher (or deeper) levels of potential. Concomitantly, the reasonable satisfaction or fulfillment of basic needs provides a "cure" and permits a *resumption of growth.*

There are four considerations based on Maslow's theory of human development which are directly related to how we assess the human crises of the final quarter of the twentieth century and the viability of human future:

1. With two thirds of the world's people barely

able, if at all, to meet physical survival needs for food, shelter and health care, and with the priorities of almost all national societies given to security needs, the human community is still at a relatively early stage of human development.

2. It is possible to view the present sense of malaise and frustration in the human community as related to the *deprivation* of two basic needs on a mass scale. That is, the potential for fuller human development has been straitjacketed by the inability to realize basic *survival* and *security* needs (the first two stages of Maslow's human development model).

3. This does not mean that human nature is evil or that the future is closed. Quite the contrary. It indicates that a concerted *cooperative* effort to meet these basic needs in the world community can open human history to higher stages of actualization.

4. Because the successful negotiation of the stages of human development are greatly affected by social institutions, we need a healthy social framework within which to *become*—individually and as a species—all that we can be. But it is precisely the lack of such social structures on a global level that, in an interdependent world, straitjackets and presents the greatest obstacle to human development.

THE TRAGEDY OF THE IK

The integral relationship of social structures and organization to fuller humanization can be illustrated in the case of the Ik, formerly a small hunting and gathering society in northeastern Uganda.[9] Of late the Ik have been used as "proof" and star example that homo sapiens is fundamentally a hostile animal. But that is too facile a judgment on these very human people and on our species.

From the stories, songs and accounts of older Ik, it would appear that not too long ago Ik society was composed of happy, generous people whose environment traversing the valleys and slopes of a mountainous terrain provided sufficient food in the form of wild game and plant life and whose relationships were marked by mutual care and cooperation. Then the Kidepo Valley in which the Ik had found their best hunting was declared a national game park by the Uganda government and the Ik were forbidden to hunt or graze cattle in this protected territory. They were given the option of relocating to another area where the government would provide them with essentials for launching a new life as farmers. They did not take this option, choosing instead to scratch out their survival on the parched and nonproductive slopes of surrounding mountain sides.

The loss of their hunting grounds and a series of droughts led to remarkable changes in the behavior of the Ik—remarkable for both the rapidity of the change and the resulting negative quality of human interaction. The degree of social deterioration and dehumanization was so startling that anthropologist Colin Turnbull, who lived among the Ik for several years, was led to remark:

> The Ik teach us that our much vaunted human values are not inherent in humanity at all, but

are associated only with a particular form of
survival that we call society; and that all, even
society itself, can be dispensed with.[10]

For in the resulting competition for scarce food,
Turnbull observed a society in which all other values
were dispensed with. Family life, love, affection, truthfulness, compassion appeared dysfunctional to the imperative of individual survival. Food was gathered
alone, not in a group, for fear that someone stronger
would snatch the find. Pregnancy and babies were seen
as threats to a woman's capacity to compete, and children from the age of three were put out of the house
and left to fend for their own survival. Mothers often
left young children near cliffs or other dangerous
places. A child who got too near a fire would not be
protected and if burned would be laughed at.

Parental love appeared to be an impairment to survival, and those vestiges of it left from the former ways
of life sometimes proved to be fatal. Turnbull relates
the case of an older couple with an adolescent daughter.
The couple, retaining habits from their previous way of
life, had continued to care for their daughter, supplying
her with food. Then, realizing she was not prepared to
compete with other aggressive youth and to survive on
her own, and lacking the means to continue feeding her,
they shut her in a house and left her to starve inside.[11]

The ill and the aged were not cared for. There appeared to be no love between couples and couples could
not explain why they married since they seemed to find
no pleasure in any aspect of their marital life—neither
in sex nor companionship. There were left none of the
usual group activities that bind societies together and
almost no communication between persons.

The story of the Ik is pivotal. It is pivotal not, as many imply, because it is proof that the fundamental nature of homo sapiens is one of hostility and competing, compassionless ill will, or that all our most prized values are not part of our nature at all, and may even be dysfunctional to our survival. The story of the Ik does not prove any of these things. What it does prove is that the failure to probe humanizing alternatives and to make *conscious*, *positive* adaptations can result in human tragedy. The case of the Ik is pivotal because of what it tragically tells us about human potential unrealized and not because it is a test case of the outer limits of human nature. And, finally, the case of the Ik is pivotal because, in a way, it is a paradigm of existent world society.

Let's examine each of these points briefly:

Failure to Make Humanizing Adaptations

The Ik had choices. The fact that older members of the tribe could recall a happier, fuller human life before the government decree that changed their habits is indicative that as a society they need not have been conceptually locked in. That is, older members of the group could remember alternative forms of human relationship.

The Ik could have chosen to relocate. Although this would have been a very difficult adaptation, without much time to accomplish it, there are human groups who have successfully made even more difficult adaptations. They also could have rejected the restrictions on their hunting and staged some form of protest, as did the neighboring Turkana who ignored the government regulations and persisted in grazing their cattle in the park. Or, accepting the new restrictions, they could have reorganized among themselves in a way to more efficiently provide for their common needs and survival instead of mitigating against it by competing as isolated individuals. Perhaps there was a failure of imagination or analysis or strategies, or effective leadership, or all of these. We will perhaps never know why they chose as they did, or failed to make a choice, but it is clear that there were other options and that, for whatever reason, they did not act on them.

Instead of *choosing* to work out their survival *communally*, they allowed themselves to socially disintegrate to the extent that, as isolated individuals, each person was perceived as a threat to the survival and security of the others. The failure to initiate a cooperative approach led to critical threats to both individual and group security—to the point where the tribe is now threatened with extinction.

A Frustration of Human Potential

The social deterioration and the dehumanized state of relationships among the Ik does not mean that they, or humanity, are basically evil or hostile. The negative and socially destructive behavior the Ik demonstrated can more accurately be assessed as a *frustration* of their intrinsic nature rather than as descriptive of it. Their needs and potentialities as human beings were straitjacketed at the most fundamental level of human development—that of survival. And with this basic need unmet, all other needs and potentialities were also being frustrated.

In speaking about the causes of the demise of the Ik, Turnbull described their destructive individualism as a "machine they have constructed to enable them to survive. They have not created it willingly or consciously. It has created itself through their biological need for survival. It is that survival machine that is the monster."[12]

Their failure to develop an adequate social framework to ensure the survival and security of the group as a whole left individuals from the earliest age on to devote their whole time and preoccupation to survival needs, leaving almost totally unmet the other basic needs in the ladder of humanization. The Ik were a very loosely knit society with no strong organizational framework. The lack of effective social structures to secure their common survival needs was a major obstacle to their return to a state of human health and growth.

The Ik, a Paradigm of World Society

Our individual competing nation-states may well be like individual Ik who, instead of working together as a social entity to ensure their mutual survival and security, mitigate against it by a dysfunctional attachment to individual national interest and sovereignty. Despite some evidence of compassion in relationships between nation-states (such as in famine and flood relief or technical assistance), the force that determines almost all public and foreign policy questions between states is not one of interest in the greater good and survival of the species as a whole, nor the quality of our life together on the planet, nor the greater development of human potential, but, rather, what is in the "national interest" of each competing state. Alliances are made and broken on that basis. And the logic motivating this type of behavior among nation-states is that of survival.

If, in the present world system, a nation cannot compete for scarce resources or monetary balances or armaments in the balance of power that determines who will have an inside edge, then that nation may not survive. Similar to the Ik, other human needs and potentialities are being frustrated in this all-absorbing focus of nation-states on this fundamental need to survive. On a mass scale there is a failure of imagination to realize that survival depends now on mutual planning and global cooperation within a system of law capable of ensuring true security to all nations.

Like the Ik, we are experiencing growing alienation, frustration, and a sense of powerlessness along with the erosion of once-prized values. Today's widespread escalation of violence, mental illness, suicide and other manifestations of human deprivation are symptomatic of the failure of existing social institutions to provide a positive framework for Becoming more fully human.

Like the Ik, we face the option of a major humanizing adaptation or of further dehumanization and social deterioration. Fortunately we have a slightly longer time frame to make the adjustment and the change can be more gradual and more self-determined than the appearance one day of a government decree. Nevertheless, on a global scale, the demise is no less significant in terms of our future well-being than it was for a small band of our species called Ik.

Will we fail, like the Ik, to make positive social adaptations, or will we use the imaginative, rational and decision-making capacities that are our inherent tools of survival, to create humanizing social structures on a global scale, freeing us again to Become more fully who we can be?

A Partial Paradigm

It is important in presenting the Ik as a paradigm

of our present world system of competing nation-states to point out that the comparison is only partially accurate. One disparity in the comparison is that the Ik were not as interdependent for their survival and security as most nations in the modern world, a fact that leaves today's nation-states even more vulnerable than individual Ik. The gathering of more than enough food from slopes by one Ik could be a threat to the survival of others, but for the most part it was possible for a strong individual to survive, albeit at a low level of human development, in the competing-individuals framework of Ik society.

That is not true for today's nation-states. The interdependencies between nations leave them more vulnerable in multiple ways. A nuclear attack anywhere affects the whole species. Depletion of the ozone leaves us all vulnerable to skin cancer. The pollution of the oceans and resulting destruction of oxygen-producing phytoplankton means less oxygen for us all. The devaluation of the American dollar, while it can be undertaken unilaterally, affects global economic security. And an increase of cost in Arab oil increases inflation everywhere, affecting the capacity of people to provide for their basic needs. A unilateral decision by one nation to change the flow of a river within its borders would vitally affect the security of neighboring states also dependent on that river. The list is endless. In short, all nations are vulnerable to the decisions and activities of other states.

Another disparity in the comparison is that, despite the serious problem of finding sufficient food, the Ik had a greater measure of security than most nation-states since their relative isolation and governmental protection provided a certain measure of safety from external threats of other groups. If the Ik, by an act of their collective will, had either reorganized themselves to work out shared methods of providing for their mutual physical needs, and/or relocated to other areas more conducive to survival, history could have reopened for them and they might once again have applied their energies to other human needs such as belonging, love, esteem, etc.

Historically, those nations and civilizations that have been freed from external threats to their security and safety have had the relative freedom for fuller human development. But except in the few cases of still existent primitive groups such as the Tasaday (whose isolation is now protected by the Philippine government against advancing lumber companies), modern transport, communications and weaponry technologies have ended forever the once effective protection afforded by favorable geography against threats from "foreign" groups. Nor are the large armies and empires of the past any true assurance of group security. The proliferation of nuclear weapons and the growing production and trade of armaments allow no nation the luxury of feeling secure against external threats. Nor is the fear of outside threats limited to armed attack from another group. It is often much more difficult to provide security from *economic*, *monetary* and *resource* threats than from military threats.

Because of the end of any effective isolation, the nature of these threats to national security is now constant, precluding the possibility of great periods of relative security in which other human pursuits can flourish. Because these multiple threats are constant, and because there is no global security system adequate to deal with them, nations must now be constantly mobilized to ensure their own survival.

Priority, therefore, is not put on health care, education, environmental needs, the arts and the quality of human life. Justice, peace, truth, beauty and other values at the higher stages of human development are subordinated to values that reinforce this mobilization for survival and security in a nonsecure world. Unable to fulfill their security needs in the present world system, nations and their citizens are straitjacketed at the security stage of human development; thereby they are constrained from significant realization of the higher stages of human potential outlined by Maslow.

The Masculine and Feminine of National Security Values

A particular pitfall of the group security drive and one which has been particularly restrictive on human development is the strong emphasis it has led human groups to place on the values of "competition," "strength," "hardness," "cunning," "shrewdness," and other so-called "masculine" virtues. In most societies, women, who have not had a significant role in providing group security from outside threats, have not been ascribed with these qualities and have been relegated to "inferior" roles not considered as equally vital to the tribal or national life. In some cases where other factors were favorable, this has "freed" women to develop other aspects of their human potential, their capacity for love, affection, warmth, intuitive and esthetic sensitivities, etc., qualities subsequently ascribed as "feminine." The fact that these qualities are part of the genetic potential of all humans, and that a role reversal, such as among the Amazons, could totally reverse the traits ascribing "feminine" and "masculine," has been obscured until very recently.

Alienation

While there is a compelling "logic" for nation-states, in our present world system, to put national security as the top priority, the cost to the quality of human life experienced by its citizenry is great. The frustration of other human needs and the low priority given to other very important human values results in a sense of emptiness, incompletion and alienation.

This growing alienation as well as frustration and powerlessness is easily observed in modern societies. Drug addiction, alcoholism and materialism cannot just be attributed to a lack of discipline or the breakdown of law and order or to human greed or depravity. They are part of the human hunger for something "more" in life, something we unconsciously know is absent. Drug addiction and alcoholism have often been associated with misguided spiritual thirst, with a longing to be in touch with something more meaningful, and with a desire to escape from meaninglessness or to rebel against emptiness. So too, excessive materialism may also be a misguided search for "having more" in lieu of "being more."

There is a strong relationship between the social and human deterioration so widespread today and the deprivation of meaning and other human needs suffered in a system dominated by the security imperative. Unfortunately, in a world system in which there are no other adequate structures through which to provide for national security needs, then it is "logical" and imperative that individual nation-states look out for their own survival even at the cost of the greater common good and fuller human potential.

Today, if we are to humanize the fabric of world society and move away from alienation toward full human development, the organizing principle must be a recognition of *human interdependence*. Other approaches to security have been tried and led to dehumanization.

Coexistence has delivered an Ik-like existence. It may have served toward national survival to date, but it has not been a humanizing force. Nor can it guarantee survival in the long run.

National self-sufficiency is also failing to provide a humanizing direction in the human community. It is failing because it is based on a fiction. It is a modern impossibility. Chasing this impossible dream saps the human community of the energy and cooperative approaches essential for the fuller development of the human community.

Unlimited national sovereignty has also contributed to an Ik-like world—one incapable of ensuring either a humanizing environment or human survival. Excessive individualism in the formulation of national policies (disguised under the euphemism of "the national interest") mitigates against the best long-range interest of its own citizenry as well as the interest of the whole human community. The national interest is no longer separable from world interest.

CONCLUSION

The evidence upon which to build negative theories about human nature has certainly not been lacking in human history. But the final evidence is not yet in. Though the exceptions have often been short lived or found in great isolation, they have been and are still among us as very real signs of our potential and our call to greatness as a species.

One reason that human nature has so often been

sold short is that the social system and environment in which a vulnerable human nature could reveal its full potential have for the most part been lacking in human history. Also lacking has been a holistic analysis from which to assess adequately the history of human development, the obstacles restricting that development, and the directions and options open to us in the future.

The need in humans for security is inherent, but it need not be realized by utilizing our destructive capacities. It can as well and with more certitude be won by utilizing our inherent capacity for bonding to build institutions that ensure true security for the world community as a whole. There is now no choice but that our security be ensured in institutions that are *global* and that are built on a commonly shared sense of the interdependence of all who inhabit this one earth.

The relationship between a more human world order and personal human development is underscored in the following premise by Maslow:

> The equally Big Problem as urgent as the one I have already mentioned is to make the Good Society. There is a kind of feedback between the Good Society and the Good Person. They need each other, they are sine qua non to each other. I wave aside the problem of which comes first. It is quite clear that they develop simultaneously and in tandem. It would in any case be impossible to achieve either one without the other. By Good Society I mean ultimately *one species, one world.*[13] (Emphasis added.)

The following several chapters will explore the nature of the National Security State system and the straitjacket it imposes on positive human development in more detail. Subsequent chapters will consider alternative global structures. What is important here, and in the remaining chapters, is to keep in mind that human history is not closed but open, and that the task of our times is not to condemn ourselves in a one-eyed view of our nature. It is, rather, to examine the human conditioning and structures which preclude the full development of our positive potential as a species and to find adequate ways to respond to the challenges and opportunities before us.

3

The National Security State

> The new far-reaching world situation is so
> new and so dangerous that all histories up to
> this point must be considered at most prehis-
> tories of this new future . . . what is past is
> but a prologue to the future.
>
> Jurgen Moltmann

The half-decade immediately following World War
II was a watershed in human history. It engulfed
humankind in a state or powerlessness that is still only dimly
comprehended.

A song that U.S. citizens sang to the top of the
"Hit Parade" during World War II can help identify
the nature of this watershed. Entitled "When the Lights
Go On Again All Over the World," the song expressed
expectations of new human development and empowerment.

Those who lived during World War II vividly remember the blackouts that cloaked European cities
from the deadly eye of enemy bombardiers. We remember the stirring films of beleaguered Londoners,
living in fear of the death that rained from the skies.
And we remember the vigilant eyes of our fathers,
uncles or neighbors who, with their air raid warden
armbands, made sure that we were all obeying the rules
as U.S. cities staged periodic air raid drills.

But those of us who sang this song were not just thinking about the *electric* lights that were not shining. We were also singing about other lights that were out. We were singing about unmet social and economic needs that were being postponed until the war would be over—tabled in favor of a *temporary* mobilization of resources, personnel and institutions for the war.

The key phrase on our lips during World War II was "for the duration." New housing could not be built for the duration of the war. Similarly with improvements of health care, of education for the underprivileged, of care for the elderly and for other social justice priorities. The litany of unmet human and domestic priorities was a long one. BUT, when "the duration" would be over, then. . . .

The mobilization of the wartime years, however, did not only mean a postponement of human and domestic priorities and a tabling of positive human developments. The wartime mobilization also meant, morally and humanly speaking, steps backward for humankind as higher human and religious values were rejected on the national level as dysfunctional to "victory over the enemy."

During the wartime period from 1941 to 1945, the American people—and citizens of all Allied and Axis nations—tolerated, with much reluctance, the morally degrading and dehumanizing results of national security mobilization. (The emphasis is on "tolerated," in contrast to "embraced.") Because the results of the mobilization were temporary, i.e., only for the "duration," they were seen as bearable. Public opinion was manipulated; government policy was made in secret; dissent was crushed; nationalistic myopia was fostered; the right to privacy was violated; foreigners became suspect; "enemies" were hated; government lying was accepted as a necessary evil; national morality was synonymous with "my country, right or wrong"; technology became king; and military budgets were sacred.

The expectation was that, after "the duration," things would return to normalcy. *Normalcy* meant "the way things used to be," when we were not faced with external threats and could pursue our personal and national goals with relative freedom from fear of external interference. Personally and nationally, self-sufficiency and self-reliance could again be an American motto and objective. This expectation of a return to normalcy was based on the historical reality of a recurrent cycle of military mobilization and demobilization. Following a war, the security imperatives constricting national life could be loosened and a period of demobilization and relative security would permit a nation and its citizenry to absorb itself with other human objectives and needs.

But the destruction of Hiroshima and Nagasaki in an atomic cloud were to change forever the security imperatives of individual nation-states, breaking the cycle of mobilization and demobilization. No major nation now could afford to demobilize because, should other nations fall privy to new and terrible knowledge and skills, there would be little lead-time with which to regather forces against possible instant attack. A constant mobilization of national resources (human, monetary and weaponry) and of the national psyche was essential to national security. Military security became a motor that needed to be constantly turned on and operative. This motor was to energize an armaments spiral that would assert a tighter and tighter stranglehold on human evolution.

But military preparedness was not the only national security motor that was to dominate life in the second half of the twentieth century. The postwar world witnessed a gradual but steady escalation of economic and resource interdependencies and a corresponding competition that would eventually pose even graver threats to national security and render a return to national self-sufficiency an impossibility.

Thus there are now three national security motors: *balance-of-weapons competition, balance-of-payments competition* and *competition over scarce resources.* The ability of a nation to compete in all three of these areas is vital to the security and well being of its citizenry. Lacking global institutions capable of providing individual countries with security in these areas, nations of the world—rich and poor, capitalist and communist— must mobilize themselves according to the priorities of national security rather than the priorities of human development. The local citizenry everywhere is increasingly besought to relinquish personal freedom and personal sovereignty to its national government in return for group security.

Ironically, it is a security that—in today's interdependent world—no government in itself or through regional alliances is able to ensure. Also ironically, it is the relinquishment of our personal freedom and personal sovereignty that breeds much of the alienation, frustration and violence that are also feeding today's insecurity spiral.

The individual National Security State is the basic unit of the existent international order in which states compete against each other for dominance and security in an Ik-like, insecure world. In this order, human persons are not central. Rather they are utilized as tools and tally beads in international competition where aggregate figures count for more than personhood. Anonymously they are strung out on the thin thread between individual national survival and collective global survival.

The above considerations are the focus of this chapter, which attempts to describe the nature of the National Security State system. We have chosen to present this analysis in the skeletal framework that follows, leaving further analysis and elaborations to following chapters. Such a capsule-like framework, unburdened with more lengthy historical footnotes and examples (of which the reader may already be well aware), may best serve our purpose at this point. An advantage of this format is that it provides an opportunity to define terms and concepts as they will be used in the remainder of the book. A disadvantage of such a skeletal format is that the analysis may appear simplistic and reductionistic when it is actually complex and open, and thus its conclusions may be prematurely dismissed. We thus ask the reader to suspend judgment about the conclusions in this sketch until considering the content of following chapters.

Feast or Famine: Mobilization and Demobilization

Prior to the nuclear-missile age, nations experienced an ongoing series of armament and disarmament cycles. Wartime was a period of *mobilization*: citizens, institutions, resources, leadership and values were mobilized for national security goals. The result was "feast" for the national security sector of society. During this feast period, human and domestic priorities were logically subordinated to national security goals. Other human needs and humanistic/religious values were tabled "for the duration" in favor of national security values and priorities. Peacetime brought *demobilization*: the national security sector experienced relative "famine" as human and domestic priorities regained a priority position on the national agenda.

Zero Lead-Time

The above mobilization-demobilization cycle was possible in the past because nations used to have months of "lead-time" to mobilize citizens, institutions and resources for war. But the advent of nuclear missiles changed that. Nations today have only seconds in which to react—which translates into "zero lead-time." The only strategic mobilization that counts today, therefore, is that which exists *before* a nuclear button is pushed.

Constant Mobilization

In today's "zero lead-time" world, the national security mobilization of society can no longer be temporary, i.e., cyclical. In order to survive the monetary, resource and military competition of today's interdependent planet, national elites must marshall institutions, resources and public opinion in a *constant* mobilization for national security goals. Such survival demands that priority be given to whatever policies are deemed necessary to ensure the nation's ability to compete in the existent lawless global arena. Those human values and domestic priorities that conflict with national security goals become expendable. For if utilized as criteria for public policy, such values and priorities would subvert the ability of a nation to survive the competition of the present interdependent but fragmented world.

Triple National Security Motor

The constant mobilization of the national security state is energized by three motors:

1. balance-of-weapons competition
2. balance-of-payments competition
3. competition over scarce resources

Balance-of-Weapons Competition

Despite much talk about disarmament and arms control, in the present system of politically independent nation-states, only peripheral limitations will be placed on the arms race. At least four factors directly underlie the competition for weapon supremacy:

1. the uncertainty of governing elites who can never be sure what policies future leaders of other nations will embrace;

2. the collision course between the depletion of the world's resources on the one hand, and the escalation of technological/industrial economies on the other—an escalation substantially energized by nation-state competition and by the inability of sovereign states to seek *unilaterally* an equilibrium growth pattern based on the criteria of social justice and the quality of life;

3. future power scrambles as Third World governments and societies collapse from their inability to handle the pressures of population, unemployment, poverty and institutional breakdown without transnational institutions based on social justice for all humankind;

4. the escalatory nature of today's sophisticated weapons technology which makes existing weapons systems obsolete almost before they become operational.

Balance-of-Payments Competition

Without a supranational authority to assure multilateralism and justice in international economic and monetary relations, countries must at all costs avoid a chronic deficit in international monetary transactions. A sustained imbalance of trade in which imports exceed exports, for example, will deplete a country's monetary reserves of gold and foreign currency. The result of this depletion—as monetary reserves are used up to offset this trade deficit—is grave instability of the national currency, exposing a nation's domestic scene to inflation, unemployment and societal breakdown. A nation's security as well as its legitimate welfare is involved.

National institutions and resources, therefore, must be mobilized to produce those types of goods which are able to sell on the world market and thus bring foreign currency into national banks. Government fiscal and monetary policy—as well as government subsidies and investment in research and development—is increasingly determined by this criteria of global competitiveness. The result is a logical subordination of domestic priorities to international payments goals. Production and services that do not bring in foreign monetary reserves, e.g., housing, health, urban renewal and care for the elderly, are placed on the back burner of national agendas. This happens not only in the U.S., Soviet Russia and other major powers involved in world trade, but it also causes Third World countries to expend their scarce resources on production that will attract foreign reserves, rather than meeting dire local needs.

Balance-of-payment goals are thus no longer the peripheral concern that they were in the limited world trade era prior to World War II or even the years immediately following the 1944 monetary agreements of

Bretton Woods. In today's interlocking global economy, balance of payments has become as much a matter of national security as competition over weapons balances.

Competition Over Scarce Resources

A country is insecure to the degree that it is dependent upon outside sources for scarce primary resources. Lacking global institutions with effective authority to assure an equitable access to and distribution of scarce resources among all nations, national leaders have little alternative but to mobilize their finances, technologies and productive institutions for the goal of becoming as resource self-sufficient as possible. Other priorities—e.g., unmet needs of housing, education, pollution control and urban renewal—are subordinate. An example is the priority being given by all nations to as much "energy independence" as possible.

This priority of resource independence is organically linked to balance-of-payments competition. The quintupling of crude oil prices illustrates this linkage, causing most countries to give priority to energy-related industries rather than social justice needs of their citizens.

Even after stressing the need for the curtailment of the rapacious consumption of resources by the industrially "developed" nations and by economic elites within "developing" nations, the logic of mobilization for resource competition remains. Simplifying life-styles among more affluent sectors of the world could significantly decrease the pressure felt in those countries which import only a small percentage of certain resources; but most countries would remain in grave resource insecurity even after such conservation policies.

Lacking equitable access to and distribution of scarce resources among all nations, national leaders have little alternative to such mobilization or to unmet domestic needs that flow from it.

National Security State

Modern national society is a complex resulting from an informal, de facto alliance among government, industry, military, big labor, educational and communications institutions. National security imperatives—spelled out in terms of monetary and resource as well as military insecurity—provide the primary centralizing force of what is popularly known as the "Corporate State." The chief function of this corporate society, directly or indirectly, is now national security. This multiple national security function—expressed in a constant mobilization of leadership, institutions, resources and values—is beginning to dominate all nations: rich or poor, capitalist or communist.

"National Security State" is spelled in capital letters to designate the precise reality of a full-blown and constant mobilization. It is thus distinguished from previous, pre-World War II realities of temporary cyclical mobilization as described in terms spelled in lower case letters such as "the national security tribe," "the national security kingdom," "the national security city-state," and the "national security state."

National Security Straitjacket

The constant mobilization for national security required for national survival acts as a straitjacket on those domestic priorities which do not contribute directly to national security competition over armaments, monetary balances and scarce resources. It also makes subservient the individual needs of citizens, whose personal lives are highly determined and made anonymous by the *aggregate* figures and goals of such competition. Fuller human development and the realization of such higher human values as justice, peace, unity, truth, etc., are restricted and subverted by dominance of security priorities.

National Security Logic

Today's constant mobilization is not primarily the work of demon men. It is, rather, the logical outcome of the competition that, in an interdependent world, is inherent to a system of totally independent sovereign states. The security of every country depends upon a balance of weapons, a balance of international payments and adequate primary resources—goals which increasingly depend upon the mobilizing policies of governing elites. It is a logical responsibility of those in power to provide for the security of their countries when such security is not provided for by institutions beyond national borders.

Corporate Society

Corporate society is the complex resulting from the informal, de facto alliance among governmental, industrial, military, big labor, educational and communications institutions. These institutions no longer operate independently, with only erratic interaction. National security imperatives of today's interdependent but fragmented planet are forging a formerly loose conjunction of these institutions into an interrelated corporate body. A primary centralizing force of this corporate complex is the nation-state's drive for international monetary, resource and military security.

Thus the corporate society becomes the Corporate State.

Rule by Elite

Decision-making power logically (i.e., necessarily) flows to the elite who control the central institutions of this National Security Corporate State. These elites are twofold: political leaders (and their advisors and ministers as spelled out in Chapter Five) and the officers and advisors of the large economic corporations who provide the aggregate power needed to survive the military, monetary and resource competition of the unregulated global arena.

A major reason for this flow of power away from local grass-roots people is the escalating complexity of decision making inherent in armaments, monetary and scarce resource competition. One dimension of this complexity is the escalating nature of the vertical technology needed for such national security competition, making it necessary to give technologists a virtual blank check in order to keep abreast of technological advances in competing countries. A second dimension is the further complexity of having to deal with political-economic-monetary relations with some 150 separate sovereignties, each with its unpredictable policies and with multiple relations with the other countries—all of which would become more manageable and stable if dealt with within a frame of global institutions based on justice and endowed with effective authority. A third source of complexity is the interplay of escalating crises on the home scene—crises that result from unmet domestic needs which are subordinated to national security priorities.

Added to these complexities is the need for secrecy

(and the manipulation of this need) in dealing with some aspects of national security policy. Taking all of this into consideration, it is not difficult to understand why the basic decisions that most centrally affect the citizens of National Security States are increasingly determined by the judgments of a new technocratic elite and the political leaders whom they directly or indirectly serve.

National Security Values

The values which the nation-state professes to protect—the security and welfare of its citizens—are certainly humanizing values; i.e., their securement would permit people to more fully realize their human potential. In practice, however, the imperatives of nation-state competition undercut not only these values of human security and welfare. They also undercut the human-centered values of truth, universal justice and love, freedom of individual conscience and human solidarity which, if allowed to become more than tokenly operative, would subvert the national security mobilization demanded by today's system of totally independent sovereignties. Instead, unrelated economic and armaments competition engenders and reinforces such dehumanizing forces as aggregate power, secrecy, ethnocentrism, competitiveness, impersonalism and other machismo "virtues." In the real world of today's competitive nation-state system, these end up being "national security values."

Legal Justice/Social Justice

As used in this book, legal justice is conformity to laws passed by a legislative body. Such justice may have no relationship to *social* justice which is confor-

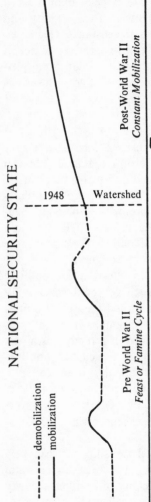

NATIONAL SECURITY STATE

- - - - demobilization
——— mobilization

1948 Watershed

Pre World War II
Feast or Famine Cycle

Post-World War II
Constant Mobilization

Balance of Weapons (1948)
Balance of Payments (1965)
Scarce Resources (1973)

TRIPLE NATIONAL SECURITY MOTOR:
(Driven by need to survive in an
interdependent but lawless
global area)

Competition Over

NATIONAL SECURITY PRIORITIES: Humanistic-Religious Values are Subversive.
Domestic Priorities are Logically Subordinated.

NEEDED: A GLOBAL SECURITY SYSTEM

WORLD ORDER INSTITUTIONS are essential to:

1. Turn off the National Security Motor by ensuring the military, monetary & resource security
   of all national groups;

2. Put human needs at top of national agendas.

mity to *natural* laws that do not depend upon human legislation, i.e., inalienable rights to food, dignity and self-determination. In fact, in many instances, legal justice is in direct conflict with the imperatives of social justice. A major task of our times is to develop a process and system in which the criterion of legal justice is social justice.

Sovereignty

A synonym for self-determination, sovereignty means basic autonomy in decision making. One can distinguish between personal and national sovereignty.

Personal Sovereignty: A core heritage of Judaic-Christian philosophy is the supremacy of personal conscience. Building on this heritage, and on Roman and British Law, Western political philosophers made the state the guarantor of personal sovereignty.

National Sovereignty: The question for political philosophy was, "How can such personal sovereignty be assured?" In a period that lacked the global unities needed to guarantee *universal* personal sovereignty, ultimate political power was placed in a regionalism (determined by local unities of language, custom and history) that in Latin had traditionally been called a "natio." Hence the double concept of *nation-state.* Since the Treaty of Westphalia (1648), national sovereignty has been the universally accepted basis for European, and finally global, politics.

This is the theoretical relationship between personal and national sovereignty and between personal and national autonomy. The reality of national security politics, however, precludes the realization of personal sovereignty. Although a long evolutionary process after Westphalia had brought forth significant gains toward genuine participation of citizens in decision making, the emergence of the National Security State after World War II has aborted this process toward egalitarianism. The logical need for and the complexity of providing for national security priorities has led to an increasing transference of power to national security corporate elites—making a myth of the *personal* sovereignty that the nation-state was originally designed to protect.[1]

The imperatives of nation-state competition in an interdependent world have also made a myth of *national* sovereignty. This is especially true for "developing nations" whose dependence upon the industrial West and whose powerlessness to influence international monetary and economic structures de facto truncates the sovereign self-determination that they embrace so passionately in theory.

This powerlessness, however, is not limited to "developing" nations. The more affluent nations also find their self-determination truncated. Constant mobilization for national security drastically limits their ability to adequately respond to the multiple crises which are threatening domestic stability. Multiple interdependencies in today's planetary world make it impossible for any nation to reorder domestic priorities unilaterally.

Alienation

Alienation is a state of deprivation where human needs and potentialities at basic and higher levels of meaning are frustrated and unrealized. Persons become alienated from their own true being (who they could *Become*) when they lose power over the central choices affecting their lives and the processes of *Becoming* —i.e., when these choices are determined by external forces rather than internal conscious direction.

As personal sovereignty is lost, a person becomes alien to his or her true self, thereby losing personal identity. Thus, persons who surrender choices to mass commonality and conformity may become alienated from self, losing their personhood, even though they are not isolated from society. By the same token, other persons may be isolated from society just because they were able to preserve their personal sovereignty and identity and were self-actualizing.

We recognize that some find a certain identity in their national citizenship. An identification with one's nation is an effort to feel a sense of community with others, a way of identifying with the human community. But as citizens lose power over the central decisions that determine their lives, this national identity is becoming increasingly shallow. Having become impersonal objects rather than subjects in a society mobilized for corporate security goals, the benefit of having a national identity is greatly undercut by the loss of personal sovereignty.

Except for limited consumer choices (and even these choices are affected by powerful external forces), decision-making power is moving increasingly into the hands of a national security elite. As a result, the personal alienation of citizens in National Security States is escalating rapidly. The rising incidence of violence, crime, drug addiction, alcoholism, family breakdown, mental illness, suicides and other symptoms of dehumanization and alienation are critical signs of the growing severity of this problem. Aggregate goals of nation-state competition have subordinated human persons to serve as anonymous pawns of national and international policy making. Alienation, defined as the powerlessness of individual human persons to participate in the shaping of their own destinies, is the dominant characteristic of today's national security societies. It is sapping persons of their will to life, their faith and hope in themselves, in humanity and in a Ground of All Being, while simultaneously breeding despair, hostility and a collective death wish.

Interdependent World

We are witnessing the final death throes of the principle of national self-sufficiency. The embryonic interdependencies that began to emerge 150 years ago with the Industrial Revolution are now in powerful bloom. Yet, at a time when national societies are mutually dependent on each other for goods and resources, political institutions continue to operate as if national self-sufficiency were still possible. The result is a multiplication of global and domestic crises as new wine remains in old skins.

The new global interdependencies are the logical result of the evolution of industrial economics. When needed resources and specialized trade are not available within national boundaries it is natural to reach out for them beyond national geographic limits. The alternative to such outreach is a return to a rural, agricultural economy which is, for the industrial world, an impossibility. There is no going back to the land on any massive scale. Although we can depend on science to create synthetic materials to replace some natural materials which now must be sought elsewhere, such breakthroughs can be only a partial solution. And even to achieve these limited alternatives, massive amounts of money would be required, e.g., to develop hydrogen to replace oil as a source of energy.

This need for resources and goods from other parts

of the world is the same for all the more industrialized nations regardless of differences in economic systems. The Soviet Union is as much caught in this historical reality as the United States. The escalating need for oil and the resultant scramble to secure sources in Third World areas is but one example of this interdependency and the tensions that result from it.

The peoples of "developing" nations and of the more affluent nations alike are hurt by the lack of adequate transnational institutions to cope with problems of interdependence. Preoccupation with a desire to establish their own autonomy has caused some people to dismiss too quickly the importance of building the transnational structures which would be empowered to establish and enforce laws and regulations according to criteria of common good and social justice for the total human family.

It is only through the creation of such duly empowered institutions that peoples of "developing nations" will be enabled to hold accountable the multinational corporations and other transnational forces which have such powerful effects on their welfare. Rather than seeking such a world order, many African, Asian and Latin American leaders hold on to the outmoded principle of unlimited sovereignty, hoping instead to break their dependencies by slaying what they consider to be the demons—corporate capitalism, Western imperialism and racism. This demon-focused effort to break free from the growing interdependencies in order to achieve an illusory self-sufficiency results instead in a guaranteed ossification of such dependencies as transnational forces expand and consolidate power without dependable and human-centered national or global restraints.

Citizens of the more affluent, industrialized world also are victims of the tensions and conflicts which grow out of the dichotomy of being dependent but making policy decisions as if they were autonomous. Some global crises have intensified for lack of transnational institutions with sufficient power to deal with problems and needs that cross national boundaries. These include environmental destruction, the energy crisis, monetary instability and the arms race.

But more often overlooked are the negative effects on *domestic* institutions which are deteriorating because of the time, taxes and talents given to national security priorities instead of to domestic needs. National leaders have no choice but to focus on national security goals when confronted by the ever-present economic and military crises that result from unchecked global competition between nations operating on the principle of total independence. Lacking transnational institutions to deal with cross-national forces in an orderly and equitable way, national leaders have reacted by mobilizing their citizenry for international military, resource and monetary competition. Such mobilization has been the cause of a recurrent draining of time, talent and money away from domestic priorities such as housing, education, transportation, ecology and urban decay.

Nation-State System

The nation-state system is the existing reality of sovereign states making decisions independently. The term must be qualified, however, for the fact is that no "system" exists in the sense of the dictionary definition: "An assemblage of objects united by some form of regular interaction; an organic or organized system." The present balance-of-power relationship is characterized mainly by the regular interaction of conflict competition.

World Order

Two types of world order must be distinguished. The first is the order that presently exists on the planet, an order of dependent relationships between allegedly independent sovereignties that are dominated by raw economic, monetary and military power rather than by law. The operative principles of this order are national interest and security. The second type envisions an order of relationships determined by law and based on universal social justice for all persons; an order whose operative principles embrace the centrality and sovereignty of the human person. It is this latter meaning that we intend in the following pages—the meaning that provides the title of this book.

Central to this type of world order would be functional public authorities endowed with the legal machinery and economic and political power needed to secure peace, economic well-being and social justice for all persons. World order would not necessitate the elimination of nation-states. Nor does it presume a world federal system, although federalism is one of the possible models. Nor would it necessarily mean that all nations would function with the same system of internal government. What it would mean is that certain functions would transfer from national levels to the planetary level, e.g., peace-keeping, transnational ecological protection, regulation of world trade and of an integrated monetary system, regulation of the uses of the seas, and some global taxation. Most other functions would remain the responsibility of institutions at the present level of the nation-state.

But because national security mobilization would not be necessary in a world order that has eliminated competition over armaments and regulates competition over scarce resources and international payments, much power presently centralized in federal national security bureaucracies of nation-states could become *decentralized*. Resources, talents, and leadership commitment now tied up by national security goals would become available for resolving local problems according to local rather than national criteria and control.

Decentralization

Decentralization, therefore, is a central dimension of the world order framework this book embraces. Far from becoming a monolithic government, a just world order could provide for the decentralization of artificial and unmanageable superstates into more representative, cultural or regional groups.

It is the security imperative in today's National Security State system that, more than anything else, demands an increasing centralization of power in the hands of security elites. This centralization will increase as global interdependencies increase. For totally sovereign nations have no other way to respond to the pressures and conflicts engendered by unregulated global forces than by placing much power in a strong central authority.

In a world order based on justice under law for all, however, a limited number of functional transnational institutions could be empowered to deal with each area of global interdependency according to the merits of its *natural* dynamics and separated from the complications "logically" bred by the principle of absolute national sovereignty.

Multi-Issue Coalition for World Order

The fear of nuclear annihilation was once the overriding rationale of many people who called for a system of world law. Removing that threat was considered sufficient motivation for the establishment of effective transnational institutions. But for persons never immediately experiencing the destruction of war, or who did not personally believe nuclear weapons would ever be employed, this fear did not have sufficient motivating power to make world order a priority issue for personal commitment of time and finances.

The global interdependencies that have burst forth since Hiroshima, however, have made it to the *self-interest* of people from every walk of life to commit time and finances toward the development of a new world order framework. The energy crisis, exploitation of the oceans, pollution of atmosphere and waterways, the recurring monetary crises, world hunger and poverty, resource depletion and peace-keeping are global crises which can be adequately handled only through transnational bodies legally empowered by and held accountable to the world community.

In addition to global crises, however, there are urgent domestic and personal reasons for working for a new world order. Alienation, addiction, increasing crime and violence, urban decay, inadequate health care, mental illness, education, housing, transportation, environment, racial justice, women's rights, civil liberties and elite rule are issues that affect and concern the daily life of the average citizen. The resolution of each of these locally felt problems is largely frustrated by national security priorities.

These self-interest as well as altruistic reasons for developing transnational institutions provide an unprecedented basis for building a grass roots, people's *coalition for world order*. A key task in sparking this coalition is to help people see specific connections between the particular issue concerns that frustrate them and the national security straitjacket that is blocking their efforts to have these specific issues attended to.

Besides an awareness of the causes of their problems, another important aspect of a multi-issue coalition for world order is the *involvement of people* in considering and developing their own alternative models and strategies, a task which should not be left to academics or politicians alone.

There are a significant number of leaders in the U.S. Congress and in other nations of the world who have for some time been convinced of the need for effective world law to achieve world peace.[2] But they do not campaign on such a platform nor act upon it in legislative chambers because they reason it would be political suicide to do so if "the people are not ready." An intermediate goal of a people's coalition of issue constituencies is to make the leaders aware that "the people *are* ready"; and that more than peace is at stake.

A basic rationale of this coalition—a coalition already in formation—is that of self-interest and true human security. Experience in this coalition building, however, shows that working for a just world order is more than merely a question of individual self-interest. It responds to the human need for meaning and our collective sense that as a species we can *be* more. It responds to our need to know that history is not on a dead-end track. It is a basis for hope and belief in the possibility of a more human future. And for some, such as ourselves, it is a basis for faith: in the human person, in our species and in the immanence of a Loving God.

CONCLUSION

The first step in the building of a more viable human future is to identify all the sources and causes of our present powerlessness. The analysis presented above and developed in subsequent chapters is an attempt to identify a central cause that has been largely overlooked.

Although this analysis is relatively simple, it is not simplistic. That is, we are not suggesting that the national security straitjacket is the total summation of all that causes the human crises of our times. Although we see the National Security State system as a major obstacle to a resolution of the multiple crises facing us, its removal will not bring an automatic reversal of alienation, violence and injustice. But the removal of national security imperatives will open human history once more to the possibility of true human security and development. It is an analysis that has not yet been included sufficiently in assessing the human dilemma. The failure to do so has led to counterproductive name-calling and polarization in the human community. Further, it is a failure that has led us down dead-end streets in search of a better band-aid to place on wounds that are in need of major systemic diagnoses and care.

Changing the people who rule, or even changing the form of internal national government, will no longer provide more than minor and temporary relief. For the problems of the human community are beyond the capacity of any one head of state or a particular political party or ideology to provide a cure.

4

The Powerlessness of Heads of State

> The significant thing about the present crisis is that the nation-states—even the most powerful—are no longer able to fulfill the purpose for which they were created.
>
> Emery Reves

To speak of *citizen* powerlessness is to touch upon a reality easily understood by most people. But not so when it comes to a discussion of the powerlessness of the President of the United States or other heads of state.

The powerlessness of which we speak is not the powerlessness of leaders to make unilateral decisions. Not a powerlessness to make war. Not a powerlessness to oppress millions of their own citizens and the citizens of other countries. Not a powerlessness to ravage the earth's environment and scarce resources. For, in varying degrees, the leaders of today's nations *do* wield such power. Theirs is a power unprecedented in history.

The powerlessness of which we speak exists *despite* such unprecedented power. It is the increasing powerlessness of even the best intentioned of national leaders to move person-centered, social justice priorities up from the bottom of their country's agenda.

REORDERING PRIORITIES—WHAT CRITERIA?

What are the criteria by which governments should determine priorities? From the perspective of the persons who comprise the citizenry, the criteria would include:

1. *The Sovereignty of the Human Person*

The human person is central. The state exists for the person, not vice versa. The state is servant, not master. Government and public policy exist to guarantee the inalienable social, economic and political rights of citizens and to assure them the access to the means toward full human development.

2. *Participation in Decision Making*

Personal sovereignty means having a significant and effective voice in the decisions that affect one's life. A corollary here is that decisions should be decentralized as much as possible; and that when interdependence demands that decisions be made at national (or global) levels, that they not be made apart from the input of and accountability to the people.

3. *Response to Unmet Human Needs*

The human needs which cannot be met at the level of personal and local community initiatives may vary in different areas of the world. But everywhere the growing complexity of modern life makes it increasingly difficult for persons to meet basic needs without government leadership and initiatives.

The following issues, which concern people the world over, need the priority attention of governments (though the philosophies and methods used to respond may vary):

—Hunger	—Care of the Aged
—Housing	—Racial Justice
—Health Care	—Women's Rights
—Education	—Religious Freedom
—Employment	—Penal Reform
—Environment	—Urban Planning
—War Prevention	—Population
—Crime Prevention	—Democratic Participation

    —Prevention of Alienation and Addiction

Most political leaders would insist that they personally embrace the above agenda. Pragmatically, however, these issues are increasingly subordinated to national security priorities (or in some cases, such as the National Defense Education Act following Sputnik, or employment related to defense construction, they are tied to national security directives).

Because no global security system exists to provide security vis-a-vis competition over weapons, monetary balances and scarce resources, first priority is given to policies which enhance a nation's ability to survive such global competition. The above priorities are consequently relegated to the back burners of national agendas. In the existent global system, a change in heads of states or ruling political parties can do little to effect a substantial reordering of priorities.

This is not to say that changes of leadership cannot make a difference or provide some minimal gains—and, in certain limited areas, even significant gains. But the basic dilemma that ties the hands of national leaders remains unchanged despite ideals or ideology. Even the most highly motivated new leaders, committed in principle to the above issues, inevitably face the same dilemma as their predecessors: in the present world system, national policies developed primarily around the above criteria would threaten the ability of their nation to survive. Without a transformation of the present system, every nation must ultimately depend only upon itself for its monetary, economic and military security. This fact increasingly dominates the formulation of public policy in all nation states.

IN THE UNITED STATES

American citizens today are confronted with the ultimate irony. On one hand, the American president has the power to rock the world nuclearly and monetarily. Yet, on the other hand, the same president stands largely impotent when it comes to leading the American people toward a resolution of domestic challenges.

What Happened to the U.S. Housing Commitment?

The status of *housing* programs in the United States provides a case in point. In 1949 a national commitment was made through the Wagner-Ellender Housing Act to provide "a decent home and suitable living environment for every American family." Today, nearly thirty years later, there is little possibility of this commitment being realized. One reason is that most housing advocates limit their efforts to strategies that flow from a *micro* analysis of local, state and national politics. What they do not adequately take into account is the relationship between global economic and military competition and the present deterioration of housing programs.

At the time the housing commitment was made, Congress was still operating in the optimism and assumption of postwar demobilization. In the belief that peace treaties with Germany and Japan had enabled the "lights to go on again all over the world," it was assumed that the United States—and humanity in general—could move toward significant gains in domestic development programs.

But in 1949 the Cold War and superpower confrontation began to heat up. The Soviet Union's detonation of its first atomic bomb coincided in time with the new housing act. As did Mao's 1949 takeover of China. And the Korean war was about to explode. It was the beginning of the rise to ascendancy of the National Security State.

Some congressional leaders were already aware in 1949 that remobilization for the nuclear arms race would affect the new commitment to adequate housing for every citizen. But few could foresee the future in which the armaments race would be only one of three engines for a mobilization of resources, leadership and institutions for national security goals.

The international monetary system fashioned at Bretton Woods in 1944 was still young and working well enough in 1949. The technological interdependencies of global communication and transportation systems that grew from technological breakthroughs during World War II had not yet brought forth the *world* economy that we experience now in the final quarter of the twentieth century. Foreign trade was expanding, but still relatively peripheral to the U.S. economic scene. But by the mid-1960s, the International Monetary

Fund (established at Bretton Woods to prevent international economic collapse) was beginning to break down, unable to deal with new economic and monetary interdependencies that it had not been designed to handle. Balance-of-payments deficits which the United States had been suffering since the early 1950s began to be a grave national security concern and United States leaders began to shuffle national policy priorities accordingly. A second national security motor was starting.

By the late 1960s and early 1970s, in Richard Nixon's first administration, this concern began to increase. The U.S. trade balance, which had enjoyed a healthy surplus, began a steady decline, moving from a $4.9 billion surplus in 1965 to an alarming $6.8 billion deficit by 1972,[1] an $11.7 billion drop. And balance-of-payments deficits further deteriorated from a $1.3 billion deficit in Official Settlements Balance in 1965 to a $10.3 billion deficit by 1972.[2]

Apart from political philosophy and regardless of who would have been president, such steady declines necessitated a strong presidential hand in developing policies that would stimulate the production and export of goods that could bring in valuable foreign exchange.

Nixon underscored this economic imperative in his Economic Report to Congress in January, 1973. "International competition is shifting from military and political arenas to *economic*." Stating that our exports had not kept pace with imports, he continued, "We have not been able to sell enough to pay our overseas expenditures, and so we had to pay by incurring more and more short term debts abroad. This is not a situation that can go on indefinitely."

Production of housing does not produce critical foreign exchange. For houses are built for domestic consumption: whereas armaments, electronic computers, communication and transportation technology can be sold abroad and thereby provide foreign currency. Accordingly, government policy was fashioned to facilitate the production of these latter *strategic* goods—through research and development grants, tax credits, guaranteed loans and other preferential assistance.

Meanwhile, on January 8, 1973, following his reelection for a second term, President Nixon called a moratorium against further progress on the housing commitment. And in his 1973 budget proposals, while an increase of $4.2 billion was proposed for the military, more than 100 federally funded domestic programs were cut or limited. Among these was rural housing while new commitments for low-income and moderate-income urban housing construction were suspended.

With presidential priority being given to balance-of-payment and balance-of-weapons imperatives, and with the burden of stabilizing an inflationary economy and keeping the federal budget in line, the president's domestic program was perhaps best summed up by the slogan he used in his 1973 inaugural address: "Ask not, what will government do for me, but what can I do for myself?"

Unfortunately, many of the older cities, already overburdened with swelling welfare rolls, unemployment and inflationary costs that made dilapidated housing almost impossible to replace, were in no position to do it by themselves.

International economic and military competition, of course, do not wholly explain the deterioration of the national commitment to housing. Other factors were also at work, e.g., the self-serving coalition between the construction and banking industries which have dominated the policies of the Federal Housing Administration. But the influence of balance-of-payments and balance-of-weapons imperatives on the depressed housing market was major.

The oil-money crisis of 1973 triggered the third engine of the triple national security engine, namely *competition over scarce resources.*

The additional strain placed on a floundering global economy and on national priorities was soon evident and predicted to get worse. Referring to this emerging problem of scarce resources, the Committee for Economic Development stated in a July, 1973 report:

> Perhaps the most serious emerging problem stems from the possibility of major worldwide or regional shortages of various raw materials and the impact of such developments on the payments positions of industrial countries. The most dramatic changes in this area are occurring in the field of energy, particularly petroleum. It has been estimated on the basis of current trends that by 1980, the industrial countries of the Organization for Economic Cooperation and Development (OECD) may have to import more than $50 billion of oil from the 'oil producing' countries. For the United States alone, such imports could easily reach $18 to $24 billion, compared with $4 billion in 1972. According to the President's Council on International Economic Policy, the net direct effect of oil transactions on the

U.S. current account balance in 1980 could amount to an outflow of from $5 to $10 billion.[3]

The launching of "Project Energy Independence" was a direct result of such forewarnings of future economic insecurity. As another top priority for presidential attention it was a further blow against hopes of resurrecting the failing national housing commitment. It resulted in billions of new dollars being diverted, directly or indirectly, to energy-related industries. This was true even before Gerald Ford's proposal for a new energy facility projected at billions of additional dollars. The commitment to energy-related priorities continues to dominate President Carter. The 1949 commitment to "provide a decent home and suitable living environment for every American family" stands as good as buried.

Each year in New York and other U.S. cities, thousands of houses and apartment buildings are lost. Very few are being replaced. If sections of the Bronx, Newark, Chicago look bombed out—victims of a war —that is because they have been. It is a war for national survival in a lawless global arena.

Housing is not the only U.S. victim of the ascendency of the National Security State. Similar time frame scenarios can be outlined for most other issues. Global Education Associates, for example, is preparing monographs on most of the seventeen issues listed above. Significant progress on these issues will not be made without a change in the world system.

IN THE SOVIET UNION

The leaders of the Soviet Union (as we will discuss more fully in a later chapter) are also caught in a straitjacket of national security mobilization, prevented by the logic of the National Security State from giving person-centered priorities and full human development a center place on the Soviet agenda. *Corporate* goals— capable of ensuring the nation's ability to survive the military, monetary and resource competition of a lawless global arena—logically take precedence over personal development goals. The new class of Soviet elites[4] who determine and implement these corporate policies are rewarded with special economic and social status in proportion to their contribution to national power, prestige and other security-related goals.

It is theoretically true that the USSR's socialist frame embraces a philosophy of economic justice more explicitly than the capitalist frame of the United States. The destitute, impoverished and hungry that are found among minority groups, elderly and other sectors of U.S. society are rare in Soviet society, thanks to government guarantees of minimal food, housing and health care. But other areas of human need, including self-determination, are subordinate to the corporate security goals of Soviet society. The relationship between this subordination of human development goals and the imperatives of national security and elite rule in the Soviet Union will be explored more fully in Chapter Six.

IN OIL-PRODUCING NATIONS

Oil-producing nations, with their critical oil reserves and resultant surplus of monetary reserves have already illustrated their potential to destabilize the world's monetary- and resource-patterns. Operating as a bloc through OPEC (the Organization of Petroleum Exporting Countries), they have made the industrialized countries painfully aware of their power.

These monetary surpluses are providing OPEC nations the capital to give greater attention to basic material needs such as food, housing and health care. Local development programs are lowering unemployment and gains in education for youth and adults are also being made.

Yet despite these domestic gains and their new international clout, the security of oil-producing nations is tenuous. Escalatory policies to strengthen national security are limiting those gains and keeping full human-development goals near the bottom of national agendas. The London-based Institute for Strategic Studies noted in a September, 1975 report, that Iran's military spending tripled in a year, from $3.2 billion to $10.4 billion and that Saudia Arabia's increase was more than threefold, from $1.8 to $6.3 billion. Ruth Sivard reports that in the Middle East, as a whole, military spending increased more sharply than anywhere else in the world—eightfold in the fifteen-year period 1960 through 1974, and it is still rising.[5]

The need for military preparedness of Arab oil-producing nations is not just related to Israeli-Arab tensions. Another threat to the OPEC nations appears in the possibility of military intervention by some industrial nations. The likelihood of such intervention can be expected to increase as the costs of nuclear alternatives to oil continue to escalate and as public concern about the dangers of nuclear power mounts, forcing industrial nations back into greater vulnerability to OPEC whims. Should an economic squeeze caused by oil politics and/or world economic instability become acute, and as international tension mounts in its wake, the eventuality of such armed intervention cannot be ruled out. Such a possibility was demonstrated when

Secretary of State Kissinger warned that military force might be used if industry in the West was "strangled." The implications of such intervention on the security and well-being of oil producing nations are self-evident.

But military threats are not the only insecurity affecting the oil producing nations. Also at stake is their *economic* security. Time threatens their newly found economic ascendancy. The eventual depletion of their own oil reserves, paralleled by the discovery and exploitation of other potential sources (such as in the North Sea), will diminish the economic power that OPEC nations have been able to wield in the industrial world, particularly Western Europe and Japan.

Further, the 1974-75 recession of the industrialized world illustrated the dependency of OPEC's large monetary reserves upon a viable world economy. World demand for oil was drastically reduced during this recessionary period. The message was clear: a major world recession or a breakdown of the international monetary system could undercut OPEC's newly found affluence and power.

Finally, OPEC countries, to different degrees, are themselves dependent on other countries for critical resources, for technology and for food. Given the balance-of-power rules of the present global system, little is assured. Alliances change, with former allies becoming enemies. Economic stability can quickly give way to instability. Lacking a global security system (i.e., lacking those functional agencies with the effective authority needed to regulate economic, monetary and military forces according to the principles of social justice and the common good of humankind), there is little alternative for OPEC nations but to also become National Security States.

The leaders of oil-producing nations and the super-powers, therefore, are in a similar bind. Although the degree and style may vary, essential characteristics are the same. Corporate goals dominate. Decisions are made by national security elites. Person-centered, full human-development goals remain on back burners of national agendas, subordinated to production and corporate policies that give the respective nations the ability to deal with military, monetary and resource competition. Lacking an effective and just world order, OPEC leaders—whoever they are now and whoever they *will be*—are substantially powerless to drastically reorder these national security goals and priorities.

IN THE NON-OIL "DEVELOPING" NATIONS

The powerlessness of the non-oil-producing nations of Africa, Asia and Latin America, especially the so-called "Fourth World" countries whose average per capita income is less than $200, leaves little to the imagination. Faced with massive economic poverty, their powerlessness is further underscored by the critical fact that they are victims of economic policies determined by powerful, wealthy industrial countries and, more recently, by oil-producing nations and multinational corporations.

Terms such as sovereignty, independence and self-reliance are, in varying degrees, contemporary delusions for all countries. This is especially true, however, for Fourth World nations. Despite attempts to gain strength by acting in blocs, they have few bargaining chips in the world power game. Their voice goes largely unheeded in the councils affecting the global forces that dominate their domestic scenes. What gains they have been able to achieve through their strategies for a New International Economic Order have been largely minimal.

This powerlessness in the global arena, however, does not mean that Fourth World countries are not National Security States. Their leaders are caught in the same national security logic as the rest of the world and left powerless to effectively concentrate on human development priorities. They too are burdened with increasing military budgets, with the need to give priority to production of goods that bring in foreign reserves rather than of goods that respond to the basic human needs of their citizens, and with the need to expend large proportions of their budgets in search of scarce mineral resources and foreign technology.

For example, balance-of-payments imperatives have led Kenya, a nation rich in agricultural potential, to *export* beef while large numbers of her children suffer from protein deficiency. Huge tracts of excellent land are given to the production for export of tea and coffee which provide no nutritional benefits to her population but do ensure Kenya a more favorable balance of trade in the international market place.

Egypt's balance-of-payments needs cause this struggling nation to put priority on cotton production and export rather than on food. The pattern is similar throughout the "developing" world.

Balance-of-weapons competition is becoming another major cause of powerlessness in the "developing nations. Military spending in these countries of Africa, Asia and Latin America has almost tripled in the last 15 years, jumping from $15 billion in 1960 to $39 billion in 1974.[6] According to Ruth Sivard, former chief economist of the Arms Control and Disarmament

Agency, this increase is "twice as fast as the economic base to support them."[7]

The military expenditures of "developing nations" are modest when compared to the big spending countries of NATO and the Warsaw Pact. But they are costs that poorer peoples of the world can hardly bear, given the burden they already carry. Peru is an example. Although Peru spends only $26.00 per capita on military[8] (small compared to U.S. expenditures), it is money sorely needed in human services. Hugh O'Shaughnessy describes it this way:

> There can be little argument that Peru could put to good use on social programs any money that could be diverted from the military. The average Peruvian is miserably poor; the average annual income in the country is around $350. About one in three Peruvians cannot read or write and one in eight, up to two million people in all, live in urban slums. Perhaps a third of Peruvians are chronically out of work or employed only part time.
>
> Large tracts of the country are inaccessible except by mule or canoe. To pay its way internationally, Peru has to rely on sales of fish products, minerals and cotton. Peru suffers when the world recession hits the prices of its minerals or when the shoals of fish disappear from its coast.[9]

Why should a country threatened by problems such as these be giving priority to the military? Without a global authority to regulate the border disputes and other interstate tensions that continue to threaten Latin American countries such as Peru, they have little choice but to arm in their own defense, even at the expense of other human needs.

The insecurity of small nations such as Peru is providing a major source of income for industrial nations who export armaments. And with rising costs of oil imports and other balance-of-payments factors spurring them on, increasing numbers of industrial nations are competing over the growing armaments market they find in the "developing" world. The United States, with a total of $12 billion estimated for overseas sales of armaments for 1976 and billions again projected for 1977, is the biggest armaments exporter—but by no means the only pusher. Russia, France, United Kingdom, China, Poland, Czechoslovakia, to name a few, are also included.[10]

Despite the very serious questions of ethics and ultimate wisdom involved in armaments proliferation, the pressures on industrial nations to jump on the arms trade bandwagon and share in this lucrative source of foreign currency are difficult to resist, especially in face of hard-pressed national economies and of increased monetary deficits due to increased oil prices. West Germany, which had developed a policy in the aftermath of Nazi mobilization to stay clear of the arms trade, recently gave in to balance-of-payments pressures and substantially increased arms exports. And in 1975, Israel seized the opportunity to increase her armaments sales by $100 million, from $90 million in 1974 to $190 million in 1975.[11]

It is this competition over balance of payments which makes it so difficult to contain the arms race. A principal argument used against efforts in the U.S.

"IT HELPS THE BALANCE OF PAYMENTS"

Congress to set ceilings on armaments sales overseas is that prospective buyers will just go to Europe or the Soviet Union instead. "If they don't get it from us, they'll get it from someone else," is the well-worn retort.

Such reasoning is not without basis in fact. "In 1965 when Washington refused to allow the Peruvians to buy Northrop F 5-A's, they bought French Mirages. During 1967-72 Argentina, Chile, Colombia, Peru and Venezuela spent $1,213 million on arms from Europe."[12] And when Peru met hostility in the U.S. Congress and was simultaneously made a better offer by the Soviet Union, they purchased Soviet tanks.[13]

It will be extremely difficult to get each of the armaments exporting nations to limit overseas armaments sales without reciprocal limits set by competing exporters. Outside of a world juridical framework in which armaments sales would not only be curbed, but armaments would no longer be necessary to ensure a nation's security, effective curtailing of the armaments spiral in "developing" nations is virtually impossible.

But "developing" nations are not only *buyers* of armaments. Increasingly they are producers as well. With one-fourth of all "developing" nations now assembling or producing major weapons, the military has become the fastest growing sector of some fragile economies.[14]

The rapid expansion of armed forces in developing countries is another concern. According to Sivard, the "developing" countries have had such a concentrated buildup of their armed forces that "there are now four soldiers in the regular forces to ten workers in manufacturing industry. In developed countries the ratio is about one to ten."[15]

Decline of Democracy

The rapid increase in armaments purchases and production, along with the high per capita ratio of soldiers, is beginning to have disastrous effects in the "developing" world, not only in terms of inadequate attention to social needs such as health care and education, but also because of its disastrous effects on democracy. At the present time, two-thirds of Latin America and thirty-four countries of Africa are ruled by military governments.[16] This ascendancy of the military in the developing world can be attributed to a variety of factors, including: 1.) personal ambitions of men such as General Amin in Uganda; 2.) the struggle for ideological and economic control, such as the 1973 CIA-supported military coup in Chile; 3.) and the logical, i.e., genuine, security imperatives which have historically given military leaders preeminence in national decision making. But, whether for legitimate or illegitimate reasons, the manipulation of "national security logic" becomes a tool for justifying and maintaining military domination and suppression of a large part of world society. Armies are retained and kept strong for the purported reason that without them enemy attack would be imminent. An important aspect in preventing military domination is to remove this "logic" for arming and maintaining armies, by eliminating the threats to security posed in a system where each nation needs to be a law unto itself.

Detente between two superpowers offers no solution for a *global* armaments spiral. Only in a global security system empowered to provide for disarmament on a global scale, will the need for defense systems be curbed and the eventuality of military takeovers be checked.

But the decline of democracy in the "developing"

world is not due only to increasing *military* domination. Not all national security elites come in uniform. Monetary and resource competition are also grave threats to a nation's security and the "developing nations" are especially vulnerable. The need for strong government approaches in these areas to ensure national viability also means the "need" for national governments to have more centralized power and opens a nation to elite rule.

Given the security imperatives facing "developing" nations in an insecure world system, it is not surprising that elite rule has so widely characterized their governments. India is a case in point.

INDIA

Why was the world's largest democracy marshaled into elite rule? Many reasons have been speculated. It is not our purpose here to list or sort them all out. Rather, we want to suggest that few of these speculations give adequate attention to the degree that the *logic* of national security was responsible for Mrs. Gandhi's elite rule. We suggest that the triple national security motor was substantially, though not exclusively, responsible for India's centralized mobilization.

1. *Competition over Weapons*

India is a member of the world's nuclear club and is expanding its military establishment. By 1973 India's federal budget allocated twice as much on military as on education; and health care was allocated only one-fourth as much as defense.[17] It is easy to decry such military expenditures, made in face of grave hunger and extreme poverty. But objectivity must recognize that lacking an effective global security system, Mrs. Gandhi was quite logical. In a balance-of-power world where only military, monetary and economic power has weight, Nehru's "moral power" had little force. And where there was no assurance of help from allies whose own individual self-interest goals lead to changing alliances and unpredictable diplomacy, India could not be certain of anyone's aid in the event of an attack by China or Pakistan.

Further, the new prestige won by India on becoming a nuclear power seems to have significantly enhanced her political and economic influence, especially among Third and Fourth World nations.

2. *Competition Over Balance of Payments*

India has been a major victim of the balance-of-payments dynamics of the international monetary arena. The quintupling of oil prices devastated her foreign reserves. She stood virtually powerless, therefore, to import the fertilizer, technology and transportation and storage facilities needed to become self-sufficient in food. She also lacked the reserves to compete with the Soviet Union for surplus U.S. grains to feed her people. Lacking a global security system, including a world order agency to provide special access to needed monetary reserves, it became *logical* for India to use much of her scarce capital, technology and foreign currency to produce goods that would sell overseas (including moderate-scale weapons from her new military arsenals) rather than concentrating on housing, health care, family planning, cottage industries, rural development and public works projects for her massive unemployed. The logic is that the latter expenditures do not bring in precious foreign reserves. So there was not necessarily a contradiction between Indira Gandhi's professed com-

mitment to social justice and socialist institutional reform and her alliances with large corporate capitalist
industries. Human-centered social justice reforms do
not provide India with precious foreign reserves. But
corporate economics does.

3. *Competition over Scarce Resources*

The oil-money crisis exposed India's insecurity vis-
a-vis the resources needed to develop a viable economy.
Lacking a global security system to guarantee her an
equitable share in the natural resources of the earth—
and/or the financial and technological wherewithal to
exploit her own untapped resources—it became logical
for India to give top priority to the corporate industries
(foreign and domestic) that could explore and capitalize
on mineral resources within her own borders.

It is easy to condemn Indira Gandhi or members
of her family for dismantling much of India's hard-won
constitutional democracy. It is also easy to decry her
tolerance of corrupt people in the government and her
alliance with corporate industries in spite of her profession of concern for the social justice needs of her people. Despite whatever truth there is in these allegations,
justice to Indira Gandhi demands that due consideration be given to the dilemma that she faced vis-a-vis
the reality of the triple national security motor. To
reply with scenarios that project what "might have
been" if Nehru would have followed either Mahatma
Gandhi's or Mao Tse-tung's development model is not
adequate. The challenge is to respond to the social, economic and political reality that faced Mrs. Gandhi in
1975.

The burden on Mrs. Gandhi's critics — including the
new government under Prime Minister Morarji Desai —

is to put forth a relevant scenario in which India can deal with the above three areas of national security and still retain a democratic, person-centered, social-justice-oriented society that focuses on full human development. We suggest that no such scenario is possible unless it is placed within a world order context of a global security system. Only then can the triple engines of the national security motor be turned off, a reordering of national priorities be accomplished and government be decentralized.

CHINA: AN EXCEPTION?

Some may insist that China is an exception, that it *has* reordered priorities and therefore is not a National Security State. Such an assertion is partially correct. China constitutes an exceptional case study. Her unique focus on a socialist society based on rural, decentralized development has significantly overcome the social injustices that for centuries had dominated China's masses. People are now experiencing a certain local sovereignty over economic policies. Poverty, hunger and disease—traditionally widespread in China—now belong to history books.

Nevertheless, China's security is far from assured. The threat of nuclear attack from the Soviet Union is ever present, causing a major Chinese emphasis on developing a nuclear deterrent. The result is a substantial dislocation of China's resources from domestic goals. Concomitant with this military mobilization is a strong voice for army officials in political decision making. Similarly, severe restrictions on political expression and on freedom of personal occupational choice are determined not only by communist ideology, but by national security ideology as well.

Economic and monetary mobilization of citizens and production processes are increasingly influenced by national security imperatives as China becomes more active in world economics. It is true that China's development model, placing a major focus on agriculture and intermediate technology, makes her less vulnerable to global forces than most other countries. But she is by no means immune. As ambitious development plans increase her dependency on outside technology and the dynamics of global monetary and economic forces, her vulnerability also increases. As this dependency increases, China's domestic policies will be affected accordingly.

Her hostility to capitalism and her doctrine of economic self-reliance notwithstanding, China's trade deficit in 1974 was nearly $1.5 billion and is expected to reach $3 billion by 1978. Although avoiding the mention of loans, the Bank of China is obtaining what amounts to foreign loans in Europe and Hong Kong. The bank successfully encourages corresponding foreign banks to deposit significantly more foreign currency than the amount of foreign currency that China deposits with the foreign banks. What results practically is a loan without having to call it one.

In order to offset the growing trade deficit resulting from the large imports of technology for oil-processing, fertilizer and steel industries (often in the form of entire plants), China is putting increasing emphasis on the export section of her economy. One consequence of this entry into the free enterprise world market is that self-reliance is diminished. As China becomes even more interlocked into the world economy by these new interdependencies (new, that is, for her), her mobilization for economic security will grow accordingly.

THE INSECURITY SPIRAL

A comparison of the military and social expenditures of the ten largest nation-states (see tables I and II pages 95 and 96) gives some evidence of the degree to which other human needs are subservient to the overwhelming priority given national security. It is important to note that this pattern is true of the wealthiest and poorest nations alike and of the nonaligned as well as of capitalist and communist ideological defenders. Bangladesh, a country facing grave starvation, spends more on military security than on feeding its hungry. Indonesia, with only one physician per 19,391 population, spends fifteen times more on military than on health programs. Pakistan, with an illiteracy rate of 81%, spends five times as much on military as on education.

By 1977 annual world military expenditures topped $350 billion. The total escalates by billions every year. Worse, there is a backlog of orders for armaments estimated at two to three times present deliveries. Describing what this cost represents in terms of human well-being, Sivard writes:

> In addition to the growing potential for cataclysmic destruction, the arms build-up represents an immediate and heavy burden on the world economy. It is destructive whether or not the weapons are put to use in war. It contributes to inflation, retards economic and social development, and diverts resources urgently needed for human well-being. Until it can be put under control it undermines the national and international security which it is intended to protect.[18]

Worse, these dollar costs represent only *one* aspect

of national security expenditures. Time, talent and human energies expended in military security concerns are not measured here. Nor are the dollar, time, talent, and energy costs of other areas of national security involvement, i.e., competition over balance of payments and scarce resources.

Leaders of today's nation-states are not only powerless to reorder the human agenda. They are also powerless, despite escalating defense budgets, to provide security against the possibility of another world war or nuclear annihilation.

Even a limited nuclear war could result in death for hundreds of millions—and in radiation contamination for unaccountable millions more. And such a limited nuclear war would probably result in a rupture of the world economic fibre, a rupture that could result in worldwide economic and social chaos.

These two arguments for a world security system cannot be treated separately. They are integrally related. The more the human agenda is postponed, the greater the likelihood of war. Wars have often been the result of mounting domestic pressures and unrest. Remote and recent history bears loud witness to national leaders who have distracted their citizens from domestic trouble by adventurism in war. The converse is also true. For history also testifies to the power that political unrest over unmet domestic problems has for breeding a public irrationality that spills over into policies that force leaders into war. External demons are easily identified as sources of domestic problems.

Few periods of history have been so full of frustrations from unmet human agendas—frustrations complicated by rising expectations the world over. Ours is a

TABLE I

PER CAPITA RANKING

Military and Social Indicators, 10 Largest (by population) countries, 1974 in U.S.$

	Population millions	Per Cap.- GNP	Illit- eracy	Per Cap. Education	Pop. Per Physician	Per Cap. Health	Per Cap. Military
CHINA	831	$ 247	5%	$ 10	7,988	$ 2	$ 16
INDIA	600	143	64	3	4,351	1	4
USSR	252	2,789	1	166	361	63	333
USA	212	6,666	1	379	604	182	405
INDONESIA	136	164	40	4	19,391	—	5
JAPAN	110	4,107	1	163	862	174	38
BRAZIL	104	943	32	33	1,600	2	20
BANGLADESH	78	99	78	2	10,194	1	1
PAKISTAN	67	131	81	2	3,916	1	10
NIGERIA	61	365	75	13	21,884	1	14

Source: Ruth Sivard, *World Military and Social Expenditures, 1977*

TABLE II

PUBLIC EXPENDITURES

In Millions of U.S. Dollars for 10 Largest Countries, 1974

	Population Millions	Military	Education	Health
CHINA	831	13,000	8,200	2,000
INDIA	600	2,594	1,881	822
USSR	252	84,000	42,000	16,000
USA	212	85,906	80,300	38,573
INDONESIA	136	706	544	45
JAPAN	110	4,199	17,908	19,135
BRAZIL	104	2,058	3,451	167
BANGLADESH	78	92	137	51
PAKISTAN	67	690	120	48
NIGERIA	61	846	820	64

Source: Ruth Sivard, World Military and Social Expenditures, 1977.

combustible period, susceptible to irrationality on every side. Proliferation of arms sales, confrontation over monetary crises and scarce resources, a growing pattern of terrorism, fear and frustration mixed with confusion —all combine to make World War III *probable* rather than just *possible*. And in our present world system, national leaders stand powerless before this probability.

The editorial offices of the *Bulletin of Atomic Scientists* has a "prophesying clock" whose hour hand has never been far from twelve. For nearly thirty years this clock has symbolized the threat of nuclear doomsday. The minute hand advances and retreats according to the movement of world power politics and the assessment of the danger by the editors.

Believing that the threat of nuclear holocaust is greater than ever before, the editors recently moved the minute hand forward to nine minutes before midnight. Their judgment is that "time is running out."

Affirming the judgment were five experts who at a Cambridge Forum panel spoke to the question: "Are the prophets of doom mistaken?" The participants were faculty members of the Harvard-M.I.T. Arms Control Seminar. Although there were some secondary disagreements, the panelists agreed that the prophesying clock was keeping reliable time. As a result of unchecked nuclear proliferation, they estimated nuclear war in some form was a probability before the end of the century. For they did not see much basis for hope in existing political institutions and the policies they generate to provide curbs on the proliferation of nuclear weapons. Nations continue to increase their armaments in the name of self-protection. The prevention of such a probability, they felt, was dependent on the willingness of nations to relinquish some of their sovereignty.

Remarks of panelist George Kistiakowsky, former Chief of the Explosives Division at the Los Alamos Laboratory of the Manhattan Project, are worth noting. They well sum up the "Bomb" question in a way that highlights the *urgency* of a world security system.

> And it is very frightening to realize that by 1999 a device with the power to blow up a community the size of Cambridge, for example, could probably be carried on the back of any strong person.

> I used to think that one of the most horrendous facts I had ever heard was the number of American nuclear weapons stationed on foreign soil. But, confronted with the number of weapons that could be made per week by 1990 from the fissionable products of nonmilitary nuclear reactors, I am beginning to believe that proliferation (like billions of mosquitoes hatching out of billions of eggs) means infection, and is a concern to be dealt with like matters of public health.[19]

Such observations underscore the fact that not only have heads of state become powerless in the existent world system to make significant progress on the human agenda. In the face of armaments proliferation, they have become powerless to guarantee their citizenry that there will be a tomorrow in which to work on the human agenda.

CONCLUSION

It has been our purpose in this chapter to underscore the degree to which national security imperatives (defined in terms of balance-of-payments and resource competition as well as balance-of-weapons pressures) have been not an exclusive but nevertheless a major factor preventing national leaders from substantially reordering priorities. Personal sovereignty and human needs on the domestic front have been ignored or given only token attention while aggregate, corporate goals related to national power and survival have come into dominance.

Generally speaking, all countries are fast becoming National Security States. Most are already there. Each country has its own list of unmet domestic needs, subordinated to the imperatives of national security competition. The lists themselves do not differ greatly in the enumeration of issues, although the degree of urgency regarding particular issues may vary considerably.

What is common to all countries is that the criterion of human development is shelved "for the duration." The *duration* here is not a short-term reality as was the four- to six-year period of World War II during which human and personal priorities were temporarily locked away. Rather, this duration is here to stay until a global security system with functional institutions capable of dealing with rampant global forces is developed. The lights of human development will remain out for a majority of humankind until the emergence of such a world-order system.

It is important to emphasize that we are not *advocating* constant mobilization for national security. It is, rather, a question of *recognizing* the reality that present corporate priorities and elite rule are not primarily due to ideological or personal demons. The world does not need more demonology. What is needed is objectivity—not to rationalize fatalistic acceptance of the status quo, but to identify all sources of power-lessness: of leaders as well as of citizens. Indeed, the surest way to more firmly entrench the status quo is to focus too exclusively on the powerlessness of the people and to rely on demonology at the cost of a more holistic analysis.

Some of our friends have counseled us that to speak of the logic of national security mobilization and of corporate elite rule is to furnish "the haves" with the rationale needed to preserve their power just at a time when they are under attack from every side. What is needed, they argue, is even greater pressure from the people.

Such advice does not dig deeply enough in its search for a solution. As long as the obsolete world system continues unchanged, the logic of national security mobilization will remain operative as a major obstacle to goals of fuller human development and true liberation. A later chapter on liberation will stress in more detail what should already be evident, namely, that the new revolutionary elites who have seized power in Africa, Asia and Latin America have little choice themselves but to become national security elites (whose revolutionary scenarios of a "New Society" based on social justice and full human development must be substantially locked away in the closet).

To acknowledge the logic and power of national security imperatives is not to fatally accept the status quo of corporate power, elite rule and militarization. Quite the contrary. Such acknowledgment is the first necessary step to liberating ourselves from this status quo.

5

The National Security Big Six

> The consequences of being at war and therefore in danger makes the handing-over of all power to a small caste seem the natural, unavoidable condition of survival.
>
> George Orwell, *1984*

Two departments of the U.S. executive branch have traditionally been allocated the task of guaranteeing national security and safety needs: the Department of Defense and the Department of State.

With these two exceptions, all the other governmental departments were designed to concentrate on *domestic* goals. Their purpose was to assist the citizenry in meeting *domestic* needs within the context of a common good philosophy.

With this distinction in mind, let us look at the list of ministries in the United States government:

    Department of Defense
    Department of State
    Department of Justice
    Department of Treasury
    Department of Commerce
    Department of Agriculture
    Department of Transportation

Department of Health, Education and
   Welfare
Department of Housing and Urban
   Development
Department of the Interior
Department of Labor

We invite the reader to consider each of these departments in the context of the constant mobilization of
today's National Security State. Let us place ourselves
in the skin of the secretaries of the non national-security
departments, all of whom are caught in the straitjacket
of this mobilization. In what ways and to what degrees
are our objectives influenced by the imperatives and
ramifications of the triple national security motors?
How does competition over *weapons* affect our department? What influence does *balance-of-payments* competition have? What about competition over *scarce resources*?

Responses to such questions will reveal that *all* of
the "domestic" departments are substantially frustrated
in achieving their goals by the national security priorities inherent in the present world system. Straitjacketed
by constant mobilization for national security, the secretaries of the respective departments are unable to
formulate policies which can effectively respond to the
domestic priorities for which they are responsible. They
are increasingly limited to cosmetic, band-aid responses
to unmet domestic needs, compelled to react to crises
without time, energy, flexibility or resources to plan
and execute ongoing programs commensurate with the
dimensions of the domestic problems that their departments are legally established to resolve.

Four of these domestically oriented departments,

however, are more than profoundly straitjacketed by the goals of the National Security State. They have become strategic *instruments* of those national security goals. These departments are the Departments of Justice, Treasury, Commerce and Agriculture. Thus we no longer have a "National Security Big Two," namely, a partnership between the Defense and State Departments. Rather, we now have a *National Security Big Six*.

DEPARTMENT OF DEFENSE

In the bygone days of "feast or famine" cycles, i.e., of alternating periods of declared war or peace, the Department of Defense was called the "Department of War." This traditional name was changed with the advent of the National Security State. It was a change in accord with the need for *perpetual* mobilization in our zero lead-time age.

Already in January 1944, Charles Wilson, president of General Electric, called for a "permanent war economy." In an address to the Army Ordnance Association, he outlined a continuing alliance between the military and industry. More specifically, Wilson encouraged large companies to establish within their companies a special liaison with the armed forces who would be commissioned as a Colonel in the Reserves.[1] In effect, Wilson was calling for an end to the traditional cycles of military mobilization and demobilization.

Wilson's plan must not be dismissed merely as a profit seeking venture. By 1944, top political, military and industrial officials were vividly aware of the Manhattan Project and its race to produce a nuclear bomb before the Germans did. Henry L. Stimson, Secretary of War, later said that in 1941 and 1942 the Germans were believed to be ahead of the United States in nuclear development. German efforts to produce nuclear weapons had begun in 1939 with projects for separating uranium isotopes and for constructing reactors. Indeed, it was Otto Hahn, a chemist at Kaiser Wilhelm Institute, who had identified barium in uranium in 1938, enabling his refugee friend in Sweden, Lise Meitner, to announce to the world in early 1939 the theory of fission.[2] Only the increased pressure from the fighting front prevented Hitler from allocating massive resources to the nuclear bomb project.

A *qualitatively* different world was dawning. Combined with German prowess in missile development, the wartime research and development of the United States and Germany clearly pointed to an era of radically different strategic confrontations. Military and governmental planners were already looking past Nazi Germany. The nuclear-missile age was about to begin with implications for humankind far beyond the consideration of "mere" physical death—implications still not adequately comprehended in our present day.

Hitler lost the race with time. But it had been a close call. And government planners were not to forget it. Should Nazi Germany have succeeded in perfecting its V-rockets so that Hitler would have won the Battle of Britain early in the war, a drastically different postwar scenario would have resulted. Without Britain as a base, the United States would have been hard put to prevent Germany from developing a long-range missile superiority. And Germany might well have won the race to develop the atomic bomb.

Today, the proliferation of nuclear weapons, orbiting satellites and intercontinental missiles has even more firmly entrenched the "permanent war economy" that Charles Wilson called for in 1944. Disarmament proposals have proven utopian to the point where government leaders no longer bother to use the term "disarmament." The term is now "arms control." And even here there is a major qualification. The focus in arms-control negotiations is on slowing down the rate of the spiraling arms race, rather than on checking it at the present monstrous level of almost $300 billion annual world expenditures.

Jacobson and Stein speak about the problems that underlie the prevailing pessimism about arms control:

> The experience with the nuclear test ban negotiations confirms the immense difficulty inherent in the task of controlling modern technology in *an environment of the multi-state system.* . . . Constructing an agreement that has an equal range of benefits and disadvantages for many disparate partners is a task of great intellectual difficulty, and one which is made even more laborious if it must be worked out through the mechanisms of multi-governmental bargaining and complex intragovernmental processes such as those existing in the United States. . . . The fact that modern technology is subject to swift changes . . . made this task even more complicated.[3] (emphasis added)

In our present world system, no country can be sure of the intentions of rival countries. Each is aware of how often national interests and national security goals affect and are affected by their domestic decision-making processes and pressures. Each knows that decisions of other nations are equally based on competitive self-interest and local political pressures. Even in those rare cases where some significant progress is made in a particular area of arms control, such progress has little impact on military mobilization. For a treaty has no effective binding power. Local pressures, unforeseen crises or a change of leadership can easily abrogate pieces of paper if they are not enforced by legal institutions with effective authority.

The unending nature of this insecurity spiral is evident in the remarks of Roger Lewis, chairman of General Dynamics: "I don't care about what I'm being called now. But I don't want anyone to say in 1979, 'Why didn't the professionals do their job in 1969?' "

It is easy to accuse Lewis and Wilson of merely manipulating the national security rationale as a means of assuring high industry profits. In more than just a few instances, such critics may well be correct. Nevertheless, a strong logic does exist for constant military preparedness. Even when manipulation can be proven, such arguments will continue to be effective with the voters as long as the logic remains. For the logic has power on its own, quite apart from manipulation. Lacking a global security system, nations survive nuclear competition through a deterrent-oriented balance of terror. It is a balance that can be maintained only through a research and development lead-time up to ten years. Such long term economic commitments are required if a nation is to counterbalance the sophisticated new weapons being developed by its rivals. The result is a constantly *garrisoned* society.

It is important, however, to understand that more than the arms race is responsible for the United States being a garrisoned state. A central thrust of this book is to show that weapons competition is only one motor of our mobilized society. Competition over monetary reserves and scarce resources have now become coresponsible with the arms race for Wilson's "permanent war economy"—a coresponsibility that will become more clear as we examine the Departments of Justice, Treasury, Commerce and Agriculture.

DEPARTMENT OF STATE

A brief observation of the Department of State will serve as a transition to a consideration of these four new national security departments. Like its cousin, the Department of Defense, the State Department has always been a national security cabinet post. From the birth of the republic, the Secretary of State has had the official position of *preeminence* among other cabinet officers. Not only does this give the Secretary of State the seat of honor at formal occasions; he is also in line for filling the vacant presidential chair after the Vice-President and the Speaker of the House. Such preeminence symbolizes the weighty influence that foreign affairs have always played on domestic affairs and domestic priorities.

The dominant role played by the Henry Kissingers, the Andrei Gromykos and the Ahmed Zaki Yamanis of the world during the past years, however, outstrips the role that our Founding Fathers had conceived for the Secretary of State. The framers of the United States Constitution carefully fashioned a system based on representative government and a system of checks and balances. What we have been witnessing is a frightening caricature of their vision: a system in which the future not only of the United States but of the whole world is carried in the hip pocket of secretaries of state and foreign ministers. Upon their knowledge, values, bias, tiredness, frustration and emotional balance largely rides the fate of the world. "Madness" is a word that describes such a scenario.

DEPARTMENT OF JUSTICE

Unlike Defense and State, the Justice Department was conceived as a domestically oriented cabinet post. Its goal was to guarantee the observance of laws legislated by Congress. As such, it was to be the guarantor of legal justice—and therefore, presumably, of social justice. Its concern was to be the "inalienable rights" outlined by our Founding Fathers.

Since World War II, however, the Justice Department has gradually moved away from this justice goal to play the role of social controller. Its function has moved toward keeping the lid on a society whose citizens and institutions are swelling with discontent under the pressures of domestic crises left unattended. A whole chapter could be written on the evolution from Franklin D. Roosevelt's wartime concern about "subversive activities" to a cabinet post consumed with domestic political surveillance in the name of national security. It was an evolution whose outlines can be traced within the concerns and policies of the Federal Bureau of Investigation.

The history of the F.B.I. under J. Edgar Hoover spanned the period during which the United States emerged as a world power after World War I, and subsequently rose to its superpower status of today. Hoover's "G-Men" were prime instruments for uncovering spies and saboteurs during World War II. As the old military "feast or famine" cycle developed into a logical and permanent national security mobilization in the postwar world, the F.B.I. continued its zealous role of rooting out "subversives."

The concentration by Mr. Hoover and his agency on the "masters of deceit"[4] was a major influence in the emotional anticommunism that polarized American society in the '50s and '60s. But the negatives did not stop there. With personnel and finances being expended on hunting down "subversives," the essential role of the Justice Department as a guarantor of basic human rights was neglected.

The F.B.I. showed very little interest in protecting the civil rights of blacks or of the whites who gave them support in the upheaval years that followed upon the Supreme Court's order for the desegregation of schools. Upon taking office as Attorney General in 1961, Robert Kennedy found that the F.B.I. hardly admitted the existence of organized crime. Mr. Hoover had considered "foreign agents" as a greater threat than racial segregation or organized crime—and spent the human and material resources of his Bureau accordingly.

This neglect of human rights and domestic priorities, however, did not dominate the top levels of the Justice Department until the advent of antiwar disturbances and the drug culture of the late 1960s. Then, faced with growing criticism and open revolt against national mobilization for the Vietnam War, national security concerns moved beyond the domain of the FBI and the CIA and became a central focus of Justice officials. One result of this new focus was that there was little time or personnel left to enforce civil rights or antitrust legislation, or to attack organized crime at its roots.

Seeing their role through national security glasses resulted in more than a mere limitation of time and personnel, however. Since significant antitrust action could weaken the productive power of corporate empires like I.T.T., whose global networks bring in profits which enhance balance-of-payments figures and assure greater access to scarce resources, the Justice Department closed its eyes to blatant abuses by such firms or undertook only token, ineffective legal action. And, as for organized crime, a Justice Department official publicly labeled it as much less a threat to national security than the antiwar movement, asserting that organized crime is "only" concerned with "personal" selfishness, whereas the New Left was committed to radical social change. In the existent world system, built on a delicate balance of power, any significant institutional change can threaten that balance.

The result has been a Justice Department that is a central partner of the new ruling national security elite. Its role has shifted to include a major focus on *social control* in the midst of civil and social breakdown. The law it enforces is selective—neglecting laws that would lead to any institutional changes that would undermine the ability of the United States to compete in the global arena over military and monetary balances and over scarce resources. Mobilization of society to assure this competition must be maintained at all costs. The name of the game has been "status quo" or "keeping the lid on."

Watergate has not radically changed this national security focus of the Justice Department. Its aftermath exposed how close the nation had been to isolated elite rule, rationalized substantially under the banner of national security. This exposure has put certain limits on the abuses of presidential power, on the F.B.I. and the C.I.A., and on the overall functions of the Justice Department through official and unofficial watchdogging. But these limitations have proved to be minimal. Indeed, some have not been limitations at all, but rather — as evidenced in Gerald Ford's proposals to watch over the intelligence establishments — have served to preserve the ability of the two agencies to operate in secret. And little of substance has changed under Carter.

The short memory of legislators and the public was seen in the case of Daniel Schorr, the CBS correspondent who, in early 1976, presented the official government report on the CIA for publication in the *Village Voice*. The House of Representatives which had performed so admirably in the Watergate affair found its members stumbling over each other to expand the investigation of Schorr's role to a massive investigation of leaks. Part of this embarrassing reversal was rooted in the evident positive response of the general public to Ford's emotional defense of the C.I.A.'s record and his efforts to make criminal acts out of intelligence leaks. Again, the *logic* of national security and its *manipulation* proved to be an unbeatable team.

This powerful duo will remain unbeatable as long as the voters, legislators, cabinet officials and presidents have no viable alternative system before them. Although flagrant "law and order" rhetoric has been severely undercut in the post-Watergate atmosphere, the basic protection of the status-quo order remains a primary working criterion for Justice Department priorities. They are priorities not only for "positive" actions taken against threats to the status quo; just as important are the actions *not* taken:

1. Little was done to bring sanctions against

I.T.T. and the C.I.A. for their clandestine activities to "destabilize" Allende's administration in Chile—an administration which, if successful, could have established a worldwide pattern that would severely undercut U.S. balance-of-payments and scarce-resource viability.

2. Little has been done to effectively curtail bribing of foreign officials by large corporations in search of lucrative contracts—contracts that help the United States resolve its balance-of-payments deficits and retain access to sources of vital primary resources.

3. Little is being done to break the growing centralized and interlocked monopolies of giant economic conglomerates.

In such omissions, the anomaly of the title, Department of "Justice," is revealed. For increasingly, justice is in conflict with the imperatives of national security.

DEPARTMENT OF TREASURY

The Secretary of Treasury's partnership with a national security elite was drawn more fully into public consciousness on August 15, 1971. It was the date that President Nixon announced his New Economic Policy.

The "new economic policy" was, in effect, a unilateral declaration of monetary war. Declaring a "national emergency," Nixon bypassed Congress and acted by executive order to float the dollar, withdraw dollar convertibility into gold and imposed a 10% surcharge on imports. Thereby he would force other nations to adjust their currencies so that the United States could rectify its international payments deficit (which had been a continual problem since the mid-fifties). The president's unilateral action was directed at producing a substantial trade surplus to offset this deficit, regardless of consequences elsewhere in the world and human costs at home.

Present at President Nixon's side at this August 1971 declaration of monetary policy was John Connally, the Secretary of Treasury. Connally's presence was fitting. For he was Nixon's Chief-of-Staff in the new, officially declared monetary war. As such, he now served his commander-in-chief alongside Henry Kissinger, Melvin Laird, and John Mitchell, in the inner circle of the national security establishment. Connally's strategic national security role was as critical as Laird's and Kissinger's, i.e., as critical as that of the two traditional national security departments. For he was entrusted with the strategic balance-of-payments competition upon which the viability of the dollar and of the economy depended. If not resolved, mounting international monetary crises could result in domestic and international tensions capable of carrying humanity into World War III.

The warlike character of Nixon's monetary policy was set against the background of a mounting crisis of international economic competition. Among other things at stake was the viability of the dollar in the world economy. Balance-of-payments deficits had reached the stage where they constituted a serious threat to the nation's economic and monetary institutions. Nixon revealed concern over this security threat in a speech he gave on July 6, 1971.

> As we look ahead five, ten and perhaps fifteen years, we see five great economic superpowers: the United States, Western Europe,

the Soviet Union, Mainland China and Japan.
We face a situation where four other potential
economic powers can challenge us on every
front. And this brings us back home for a
hard look at what we have to do.[5]

What Nixon did "back home" was to turn up the
second national security motor: mobilization for balance-of-payments competition. His declaration of
monetary war was the more dramatic expression of this
mobilization. Following his declaration came a continuing series of less dramatic policies that gave priority to
export industries which could bring monetary reserves
into the country. Subordinated were those industries
and services that do not produce such foreign reserves.
(The emergence of the oil-producing nations as a strategic economic bloc provided an additional dimension
to this warfare, causing further escalation of this mobilization for monetary viability.)

The "warfare" nature of the new economic challenges was evident in the fact that two allies of the
United States—Europe and Japan—were now linked
by Nixon with the two nations that occupied the top
spots on the State Department's "enemies" list. This
linkage revealed more clearly the outline of the National Security State that had been building up since
1948.

Several months after making the above statement
about five economic superpowers, Nixon was involved
with a balance-of-payments confrontation with Japan,
one of the new economic "enemies," over imports of
textiles into the United States. Japan's yen was healthy,
enjoying large foreign reserves. Reports were leaked
out of the White House that, if necessary, Nixon was

ready to invoke the *Trading with the Enemy Act* as the legal authority for imposing textile quotas—a threat he did not have to implement when Japan capitulated.

Nixon's use of executive power to call a national state of emergency and make unilateral decisions in violation of the Bretton Woods agreement was not, as some supposed, the aberration of an ego starved for power. It was the logical conclusion of a man delegated to oversee the national interest. Though they varied on the specifics, the experts were in agreement that something had to be done to protect a floundering U.S. economy. The measures adopted at the Bretton Woods accord in 1944 to prevent economic collapse were obviously not working. Aronson describes the series of events which worried U.S. economists at the time:

> Mountains have been written about the events leading up to the withdrawal of dollar convertibility into gold on August 15, 1971. Clearly the devaluation of the dollar which this action portended was needed. The U.S. balance of payments had been in deficit every year except one (1957) since the early 1950's. European central banks were saturated with dollars and had no desire to accept more. U.S. gold reserves had shrunk from $22.86 billion in January, 1958, to $10.45 billion at the end of July, 1971. Total reserves had plummeted from $24.84 to $13.28 billion during the same period. In May, 1971, a major move from dollars into Deutsche marks, Swiss francs, and Austrian schillings caused the mark to be floated and revaluations of the Swiss franc by 7 percent (its first parity change in 35 years)

and the schilling by 5.05 percent. World market confidence in the dollar began to fail and it appears that the U.S. government had reluctantly concluded that it might eventually have to succumb. In mid-July the Bank of France was forced to intervene to prevent the dollar from falling to its parity floor. Pressure resumed on August 8th when the Treasury announced it would draw $862 million from the IMF for resale to France and Britain and that $200 million in gold would be transferred from the Treasury's domestic stocks to the Exchange Stabilization Fund to cover an unavoidable $191 million sale of the metal to France. The same day the Treasury conceded "serious problems exist" and the International Exchange Subcommittee of the Joint Economic Committee under the gavel of Henry Reuss issued a report which concluded that the dollar was definitely 'overvalued.'

Actually, the banks 'decided' on about August 8th, that barring a major new American initiative the dollar was going to be devalued in the near future. Therefore they began shifting massive amounts of dollars into stronger currencies for their own accounts and for their corporate customers. In the week preceding the devaluation, $2 billion moved into Zurich alone and something close to $5 billion was switched out of the dollar. Never previously had there been such an immense flow, and the European central banks were simply unable to tolerate the pressure. *Bretton Woods died on*

August 15, 1971 and was buried on December 18, 1971 when all efforts at resuscitation had come to nearly naught.[6] (Emphasis added.)

To better understand why the international monetary system designed at Bretton Woods failed and why, as a result, the U.S. (and consequently other countries) felt forced to depart from established principles and undertake unilateral actions to protect their own interests, it may be helpful to briefly review the circumstances leading up to and following from that 1944 accord.

The inadequacy of the international monetary system to deal as effectively as possible with global economic imperatives is underscored in its historical development since World War I. In 1918 the international monetary system lay broken. The major powers were paralyzed; their economic institutions were in disarray, their reserves depleted, and their currencies unstable. The United States was the exception. It had emerged as a global leader. Its people were exhilarated with the excitement of this new role. Confident in American knowhow, morality and economics, they would lead humankind *back* to "normalcy."

It was precisely this look to the *past*, rather than to the future, that contained the seeds for the subsequent collapse of the international monetary system in 1929. Rather than realizing that a new world was in the making (the beginnings of a planetary world whose political and economic configurations would be drastically different), the central banks of the United States and England led the efforts to restore international monetary arrangements according to prewar patterns. Similar to the role it would play a generation later, the United States became the banker for the world. The only difference in this first venture at economic reconstruction was that it was in the hands of private bankers, following Secretary of State Hughes's statement of American policy:

> It is not the policy of our government to make loans to other governments, and the needed capital, if it is to be supplied at all, must be furnished by private organizations.[7]

This post World War I reconstruction of Europe, then, was attempted with only *indirect* government involvement. The American government's role was advisory.

But by 1929, the free market and the profit motive of European industrialists and American bankers proved inadequate to the task. With much of the world now dependent upon American investment and demand, the post-1929 depression had devastating global effects. In the economic chaos that followed, protectionist policies escalated, spurred on in the United States by the long-standing belief that American prosperity depended upon protectionism. Such a protectionist, competitive approach to ensuring economic security for struggling European nations still not recovered from World War I was a major cause of the hostilities and anxieties that led the world into a second world war.

In 1944, as World War II drew toward a close, the Bretton Woods Conference[8] was called to prevent yet another economic collapse and to begin plans toward postwar economic reconstruction. Toward these ends, world leaders called for a "new" international economic framework.

The "new" in the framework developed at Bretton

Woods included a proposal for two new agencies: The International Monetary Fund and the International Bank for Reconstruction and Development. (Both were ratified in 1945 and by 1946 were operative.) They were established to promote international monetary cooperation and trade by: 1.) setting the comparative value and facilitating the purchase of foreign currencies for discharging international debts; 2.) making loans to member nations; and 3.) providing technical assistance in international banking.

Another "new" aspect of the Bretton Woods international monetary framework was that the comparative worth of world currencies would now be pegged to the U.S. dollar, which was tied to gold at the fixed rate of $35 to the ounce. Because it was based on the dollar, this parities principle gave the U.S. an economic advantage. But it also served to spark unprecedented world economic growth—so long as the United States had a strong economy and abundant foreign reserves, and so long as she was *disposed* to assisting other nations in trouble.

Also "new" in this second effort at global economic reconstruction was the *direct* role of government. No longer was the government's role a passive one. Its involvement became overwhelmingly critical to the national security. The zero-lead-time world of global interdependence had dawned. It was a world in which military, economic and monetary policies were intertwined. It was a world of greatly expanded world trade, spurred on by new technologies and the evolution of a global village as marketplace.

But despite the more direct involvement of governments, and the creation of an International Monetary Fund and an International Bank for Reconstruction and Development, the Bretton Woods Conference did not provide a radical departure from status-quo economics. It was still based on a market system in which poorer nations had no voice. Nor was it designed to deal with the complexities of an interdependent world, many aspects of which were not yet clear.

The inadequacies of the old rules—adjusted only minimally by parities and related band-aid procedures —were not immediately evident. The vast gold reserves accumulated by the United States right after World War II permitted it to follow an extensive foreign aid program that was central to its national security strategies. This monetary aid was closely coordinated with the development of a network of military bases and alliances. But these reserves gradually were depleted due to balance-of-payments deficits.

By mid-1971 these growing *payments deficits* (see Table III) threatened the viability of the dollar and, therefore, the monetary security of the United States. The growing seriousness of the problem was also evident in *balance-of-trade* figures which indicated drastic decline for the United States between 1965 and 1972. (See Table IV.)

It was this growing monetary insecurity that prompted Nixon's startling action in August of 1971. Disregarding the Bretton Woods agreements against unilateral action, President Nixon declared monetary war and threw the international monetary system into upheaval. Temporary measures, such as "Special Drawing Rights," remained band-aid responses as a state of confusion and unpredictable outcome moved in. As other measures failed to prevent a series of foreign exchange crises, and when the dollar was further devaluated in February 1973, European nations decided

U.S. Balance of Payments by Area, 1965 and 1972 (in billions of dollars)

	Global[a] 1965	Global[a] 1972	Western Europe 1965	Western Europe 1972	Japan 1965	Japan 1972	Canada 1965	Canada 1972	Developing Countries 1965	Developing Countries 1972
Trade Balance	4.9	−6.8	2.7	−0.6	−0.4	−4.1	0.6	−1.8	1.3	−0.9
Exports	26.4	48.8	8.9	15.0	2.1	5.0	5.4	12.6	8.4	13.9
Imports	−21.5	−55.7	−6.2	15.6	−2.4	−9.1	−4.8	−14.5	−7.2	−14.8
Current Account Balance	4.3	−8.0	1.2	−4.5	−0.4	−4.8	1.4	−0.4	1.5	0.8
Total Long-Term Capital (net)	−6.1	−1.2	−1.3	3.4	−0.1	0.3	−1.4	−1.1	−2.8	−3.3
Private Long-term Capital	−4.6	0.1	−1.2	3.5	−0.1	0.3	−1.4	−1.1	−1.3	−2.2
Basic Balance	−1.8	−9.2	−0.1	−1.1	−0.5	−4.5	0	−1.5	−1.3	−2.4
Official Settlements Balance	−1.3	−10.3	—	—	—	—	—	—	—	—

[a] The global figures cover more regions than are shown in the table.

Source: U.S. Department of Commerce, Survey of Current Business.

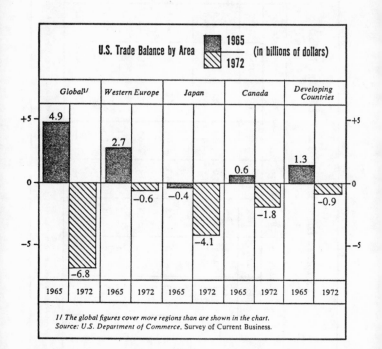

U.S. Trade Balance by Area — 1965 / 1972 (in billions of dollars)

	Global[1]	Western Europe	Japan	Canada	Developing Countries
1965	4.9	2.7	-0.4	0.6	1.3
1972	-6.8	-0.6	-4.1	-1.8	-0.9

1/ The global figures cover more regions than are shown in the chart.
Source: U.S. Department of Commerce, Survey of Current Business.

they had to float the exchange rates on their currencies also.

There was disagreement among experts as to whether the new floating monetary environment would offset further economic crises. In contrast to Milton Friedman, who was a staunch supporter of such moves,[9] Ricardo Arriazu, representing portions of Latin America at the International Monetary Fund, proffered that it did not *avoid* crises, but merely changed crises' characteristics. "Up to now crises took the form of massive movements of reserves, but now they take the form of movement in exchange rates."[10]

Aronson's evaluation supports Arriazu's premise. From an analysis of exchange rates for selected countries of Europe plus Canada and Japan and covering a two-year period from January of 1972 to January of 1974, he concluded:

> The floating system did not seem to adjust quickly to new rates and continued high volatility plagued it. Except for the British pound which gyrated extensively in the latter part of 1972 after it was allowed to float and the Canadian dollar which is inexorably linked to the U.S. dollar in the minds of most exchange dealers, all major currencies showed greater variability after the floating era began than before.[11]

If the floating system that emerged in early 1973 was of dubious merit and could guarantee little monetary security to the industrial nations of Europe, Canada and Japan, it was of even graver concern to the nations of the "developing" world who complained that its "volatility and unpredictability" was "unacceptable for their economies which relied on central planning" and that it allowed "practically no control over their own currency system.[12]

A statement issued in July of 1973 by the Committee for Economic Development (C.E.D.) looked at both positive and negative signs in the sequence of events following Nixon's action and ended up calling for significant reforms in the international monetary system.[13]

Cooperative arrangements have been worked out only under *crisis conditions* and on a *piecemeal basis*. Major questions remain as to whether cooperation will in fact persist or give way to a series of competitive depreciations of major currencies and an uncoordinated proliferation of national controls over trade and capital movements. In the absence of a clear indication that there is fundamental agreement on the rules of the game and a basic willingness to abide by a central authority that will enforce these rules, the danger remains very real that *the world will be moving toward a system of economic warfare among increasingly separated regional trading blocs*.[14] (Emphasis added.)

Just how vulnerable were the temporary gains from parity realignment and floating currencies? And to what extent was the world headed for economic warfare? The answer was soon evident. In the Fall of 1973, just several months after this statement and before its recommendations could be acted upon, the oil crisis rocked the world and threatened further breakdown of global monetary and financial institutions. The monumental power of the Arab oil nations to disrupt the international monetary system dramatically revealed its precarious nature. Holding tens of billions of dollars in monetary reserves gave the oil-producing nations a double instrument of "national economic defense." Their arbitrary shifting of these reserves could disrupt the economies of the industrial world as surely as an arbitrary turning off of the spigots of their oil wells—a reality which dramatically illustrated the fiction of national sovereignty.

If the U.S. and the oil-producing nations could act unilaterally, so might others in the future. The recognition in the U.S. that she might not always be "in the driver's seat" caused some shock waves among her citizens and a resurrection of protectionist attitudes. Instead of undertaking the concerted *global* planning essential to strengthen a world economy, there was even further intensification of the incrementalism and the "uncoordinated profileration of *national* controls over trade" against which the C.E.D. report warned. As a result, global economic warfare escalated.

The world's leaders had still not learned what Emery Reves tried to point out 30 years earlier— "collective security depends on collective sovereignty."[15]

In an obsolete attachment to unlimited national sovereignty and a scientifically untenable attachment to self-sufficiency, we have failed to develop a global authority effective to ensure monetary security for all nations. And therein lies the perpetual nature of the mobilization for economic warfare we are still engaged in.

Without a supranational authority to assure just responses to economic and monetary crises which are

beyond their control, countries *must at all costs* undertake the means available to them to avoid a chronic
deficit in international monetary transactions.

A sustained imbalance of trade in which imports
exceed exports, for example, will deplete a country's
monetary reserves of gold and foreign currency. The
result of such a depletion (as monetary reserves are
used up to offset this trade deficit) would be grave instability of the national currency, exposing a nation's
domestic scene to inflation, unemployment and societal
breakdown. A nation's security, as well as its legitimate
welfare, is involved.

National institutions and resources, therefore,
must be mobilized to produce those types of goods
which will sell on the world market and thus bring
foreign currency into national banks. Government fiscal and monetary policy, as well as government subsidies and investment in research and development, are
increasingly determined by this criterion of global competitiveness. The result is a logical subordination of
domestic priorities to international payments goals.

It is important to stress that the authors are quite
aware that there are *other* reasons besides military,
monetary and resource security imperatives for the lack
of adequate attention to housing, health care, urban renewal and other domestic programs. Volumes have
been written on such reasons, with very few practical
gains coming from the analyses and proposals contained therein. We suggest that a major reason for
these limited gains is that these volumes have not given
adequate attention to these three broad security goals.
They are goals that not only curtail the flow of financial resources toward domestic needs. They also curtail
the creative time and energies needed by national lead-

ers to formulate and implement the moderate and long range planning needed to deal with the interrelated nature of these issues.

The Treasury Department was commissioned to formulate fiscal and monetary policies which would meet such needs of citizens at home. International relations have always had some impact on its policies, but the impact was largely peripheral. But in the new world of the National Security State, these domestic fiscal and monetary policies are substantially determined by forces external to the nation.

A prime example of the effect of global economic warfare on U.S. fiscal and monetary policies was the proposal by President Ford to launch a new government energy facility to expedite energy independence. The proposal, drafted in the wake of the oil crisis under the leadership of Vice-President Rockefeller, included a staggering budget of $100 billion—this at a time when Ford was reiterating in almost every speech across the nation his intent to cut back or veto all legislation related to social services. Although Ford's $100 billion facility was not approved, his commitment to massive expenditures for energy-related industries prevailed. It is a commitment that continues under President Carter.

Ford's goal was clearly stated: "To give us control over our own destiny" by ending "runaway energy prices imposed by foreign nations."[16]

The money for such a facility was proposed in a period when the national budget was already under great duress, ensuring further that housing, education, health care, care of the aged, urban decay and a long litany of other unattended domestic concerns would be further ignored.

The irony is that even if we were to achieve energy independence by mid-1980 (at great cost to the environment and with nuclear contamination a risk still not adequately dealt with), we would still be vulnerable in regard to many other resources for which we rely on other nations. Lester Brown describes this dependency:

> The growing dependence of the United States on imported raw materials is becoming a matter of national concern. Of the 13 basic industrial raw materials required by a modern economy, the United States in 1950 was dependent on imports for more than one-half of its supplies of 4—aluminum, manganese, nickel and tin. By 1970 the list had increased to six as zinc and chromium were added, the latter when its heavily subsidized domestic production was discontinued. Projections by the Department of the Interior indicate that by 1985 the United States will depend on imports for more than one-half of its supplies of nine basic raw materials—as iron, lead and tungsten are added to the list. By the end of the century, our country will depend on foreign sources for more than half of its supply of each of the 13 raw materials except phosphate.[17]

New government agencies to insure "Aluminum Independence," "Manganese Independence," "Nickel Independence" or "Tin Independence" is an impossible absurdity. Even aside from the ethical question of just prices, the United States cannot pragmatically expect to continue obtaining such commodities at the low prices paid in the past to poorer nations.

U.S. Dependence on Imported Minerals — Percentage Imported

	1950	1970	1985*	2000*
Aluminum	64	85	96	98
Chromium	Not Available	100	100	100
Copper	31	0	34	56
Iron	8	30	55	67
Lead	39	31	62	67
Manganese	88	95	100	100
Nickel	94	90	88	89
Phosphate	8	0	0	2
Potassium	14	42	47	61
Sulfur	2	0	28	52
Tin	77	Not Available	100	100
Tungsten	Not Available	50	87	97
Zinc	38	59	72	84

*Projected

Source: *Data are derived from publications of the U.S. Department of the Interior*

As in the area of armaments, it is not only the wealthy, industrial nations that have resorted to monetary and economic warfare in lieu of a global economic security system. The example of immediate gains enjoyed by OPEC nations following their bloc action to increase oil prices is having a significant effect on the non-oil producing nations of the "developing world." Indeed, if they are not to succumb to external economic controls by wealthier nations and if they are to overcome the trade and payments deficits which threaten their economic survival, they have little choice in the present system but to organize in commodity blocs similar to OPEC and—even though their commodities cannot carry the same clout as OPEC's oil—actively move into open warfare from a more favorable position of strength.

It would not only be the Third and Fourth World nations who would benefit from a just and effective international monetary authority. Aside from the fact that strengthened economics in poorer countries means a strengthened global economy, all nations will have new freedoms to respond to unmet domestic needs *if* their monetary security is not being threatened by unilateral actions from external sources over which they have no control, and *if* world economic/monetary structures, based on social justice, provide a stable climate in which long-range planning and development can take place. Whatever insecure "advantages" the rich nations who dominate the monetary scene might have to surrender for the sake of strengthened transnational policy and authority would be well worth the price; i.e., the cost/benefit ratio would be mutually advantageous.

There have been some positive trends toward a transnational monetary authority, including the call for a New International Economic Order with more equitable trade opportunities for poorer nations that was the focus of a special U.N. session. These trends also include the resuming of discussions in Europe toward a common currency and economy, and the January 1976 accord reached in Jamaica on new guidelines for the International Monetary Fund in which the role of gold was reduced and IMF lending terms liberalized to provide greater help to "less developed" countries.

Despite such positive steps, however, there is considerable distance to go before there can be a shift in Treasury Department priorities. The present international monetary system is vulnerable to manipulation by both private business interests (especially the giant conglomerates) and by foreign governments. Thus even should the U.S. be able to overcome current trade deficits (projected at $30 billion for 1977) and alleviate the current-account payments deficit ($8.8 billion for the first half of 1977), the Treasury Department would still have to remain heavily oriented to balance-of-payments competition so as not to lose what could be a mere temporary advantage. This balance-of-payments orientation is maintained at the expense of pressing urban problems and other critical domestic needs. When the question arises as to who will receive government guaranteed loans, U.S. cities in danger of bankruptcy will receive secondary consideration because housing, hospitals, education and urban development are not marketable exports. But private firms, such as Lockheed, who win the United States valuable foreign currencies as well as supply U.S. military needs, will be given priority attention.

DEPARTMENT OF COMMERCE

The full inadequacy of the present monetary system can only be seen by also examining the Treasury Department's special ally: The Department of Commerce. Much of what has been discussed above under Department of Treasury also relates to Department of Commerce, i.e., monetary problems such as balance-of-payments and trade deficits affect the priorities of the Department of Commerce.

The responsibility of the Secretary of Commerce is to formulate those government policies and promote those industries which will assure the economic well-being of American citizens. Whether it has been true to this commitment to citizen interest or, instead, to corporate interests, has always been debated. It is a debate being energized today at a new, nonideological level by consumer advocates like Ralph Nader, Bess Myerson and Carol Foreman.

This new consumer consciousness carries within itself unprecedented opportunities for a dialogue among citizens, professional economists, corporate managers, and government officials—a dialogue that, for the first time, could transcend ideology. But as with other aspects of our domestic scene, those with the power among government elites are so consumed with national security priorities they have little time left for creative input into such a dialogue. And they fear that changes resulting from this growing consumer consciousness might threaten the ability of American industries and institutions to mobilize for such priorities.

For reasons already given, this fear cannot be dismissed simply as a rationalization of those who wish to retain privileged and wealthy status. For in today's world system, nations perceive that national survival in military, monetary and resource competition depends upon *corporate* power. Person-centered and decentralized models of economic development such as those promoted by E. F. Schumacher in *Small is Beautiful*[18] cannot assure the nation the same volume and sophistication of production that is guaranteed by large corporations. They lack the financing, the sophisticated technologies and the capacity for such production. Nor can they guarantee the rapid national and global processing and marketing of production needed for military, monetary and resource goals.

Because of this national need for *aggregate* power, it should not be surprising (even if lamentable) that the Department of Commerce has not been giving priority attention to the expansion of small businesses and industries. Instead priority is given to the needs of U.S. corporations that can produce computers, grains, armaments and other goods in large quantities for sale and consumption overseas. Overseas markets (and therefore overseas alliances, regardless of whether they are made with repressive regimes of the right or left) are given a top priority because of their multiple strategic importance for national security objectives. Subsidies are provided corporations that can guarantee: 1.) weapons for foreign as well as U.S. military establishments, 2.) foreign reserves for the U.S. Treasury and, 3.) scarce resources for U.S. industries. Large corporations are also provided loan guarantees, though similar guarantees are denied municipalities and industries seeking to respond to unmet social needs.

The case of Lockheed is an example of the government favoritism shown large corporations. While small concerns go out of business every year by the thousands for lack of capital loans, a large corporation such as Lockheed (which can produce weapons and foreign reserves) was bailed out of financial difficulties by a Federal guarantee on loans totalling $250 million. This was in addition to special Federal research and development grants that enabled Lockheed to test and develop new products. Special tax incentives are also available to such national security-related corporations.

The reasons for such preferential treatment cannot be ascribed *only* to political contributions or kickbacks. *Export* sales from the purchase of U.S. armaments by foreign governments totalled $12 billion for one year alone in 1976. Not only do such armaments exports do "wonders" for the U.S. balance of payments; they preserve the so-called balance of power by arming allies and help assure relationships with countries that have resources vital to the U.S. economy. Looked at in these terms, the viability of Lockheed is integrally related to all three areas of national security competition.

But it is not only the armaments industries that are given preferential treatment, but also other security-related enterprises such as agribusiness, energy, communications, etc.

It is such preferential treatment for security-related corporations that gives rise to assertions that the United States is moving into a "socialism for the rich and a capitalism for the poor." While government subsidies (direct and indirect) and outright expenditures to sustain large corporations have been on the rise, industries and service programs related to human needs such as housing, urban renewal, education, care of the elderly, drug rehabilitation, etc., have been cut back.

In the present nation-state system, the Secretary of Commerce does not have substantial freedom to promote person-centered, service-oriented commerce. Not that the Secretary's hands are totally tied. Should

Common Cause, the Consumer Federation of America and other consumer advocacy groups ever develop the national political clout to elect a President who would appoint a Secretary of Commerce devoted to consumer needs, some changes could be expected. But even in such a scenario, the head of the Commerce Department would still be constrained by national security imperatives.

DEPARTMENT OF AGRICULTURE

When Harry Truman first received word from Alamogordo, New Mexico, that the atomic bomb had been successfully tested, he exulted that he now had "a hammer on those boys." Those boys, of course, were the leaders of the Soviet Union.

In a similar vein, Secretary of Agriculture Butz said that the food reserves of the United States were a powerful weapon in America's diplomatic arsenal. His "food is power" formulations came in the Fall of 1974 as the world's attention was on the U.N. Food Conference in Rome.

The context of Butz's remarks was clear enough. A year earlier, in 1973, the OPEC nations had unleashed *their* diplomatic weapon. OPEC's oil embargo had rocked the world. Now it was *our* turn. The parallel is real. Thanks to the bountiful fields of its Midwest and to technology, the United States possesses a larger percentage of the world's exportable grains than the OPEC countries possess of the world's exportable oil.

Butz's remarks created shock waves among peoples of the world who were wrestling with the problem of widespread hunger and growing areas of actual famine. His comments stood in stark contrast to the concerns and principles being expressed by planners and consultants for the World Food Conference. Central to this planning was a proposal for a *World Food Authority* with adequate empowerment to develop a world food bank and to bring about a more equitable distribution of the most vital of all scarce resources.

The widespread indignation expressed at Butz's remarks was not surprising—especially as a central issue being discussed was the inalienable "right to food" which flows out of the principle of the "right to life." What was being challenged in this discussion of a basic human right was the historical assumption that food was a market *commodity*, economically similar to commodities such as coal, oil and gold.

Butz's remarks were unfortunate; and in the moral context being formulated around the World Food Conference they defended an unjust "world order." But operative beneath his remarks—and apart from his quite evident advocacy of the financial interests of U.S. agribusiness—was the imperative of national security in all three areas: balance of weapons, balance of payments and scarce resources.

That the Department of Agriculture has a national security role related to competition over armaments was evidenced in the massive grain sales to the Soviet Union. A principal rationale for these sales was detente. U.S. grain surpluses, especially of wheat, became a strategic instrument for lessening tensions between the United States and the Soviet Union. Lacking effective world law to provide security against possible nuclear confrontation, policy makers embraced detente as a priority value to be vigorously pursued. Other values, e.g., economic justice for the hungry of the world, were subordinated.

Competition over *balance of payments* was another rubric and one of the most critical factors in the Soviet grain deals. The export of food, especially of grains, ranks as a prime source of the vital foreign reserves that the United States needs to offset its balance-of-payments deficits. In defending these grain exports, Butz wrote:

> Agricultural exports, which have become this nation's major source of foreign exchange, grew from less than $6 billion in 1969 to nearly $22 billion in the fiscal year which ended June 30, 1975. This strengthened the dollar at a time it desperately needed it. . . .[19]

Competition over *scarce resources* was a third rubric under which the Soviet Union was given a priority claim on grain exports from the United States. State Department officials envisioned the sale of wheat to the USSR as leverage in reaching agreement about the U.S. purchase of Soviet oil. Not only would such oil imports lessen U.S. dependence upon OPEC oil. The United States also sought price advantages for the purchase of Soviet oil which they hoped would be lower than OPEC prices. It was expected that such lowered prices could be arranged under the banner of detente. Such a price victory would undercut the global economic and monetary power wielded by OPEC nations.

Hard-line anticommunists were not alone in their opposition to the Soviet wheat sales. Also opposed were three other groups: persons concerned about the added inflationary pressures that these sales put on domestic food prices; persons who wanted U.S. policy-makers to put pressure on Soviet leaders to loosen their restrictive internal policies; and persons who argued that such wheat should be made available to the hungry and starving in Asia, Africa and Latin America.

What was especially galling for some of these groups was an aspect of the Soviet demand for more grain not widely understood. The grain that the Soviet Union was purchasing from the United States was not going to feed undernourished Soviet citizens. Rather, the increased demand was due to a phenomenal increase of Soviet citizens clamoring for more beef in their diet: the grain imports met the increased need for cattle feed.

Persons concerned with inflationary pressures on food could accept higher prices more easily if the grain exports were being used for feeding the world's hungry. But because of the inability of the Fourth World countries to come up with the foreign reserves that could compete with Soviet reserves, the grains were sold to fatten Soviet livestock.

One alternative would have been for the United States to make American grain available to the world's hungry through foreign aid programs, either through direct aid or by making special concessions in lower prices to poor countries. This latter could have been achieved without burdening U.S. farmers if equitable government subsidies were arranged.

The successful leadership of the U.S. government in adopting the Marshall plan to respond to the plight of Europe following World War II is an historic precedent for the kind of concern and humanitarian response to global hunger that the U.S. was once capable of. In 1947, following the rallying call of Harry Truman and other government leaders, U.S. citizens observed one meatless day a week, cattle producers' grass fed their cattle, and distillery production of grain-based alcoholic beverages was cut back—all to save precious grains for a hungry Europe. The response was so successful that more than three million extra tons of grain were made available within three months—enough to feed sixty million people and help Europe get back on its feet.

In contrast, recent government leadership in response to world hunger has been almost nil. This is not a matter only of conservative politics or selfishness. Rather, grave preoccupation about balance-of-payments competition was also involved. The balance-of-payment deficits that have plagued the United States ever since the Bretton Woods monetary institutions began to break down under the pressures of global interdependence are causing more humanitarian alternatives to be shelved by our national leadership in favor of economic survival policies and other national security considerations.

Not that food is new as an instrument of U.S. national security diplomacy. Even before foreign food aid was undercut by the problem of balance-of-payments deficits, food had been envisioned as a strategic instrument of U.S. national security policy. Those nations that supported and assisted our national security goals and policies received food. Those that did not were denied such aid or were pressured to change their position. The use of the "Food for Peace" program by the United States to pursue its Indochina war objectives bore witness to the emerging national security role of the Department of Agriculture. But what has changed is the degree and open intensity to which food has come to be employed as an instrument of national security.

A replacement of the person who sits as Secretary of Agriculture at any particular time cannot be expected realistically to result in removing food from the list of strategic instruments of national security policy. Nor is there much hope that the principle of an "inalienable right to food" will become a criterion for public policy unless more explicit steps are taken to develop an effective world order.

Until such steps are taken, the food surplus of the United States will continue to be utilized as a "hammer on those boys" who disagree with our foreign policy.

Fortunately, the conceptualization at Rome of a *World Food Authority* was an important first step, even if only haltingly taken. What this embryonic world order institution needs now is true functional authority. The mandate for such a Food Authority will constitute important progress toward the *global security system* that can loosen the straitjacket imposed by the National Security State system.

Such progress, however, will not be made in isolation of other related developments. Progress toward a more just world order will occur to the degree that an agency such as a World Food Authority is developed as one aspect of a total growth process in which other world order agencies—e.g., a World Seabed Authority, a World Environmental Authority, a World Monetary Authority, a World Disarmament Authority—are developed in concert, all having the appropriate authority to deal with specific global problems that individual nations cannot handle alone. Such a global security system, which will be explored more fully in chapter nine, would eliminate the logic utilized by nations aspiring to apply a "hammer" to other nations.

BEYOND INCREMENTALISM

Political scientists speak of "incremental" policy. It is a concept used to defend decision-making patterns as "pragmatic," i.e., to separate the "wise" from the "idealists." Yet its bankruptcy as an adequate policy framework is evident in the multiplication of personal and institutional crises confronting us on every side.

Charles Lindblom describes incrementalism as a framework in which policy analysts identify situations or ills from which to move *away* rather than goals *toward* which to move.[20] A feature of incrementalism is that only those policy choices are considered whose consequences differ *marginally* (i.e., incrementally) from the status quo. No comprehensive evaluation of societies is permitted; only marginal or incremental differences are considered.

This goalless and value-barren policy framework should not surprise anyone. At least it should be of no surprise to those who comprehend the structural mobilization for interstate competition that ties the hands of national policy makers in every nation. For the bankruptcy of this policy framework is *structural*. A change of governing parties would only be able to make marginal adjustments in present security policies. Harold Lasswell spoke to this point when he said that "limited catharsis has often been obtained by railing at the stupidity or malevolence of world elites for failing to bring the current nightmare to a peaceful end."[21]

It would be different if individual nations existed in a vacuum, each a separate planet. A comprehensive evaluation of social institutions would then be possible. The logjam that currently blocks human development could then be broken. Consider the scenario of such a nonexistent world.

1. Pressures to compete over weapons technology and international monetary balances would not exist.
2. Our leaders, therefore, would no longer have to

mobilize large segments of their time and of the nation's human and material resources away from person-centered and domestic priorities.

3. Giant conglomerates like International Telephone and Telegraph would no longer merit billions for subsidies for national security research, development and production, and thus would lose a primary rationale for receiving Justice Department approval of their expanding size and power over national and international affairs.

4. Ideology and demonology would no longer be necessary to silence dissent over existing institutional injustices and to assure the continuation of national security mobilization.

5. We could expect a diminution of the polarization that results from such a defusion of ideology and demonology.

6. Another result would be that present unjust institutions and dehumanizing corporate policies would no longer be able to hide behind national security rhetoric. (For example, advocates of economic liberalism have successfully obstructed social justice by using national security ideology to block social legislation such as universal health service by simply labeling such legislation "socialist"; thereby confusing an issue of basic inalienable rights with a historic *nation-state* conflict with the Soviet Union.)

7. The President would have the time, energy and psychological and political freedom to provide the true statesmanship needed to help the American people analyze root causes of their alienation and frustration and then to move to-

ward the complex but possible task of developing institutions commensurate with the challenges of our future-shock, interdependent world.

As is evident, the key to this scenario is factor number one above. In our present nation-state system, no national leader can be free from the outside pressures to compete over weaponry technology, international monetary balances and scarce resources. Because we cannot move the United States to another planet, the only alternative by which such national security pressures can be reduced is through effective world law.

Here lies the central dilemma of the presidency— and of national leaders of other countries, all of which are also caught in the web of the national security system. Heads of states now have no choice but to follow the dead-end road of incrementalism. The majority of their policies are determined by national security goals —directly or indirectly. Such goals are opposed to integrated, long-range planning for human development. The unpredictability of the global arena permits only short-range crisis responses.

THE NATIONAL SECURITY PRESIDENCY

The powerlessness of the above six national security departments to achieve their constitutionally commissioned tasks—i.e., to facilitate the security and wellbeing of U.S. citizens—does not mean that their chiefs are totally powerless. Quite the contrary! Like the president, and through his authority, the secretaries of these departments each wield great power as part of the national security elite that is largely determining (directly and indirectly) the priorities of suburban Los Angeles, rural Minnesota and urban New York City. As part of the presidency, they share the power as well as the powerlessness of the presidency. The converse is also true: their dilemma is the president's dilemma.

The president of the United States is too consumed with national security issues to have much time or energy left to lead the American people in the task of designing institutions capable of giving human control to our runaway world, let alone of implementing that design. One prior problem, of course, is that presidential commitments to national security are often in opposition to such a design. Our concern here, however, goes beyond that opposition. It is a concern with the president's lack of human energy, time and creativity to mobilize national talents and resources to develop new approaches, new structures and new attitudes commensurate with the problems and opportunities of an interdependent, future-shock world.

The task of humanizing priorities in our technological society is immense. It requires the constant attention of the nation's best scientific and moral leadership. Part of the design is to create a national climate of trust, openness and hope. For much more is needed than abstract institutional blueprints. The scenario of such a task cannot be a static, predetermined design. It must be a dynamic process, constantly integrating projected options with the existential reality of any given time and place. And it must be placed within a *macro* frame of global interdependence.

We cannot expect such creative planning and initiative to come from the presidency given the existent national security imperatives. Nor can we expect it to come from another sector of society without close support and involvement from the presidency. For much of the power of the National Security State finds its focal point in the presidency. It is a mistake to believe that America can reorder priorities and humanize its agenda without ultimate participation by the president and the president's cabinet members and advisors. This, of course, is not to say that the energy and basic leadership cannot come from an enlightened citizen movement that comprehends that national interest is now synonymous with the human interest on a world scale and can thus convince the president and Congress that "the people are ready."

Such citizen support of effective world order agencies is essential to remove the existent national security straitjacket that frustrates the creative planning for, and realization of, domestic needs. And winning such popular support is dependent upon convincing people that the creation of a just world order is not only a fine ideal, but pragmatically integral to our self-interest and well-being.

6

The Soviet Security State

> Under this lies a fact never mentioned, but
> tacitly understood and acted upon: namely,
> the conditions of life in all three superstates
> are very much the same . . . . the same econ-
> omy existing by and for continuous warfare.
>
> George Orwell, *1984*

The world view that divides the world along ideological lines into the forces of capitalism pitted against
the forces of socialism, though still popularly held, is a
contemporary anachronism. It has outlived its useful-
ness to help us deal effectively with existent problems
or to chart our future course, either as individual nations or as an interdependent world community. Ideological differences, real as they may be, are of secondary concern when placed alongside the national security imperatives that individual nation-states hold in
common.

The global convergence in domination by the National Security State is a central characteristic of our
era. It is a characteristic marking the development of
the Soviet Union no less than that of the United States.

It is a characteristic prophesied by Emery Reves
more than thirty years ago when he wrote:

> It might advance a dispassionate approach to
> the sterile and now centuries-old controversy

if the champions of capitalism and socialism would realize that they are fighting each other in a hermetically sealed conveyance. The fight for a better seat, for a broader view, for a little more comfort is rather meaningless, as they are being carried by it relentlessly toward the same terminus. The vehicle is nationalism. The terminus is totalitarianism.[1]

THE MARXIST VISION AND THE FAILURE
OF A PROMISE

Both the Soviet Union and the United States began their experiments with a dream and a promise toward which to strive. While the emphasis in the Jeffersonian dream was on political justice, the emphasis in the Marxist dream was on economic justice. But the vision for both was a humanizing, person-centered society freed from the old oppressions that had alienated persons by treating them as objects rather than as subjects with the capacity and right to determine their own destiny.

There is a major difference between Karl Marx's vision of a humanistic, person-centered and nonalienating society and the reality that has historically developed in the Soviet Union.

Marx's view of human nature was not collectivist. On the contrary. His starting point was that *human destiny is to be free.* To be free, for Marx, meant to have the ability to determine one's own actions *from within.* To the degree that one's actions are determined by forces external to one's person, an individual is alienated. Thus, Marx shared the same central concern about individual personal sovereignty that has traditionally preoccupied conservatives.

As a personalist who saw human sovereignty trammeled by three external alienating forces—the state, economics, and religion—Marx sought to fashion the outlines of a process and society in which personal self-determination would one day be possible. Unfortunately, his socialist framework to overcome this triple alienation never adequately dealt with the question of national sovereignty. It failed to provide for the shoals of the nation-state system. In the twentieth century, the sovereignty of the individual—the underlying motivation of Marx's commitment to "communism"—would be run aground by the *sovereignty of the nation-state*. This abortion of his quest for human centrality is evident in the experience of the Soviet Union.

THE SOVIET SECURITY IMPERATIVE

The development of Soviet totalitarianism is historically rooted (in great measure, but not completely) in the structural imperatives of independent, sovereign states, each caught up in a struggle for survival and security. These imperatives have precluded significant progress toward the person-centered society that Marx had envisioned.

Right from the onset in 1917, Lenin was prevented from implementing whatever humanist vision he may have shared with Marx. On one hand, he had to mobilize men, institutions and resources to fight British, French, American and Japanese expeditionary forces who were part of the "White Army" overrunning Soviet soil until 1921. On the other, he was faced with a demoralized and fragmented nation, whose economy was broken and institutions paralyzed. Economic boycotts by the major capitalist nations contributed to this economic debilitation. Both factors made the development of a strong collective corporate society an absolute necessity—quite apart from any socialist ideology or from any personal aberrations and ruthlessness—if Russia was to survive.

A condition for survival was social discipline and cohesion. They were conditions that, in Russia's situation, could only come through a highly centralized and stern regime. The liberal democratic effort of Alexander Kerensky's government, since March 1917, had resulted in division rather than even an elementary beginning of cooperation. It was a divisiveness leading to violence and governmental breakdown. The discipline and basic social unity that enabled the United States, England and other Western European democracies to develop effective and stable governments do not suddenly blossom overnight. Russia was the first of many countries—from Italy, Germany and Spain to many of the countries of Africa, Asia and Latin America today —that did not have the time for developing the unity and social discipline that enabled the Western democracies to restrain political freedom from degenerating into license.

Lacking that social cohesion, the Bolshevik regime that picked up the pieces had to artificially create it. In his book, *Why Lenin? Why Stalin?*, Theodore Von Laue says that "after the July days, the sole question of Russian domestic politics was whether the heir of autocracy would be a dictator of the right or the left."[2] On the right, General Kornilov was convinced that Russia could be saved from Germany and disintegration only through a military dictatorship. But his coup failed, giving the special impetus the Bolsheviks needed. In November, the government of "Soviet Russia" took power.

Aware of the chaotic alternatives, we can understand why Lenin's regime began to flex its muscle. Van Laue writes: "If Russia was to survive as a Great Power, with the same universal appeal as the others— these were the harsh terms of the competition—it need- ed the discipline of cooperation under both government and an industrial economy."[3]

Von Laue then directs our attention to powerful national security imperatives which short-circuited any hopes for a Marxist-Socialist society in which human priorities and personal sovereignty could be permitted:

> Here lay the central quandary of modern Rus- sia. It was a backward country at the mercy of powerful neighbors. The essence of its backwardness rested in the fact that its peo- ple, left to their own devices, could manage neither effective government nor a productive modern economy. Was the Russian empire then to be dissolved? For the Bolsheviks, at any rate, and many non-Bolsheviks as well, the answer was a passionate NO . . . thus from November, 1917, onward *the suppres- sion of spontaneity began anew*, slowly at first under Lenin, furiously at last under Stalin. The new harness of Communist rule proved to be far tighter than the Tsarist one. *The dangers to the country were greater*, the ambi- tions of its rulers bolder, *and the progress of the "advanced" countries undiminished; they would not mark time while Soviet Russia tried to catch up*.[4] (Emphasis added.)

Thus, a powerful, centralized rule was a logical necessity, quite apart from ideology and from Lenin's personal proclivity to terrorist politics. There was little alternative, outside of a world order of global security institutions which were not then on the immediate horizon. If the U.S.S.R. was to survive in the hostile international environment of military and economic conflict, Lenin *had* to establish firm national security goals and use strong means to mobilize Russian society to achieve them. This is not to gloss over Lenin's use of terror as a means of overcoming internal opposition. Nor do we wish to downplay the influence of the "dictatorship of the proletariat." Lenin's concept of what a Russian Social Democratic Party should be was drastically opposed to the liberal, humanitarian perspective of Marx. As early as 1903, Trotsky accurately predicted what would happen if Lenin's views prevailed:

> The organization of the party takes the place of the party itself; the central committee takes the place of the organization, and finally, the dictator takes the place of the central committee.[5]

Quite apart from Lenin's terror and his concept of political organization, however, the logic of national security mobilization was powerfully operative. It has been consistently the dominant force behind Soviet corporate society and elite rule even up to our present time.

Von Laue makes this point by the very title of his book: *Why Lenin? Why Stalin?* His central thesis is that if these two men—Vladimir Ilyich Ulianov and Josef Stalin—had been two other men occupying the same roles and positions, the essential dimensions of Soviet corporate elite rule during those years would not have been substantially different. Less Terror? Yes! Less *personal* ruthlessness? Yes! Less *institutional* ruthlessness (to the degree that such a distinction could be researched)? Relatively little.

With two other men (or women) in charge, the logic of national security mobilization would have remained. The given in this scenario, of course, is the assumption that our speculative "other" two leaders would have embraced socialist goals which ideologically challenged the capitalist world strongly enough to elicit the latter's military and economic opposition. (After World War II, the imperatives of an interdependent but fragmented world would give priority to the logic of national security *regardless* of whether such an external ideological challenge did or did not exist—a point we will explore further later.)

AN ESCAPE FROM BACKWARDNESS

Given the imperatives of Soviet survival in a hostile and competitive global arena, Lenin's successor, whoever he might have been, *had* to continue developing the nation along strong corporate goals. It was in this quest for national survival that Stalin committed the Communist Party in 1928 "to be responsible for the escape from backwardness." It was to be an escape along a road in which Marx's personalist revolution (i.e., individual self-determination) would be shelved for the duration. Ironically, it was a road which pressed toward the very limited "homo economicus" that Marx so deplored in Western capitalism.

Stalin presented the urgency of this road for the Soviet Union in an impassioned and famous speech given in 1931:

One feature of the history of old Russia was

the continual beatings she suffered for falling behind, for her backwardness. She was beaten by the Mongol Khans. She was beaten by the Turkish beys. She was beaten by the French and British capitalists. She was beaten by the Japanese barons. *All beat her—for backwardness*, for military backwardness, for cultural backwardness, for political backwardness, for industrial backwardness, for agricultural backwardness. She was beaten because to beat her was profitable and went unpunished. . . . In the past we had no fatherland and could have none. Now, however, that we have overthrown capitalism and the workers wield power in our country, we have a fatherland and shall defend its independence.[6] (Emphasis added.)

Then comes a central rationale for totalitarian rule and centralized mobilization of the "New Russia's" economy and peoples.

Do you want our Socialist fatherland to be beaten and to lose its independence? If you do not want that, then you must abolish its backwardness and develop a really Bolshevik pace in the establishment of its Socialist economy. . . . We are fifty or a hundred years behind the advanced countries. Either we accomplish this or we will be crushed.[7] (Emphasis added.)

It was primarily national security imperatives, not Marxist-socialist principles, that motivated Stalin's "great leap forward." Stalin's effort was an attempt to bridge a half-century gap in a decade—a national security goal never envisioned by Karl Marx.

U.S. postwar leaders did not adequately recognize (or want to admit) this national survival thrust in Stalin's foreign policy. Missing the insecurity behind Stalin's postwar belligerence, they too facilely attributed Soviet policy to communist ideology and Stalin's mania for power. The holy crusade atmosphere of the Cold War resulted—a demonological atmosphere that divided good guys from bad guys, instead of recognizing the common national security goals that ultimately motored both sides.

BEYOND IDEOLOGY

Von Laue comments that Soviet citizens were hounded with the "dire choice between advance or extinction, familiar in imperialist rhetoric from Disraeli to Hitler."[8] With the additional historical perspective of more than a decade since he wrote his book, we can today add to Von Laue's list of leaders espousing "advance or extinction" rhetoric. The new listing would include not only the proclamations of Stalin's successors, but also those of John Kennedy, Lyndon Johnson, Richard Nixon, Gerald Ford and James Carter. All gave priority to being "number one" under the rationale of national security. All "advance or extinction" scenarios tend to be effective — even when manipulative — because they are built on logical need for security in a very insecure system.

It is within this context of national security mobilization that the important revelations of Aleksandr Solzhenitsyn's *The Gulag Archipelago* must be read. The mistake for Soviet and American readers alike would be to attribute the centralized, police-state character of Soviet society as described in the *Gulag* to Marxist ideology. Solzhenitsyn's pain and compassion were forged in Soviet prison camps and subsequent clandestine struggles. Understandably, he is deeply aware and concerned about the existent reality of citizen powerlessness. But this subjective account from personal experience and observation does not encompass the totality of the problem. It does not raise the full question of *why*—a question as important as *what*. The Nobel Laureate's conclusion that the secret police have been a vital element of the Soviet regime since its founding by Lenin, that they were not first created by Stalin during the purge period of the 1930s, that the use of police terror and lawless repression began with the seizure of power by Lenin, does not contradict our identification of the National Security State that Lenin was compelled to establish right from the start. Nor does it contradict what was a manipulated internal power struggle over who would forge the new society. Solzhenitsyn's conclusions help to document a reality that was rooted more deeply than merely in the *personal* ruthlessness of Lenin and Stalin or in the deficiencies in communist ideology.

To smugly read *The Gulag Archipelago* as a definitive defense of U.S. foreign and domestic policy vis-a-vis the Soviet Union is a premature, self-defeating exercise. It not only precludes an alternative future scenario in which Soviet society could substantially replace present national security priorities with person-centered values and policies. It also obstructs an objective *macro*-analysis of the National Security State that is emerging in the United States.

Nearly a century before the Bolshevik victory, Alexis de Tocqueville predicted that the twentieth century would be dominated by two superpowers—Russia and the United States. The context for his prediction was the logic of nation-state power which he recognized in three power factors which the two countries both had:

1. Expansive territory rich in natural resources.
2. Large population committed to hard work.
3. The potential of national unity and political organization needed to mobilize their resources and people for common national goals.

The accuracy of de Tocqueville's prediction was vividly clear by the mid-twentieth century.

Thanks to its long isolation as Fortress America, the United States was able to arrive at the destined role foreseen by de Tocqueville through the route of democratic processes. Wide oceans served to permit the Jeffersonian experiment to blossom. It also permitted a "rugged individualism" form of free enterprise capitalism to thrive, unrestricted by the national security imperatives which characterized the capitalism of the "Old World."

Able to escape the physical, economic, social and psychic devastation of two world wars; transformed into the premier world economic power through its role as the "Arsenal of Democracy"; and possessing the "nuclear hammer," the United States by 1945 was at the pinnacle of her power and freedom. Her citizens, believing that the "duration" of sacrifice that marked the war years was over, and that "the lights were on again," looked forward with expectancy (falsely based as it turned out) to a new level of humanistic priorities.

In contrast, by 1945 the Soviet Union had already been constricted for nearly forty years in the straitjacket of the National Security State. Her rise to the superpower status predicted by de Tocqueville had not come primarily from the ideology or strategies of communism. Nor from Stalin's terror or personal ruthlessness. (Indeed, scholars of Soviet history have shown that Stalin's purges were a major factor permitting Hitler's troops to so easily overrun the Soviet army during the original invasion of Soviet territory. His purges had wiped out strategic leadership in governmental and military ranks.) *More than anything else, what brought the Soviet Union to its superpower status was its national security mobilization goals and strategies.*

De Tocqueville's geo-political framework helps us see that the fundamental conflict between the Soviet Union and the United States is not ideological. Their central conflict is rather a conflict between two superpowers who, with no recourse to a global security system, have little choice but to preclude humanistic personalist goals from their national agendas in favor of national security goals.

To say this is not to deny the ideological differences between the two giants. Ideology remains a strong cause of antagonism. But not all such antagonism is based on ideology. A great deal of it is based on the historical realities of the past sixty years—realities that have substantially changed on both sides. Some of the antagonism is the product of hard-line ideologues who have readily twisted and exaggerated deficiencies of both systems. Old Cold Warriors on both sides still wield power, preventing younger leadership from effectively voicing more moderate views regarding not only their own system but also the system and motives of their chief capitalist antagonist.

TOWARD PRAGMATIC CONVERGENCE?

The voices of the nonideologues, however, are increasing. Alexander Yanov, who emigrated from the Soviet Union in 1974, speaks of a new Soviet managerial class who, though presently relatively silent, constitute a "real mass opposition to the present Soviet regime."

> At the same time, a new generation of managers has come to leadership positions in the Soviet economy, unterrorized by the punitive machine and possessing a kind of inherent sense of economic initiative, as natural to them as breathing.

> Here we have a conflict that develops turbulently between a stagnating, unnaturally centralized economy and a new social stratum of managers, intensely interested in progress.[9]

The last phrase is important: "intensely interested in progress." Obsolete ideological emphasis on highly centralized planning is an albatross around Soviet efforts to achieve goals of economic planning. Perhaps more than anything else, it explains Soviet failure in agricultural production. There is increasing pragmatic pressure to add "capitalist" incentives in agricultural and industrial production, and to decentralize economic planning and production processes. Ideological baggage from Lenin's founding father's bible still remains strong. But its influence is slowly being eroded by the type of pragmatism outlined by Yanov:

> They believe that the only way out of stagnation presumes a total reconstruction of the economy without placing economic limita-

tions on otherwise unlimited power, and presumes cooperation with western capital and
western thought. It *presumes detente*. . . .
Detente is as natural for this stratum [of man-
agers] as the "Iron Curtain" was for the slave-
holders of Gulag.[10]

Such reconstruction won't happen overnight. And
as it does take place, it will not be total. But significant
reconstruction is inevitable. How fast it comes will partially be determined by the attitudes and policies of the
United States and of China (the budding superpower
which de Tocqueville did not foresee).

One factor in the Soviet Union's present inflex-
ibility is the presence of an old guard in Soviet decision-
making circles who—besides being convinced by Stalin's "advance or extinction" scenario—were also deeply formed in Leninist-Stalinist ideology. Theirs was an
ideological formation achieved in a Stalinist society
that was isolated from the rest of the world. This formation also took place in the context of a collapsed
capitalist economic-political system, devastated by the
Great Depression. Whereas the formation of the new
managers described by Yanov took place in a substantially different context.

As this old guard dies out, one can expect more developments along the lines proposed by Yanov. Yet,
even then the change will not be sudden. For two gen-
erations of Soviet citizens have been taught to believe
that ideology was the primary reason for the highly
centralized nature of Soviet economic life. Their ideological indoctrination was based on the theory of inevitable historical forces which would assume eventual
success in achieving the revolution's collectivized

economic goals. A too-sudden admission, by a reversal of present collectivized economic processes, that ideology is not central to Soviet life and that the dominant factor in Soviet mobilization is nation-state confrontation, could have a profound debilitating effect on the morale and self-image of Soviet society.

U.S. citizens are still suffering from the collapse of their self-image as a uniquely destined and moral people. This collapse, however, is minimal when compared to what could be expected in the Soviet Union if the mystique of Soviet Communism and of its founding fathers were too suddenly replaced by the imperatives of pragmatism.

Members of the Soviet Politburo are an aging group—their average age is nearing seventy. They also are a homogeneous group. At this writing, all but two of the present sixteen members have been educated as *technicians*. Only one is an economist. (The other non-technician is a historian.) The criterion for membership is a pragmatic one—that of being able to achieve production goals. A complicating factor, however, has been the national-security confrontation with China that effectively utilizes ideology to put down Soviet influence in the "developing" world.

In accusing the Soviet Union of "revisionism," of being a tool of capitalism, of abandoning the world socialist revolution, and of being part of the industrial North which oppresses the agrarian South, the Chinese have put strong political pressure on Soviet leaders. This pressure to stay in ideological line constrains the pragmatic move toward greater market incentives promoted by Yanov and others.

Pressures against "revisionism" also come from the Soviet military. Like U.S. military leaders, ideology gives them an effective instrument in keeping military budgets the top domestic priority. Because arms production is not affected by supply or demand, or by market incentives in the Soviet Union, the market incentives proposed by the new managers have little pragmatic attractiveness to the Soviet military establishment. Also, China again constitutes a conservative factor in the stand of the military. Confronted with the responsibility of not only maintaining nuclear equivalency with the United States, but also with the antagonism and growing military might of China, with whom the U.S.S.R. shares a 4,000-mile border, military leaders oppose any "revisionism" that might weaken the mobilization and resolve of Soviet citizens.

In his essay, "Power and Ideology in International Politics,"[11] Hans Morgenthau speaks of the role of ideology in international politics. Ideological justifications and rationalizations are easily used to conceal the true nature of power policy. Morgenthau argues that it is the very nature of politics to compel national leaders to use ideologies in order to disguise immediate goals of their actions. The more removed from the struggle for power, the less likely are persons to deceive themselves by ideology. Thus the new breed of Soviet managers is less likely to succumb to the delusion described by John Adams two centuries ago: "Power always thinks it has a great soul and vast views beyond the comprehension of the weak and that it is doing God's service when it is violating all his Laws."[12]

Morgenthau concludes that ideology is essential if a nation is to attain and preserve the enthusiasm and the willingness to sacrifice without which no foreign policy can pass its ultimate test of strength.

Despite this "necessity" of maintaining a strong

facade of ideological differences, both the U.S.S.R. and the U.S. are driven by common security goals which override their philosophical differences. Throughout the sixty years of the Soviet experiment, the Marxist vision of self-realization has been straitjacketed by Soviet security imperatives. Since the death of Stalin (whose personal ruthlessness blurred other factors contributing to Soviet policy), and with the advent of the nuclear age, the launching of Sputnik and the confrontation over scarce resources, the rise to dominance of the Soviet Security State has become more visible—the public professions of communist orthodoxy notwithstanding.

A LOGICAL IMPERIALISM

Soviet backing of Marxist-oriented liberation movements in Angola and elsewhere does not belie the proposition that the fundamental conflict between the U.S. and U.S.S.R. is *not* ideological. The imperatives of national security and national interest provide enough reason for the Soviet Union to be deeply involved in Africa. The stakes are high: rich mineral resources, future markets for Soviet goods, and sources of precious foreign exchange.

Not only does Southern Africa provide possibilities of significant *positive* augmentation of Soviet economic and monetary power; such augmentation of power is doubled by the *negative* deficiency of power for the United States and China, as Soviet gains in Southern Africa become their losses.

No ideological framework is needed to explain Soviet initiatives in Africa, any more than an ideological framework is needed to explain the parallel "imperialism" in U.S. military, monetary and economic policy in Third and Fourth World countries. Which is not the same as saying that no ideology is operative. Or that it is all manipulative, all phony. As we have already stressed, one affects the other. National security needs affect the use of ideology; and ideology is a consideration in national security policy. Increasingly, however, ideology is subordinate to national security goals; indeed, we are witnessing a dynamic where the dominant ideology is becoming "national security."

One only has to visit the African continent to see how most African countries view the Soviet's recent penetration into Southern Africa. Viewed in the past as a heavy-handed benefactor, the Soviet Union's attempt to prove that it is still at the vanguard of world revolution has been thwarted by African nationalism in countries like Kenya and Zaire. They are suspicious of any new scramble for Africa that would diminish their struggle for autonomy and noninterference. Even in those countries where Soviet influence has been considerable, e.g., in Guinea, Somalia, Uganda and the Congo, African leaders have seen that the Soviet Union's presence has been and continues to be primarily motivated by its own national interest.

With the "developing" world taking the initiative toward a New International Economic Order, the Soviet Union has found itself increasingly placed in the same category as the capitalist Atlantic nations, namely, in the category of the "haves." Seen as committed to a centralized corporate economy based on heavy industrialized technology, the Soviet Union has lost the mantle of champion of world social justice to China.

Southern Africa provided a natural place for the Soviets to achieve two goals at the same time: to strengthen their national security and to convince their critics that the Soviet Union had not relinquished the world revolutionary leadership to China. Initiatives for a foothold in Angola had begun long before the departure of the Portuguese. Their backing of the M.P.L.A. thus was not a belated effort undertaken only to convince their critics that they had not relinquished their world revolutionary leadership to the Chinese. Yet the M.P.L.A. success in Angola achieved this second goal as well as the first.

It is important, however, to recognize that, whatever her motives, the Soviet Union has been on the "right" side of the overall conflict in Black Africa ever since the early 1960s when many African countries achieved independence; whereas the United States has consistently backed the oppressive white regimes of Rhodesia and South Africa. Only in 1976, under the pressures of a collapse of its policy in Africa and of Soviet successes, did the United States reluctantly begin to back into a policy for Africa that identified with the goals of racial and social justice on behalf of Black Africa.

A GLOBAL CONVERGENCE

Humankind is entering an era in which ideological rigidities are giving way to the pragmatism of nation-state competition. It is an era of *convergence*. Not so much a convergence of capitalism toward communism; nor a convergence of communism toward capitalism. Rather, the convergence is toward a model of the National Security State in which traditional ideology is a secondary factor in government policy. It is a convergence toward a corporate elite rule based on national security logic rather than ideology.

For reasons given above, including the danger of an abrupt change of self-image, both superpowers can be expected to continue to deny (for another five years or more) that this convergence is happening. Meanwhile, both have their isolated New Classes[13] who, under the rubric of national security, make decisions that profoundly determine the lives of the people.

Both have their masses locked out of the decision-making process under that same rubric. Both are corporate states dominated by corporate goals. Both give verbal homage to their principal philosophers of human liberation (Marx and Jefferson) while precluding most of the humanistic values of these philosophers from the criteria for public policy.

This is not to equate the Soviet Union and the United States. Significant differences exist. Soviet society is strong in some areas where U.S. society is weak, e.g., in the area of inalienable rights to the basic *economic* necessities of life (although priorities given to national security mobilization substantially limit the implementation of these rights). And whereas the area of civil liberties is strong in the U.S., it is seriously violated in the Soviet Union. Despite our judgment that Solzhenitsyn fails to identify the role of national security logic in the corporate Soviet society, his testimony of the brutal treatment and asylumization of political dissenters is one that must not be ignored in the meantime between now and a more just world order system.

A second area of *relatively* greater U.S. strength is that of political participation. However, it is an area rapidly deteriorating. Despite presidential elections every four years and Congressional elections every two years, U.S. voters have increasingly less voice in the national decisions that profoundly affect their personal lives. It really makes little difference whom they elect. Republican, Democrat or Socialist—whatever party elected would be consumed and dominated by the weapons, monetary and scarce resource imperatives that inherently dominate an interdependent world that worships around the altar of unlimited national sovereignty. The central decisions that determine the lives of citizens are made by the elites who run the National Security Big Six (as spelled out in Chapter Five) and by the elites in the board rooms of the big corporations that provide the National Security Big Six the aggregate power needed to survive the military, monetary and resource competition of today's unregulated global arena.

The privileges of the New Classes of both countries are based in the logic of national security mobilization. "The people," in whose name the American Revolution and the Soviet Revolution were both made, end up as the powerless in both cases. Yet the deeper irony is that, powerful as both New Classes are, they share a mutual powerlessness to significantly reorder priorities. It is an Orwellian world come tragically true.

AN ORWELLIAN WORLD

A global convergence in elite rule was foreseen and depicted in the prophetic writing of *1984* by George Orwell.

Several points of clarification need to be made about Orwell's work. He was not writing about the Soviet Union, although many people at the time and since have equated his work with Soviet rule. He was writing about the world as a whole. The world he foresaw was one giving way to a frightening rise of totalitarianism and the destruction of the human spirit.

Mistakenly, the images of crushing dictatorship depicted in *1984* have been attributed in many people's minds to a monolithic world government. But that was not Orwell's vision. Quite the contrary. In the absence of a worldwide legal system which could provide nations with security and hold them and their leaders accountable for their actions, parallel totalitarian regimes destroyed the vestiges of democracy in three superstates of the globe.

Unfortunately, (and perhaps because of the time in which it was first published in 1949) Orwell's basic message was obscured by the proximity of Adolph Hitler's personal dictatorship and Josef Stalin's ruthlessness. Vivid public consciousness of Nazism and Stalinism led readers of Orwell's book to credit his Big Brother society to a similar personalized dictatorship. But rather than being the result of a *personal* dictator who benefited from sophisticated modern technology, the Big Brother totalitarianism of Orwell's vision was the result of a *constant national security stalemate* among three large superpowers. All three fought over outlying, disputed territories, representing one-fifth of the world's population, which had valuable mineral resources and cheap labor.

Although the citizenry of each world region was manipulated to believe differently, these powers did not have fundamental ideological differences. Yet, in one combination or another, they were always preparing, i.e. mobilizing, for war. This mobilization had limited aims because none could gain a considerable lead over the others, and no superstate could effectively destroy the other, even if two aligned against one, because they were so evenly matched. In the shadow of stockpiles of atomic weaponry (constantly being developed, tested and stored, but not of practical use), the people were manipulated by the elites of their respective governments to fear an ever-present enemy attack. They had come to accept the logical need for a perpetual mobilization of their societies for national security and, lacking an alternative scenario of a global security system, this logic was an effective tool for manipulation.

This national security rationale permitted the Big Brother elites to mobilize society, effectively control it and thus maintain themselves in power. Dissidents and freethinkers could be effectively eliminated as threats to national security. The truth regarding government policy and the real issues was "adjusted" to safeguard the "security of the state." The situation was the same in all three superstates. Men could not break free from Big Brother elite rule because of the "doublethink" logic of national security.

Just an imaginative account—the fiction of a novelist's fantasy? Or accurate prophecy? In the final quarter of the twentieth century, it is increasingly clear that in predicting both the ascendancy of a New Class of elites and the national security rationale upon which they would accede to power, Orwell was amazingly on target.

CONCLUSION

Up to now, persons worried about the protection of individual freedom and the right of people to assert control over their personal lives and destinies have tended to see totalitarian rule as the result of either power-hungry devil-men or of a statist ideology—or both. Getting more concrete in the content of modern ideology, the assumption is that corporate elite rule is rooted primarily in a collectivist social ideology—an assumption that places the blame for loss of personal sovereignty on interference by government in the natural dynamics of the "market." Events of the past two decades, however, have made it apparent that it makes little difference whether a state began with a collectivist social philosophy or not. A new (yet old) imperative has taken center stage, one which serves as a centralizing magnet of power. It is the imperative of national security competition in an interdependent but ungoverned world. The result of this imperative is an elite rule throughout the world that is neither dependent upon personal deification nor upon statist ideology.

Recognition of this national security imperative exposes as a myth the argument that social planning in itself causes an inevitable loss of individual freedom and personal sovereignty. *National and international planning do not inherently breed totalitarianism.* On the contrary, amidst the anarchy and insecurity of the present system, it is the lack of a *global* framework for coordinated and long-range planning that leaves isolated, individual national societies vulnerable to totalitarian, elitist decision making.

7

Liberation for Being

> A new vision is emerging of the possibilities
> of man and of his destiny, and its implications
> are many.
>
> Abraham Maslow

The two previous chapters focused on the National
Security State system as it has affected the United
States and Soviet Union. We looked at a double powerlessness of national leaders: 1) powerlessness to reorder
priorities; and 2) powerlessness to provide true national
security.

The leadership of other major nation-states increasingly experience a similar powerlessness. But the
powerlessness of leaders in many African, Asian and
Latin American countries is even more poignant. Their
impotence within the National Security State system is
the focus of this chapter.

A Degradation of Language

Since launching the U.N. Development Decades of
the 1960s and 1970s, the peoples of Africa, Asia and
Latin America have come to be commonly referred to
as "developing" nations. We have been putting the
terms "developing" and "developed" in quotation
marks throughout the book, and in the context of this
chapter it is important to explain reasons for doing so.

The term "developing nations" was coined in the
early '60s as a nicer way of saying "underdeveloped" or
"not developed enough" or "poor." As such, it referred
to technical-industrial-economic growth, usually mea-

sured by G.N.P. We have encased it in quotes because we insist that *no* nation has "arrived," that *all* nations are developing, and that they are doing so in ways that cannot be measured by economics alone. Indeed, to continue to measure human progress by national G.N.P. scores is a critical flaw—an Achilles heel—of our day. The whole world community is engaged in a process of "becoming," which must be viewed in a wider framework of full human development.

Although not placed in quotation marks, the terms Third and Fourth World also need special comment. The distinction between Third and Fourth World nations is historically very recent, arising with the economic ascendancy of oil-producing nations. As now popularly used, it delineates between two levels of "developing" nations: those whose economic growth rate and G.N.P. have risen to somewhat higher levels (Third World) and the so-called Fourth World nations whose annual per capita income is less than $200.00. Rather than inventing new terminology, we have employed these terms when it was unavoidable. Nevertheless, we find such distinctions, based on a limited economic scale of worth, repugnant on several counts:

1. *It reduces the personal worth* of a majority of the world community to low value, measured purely in economic terms, and makes a grave error in ignoring totally the value to the world of persons who have tremendous gifts to give when assessed in fuller human terms.

2. *It depersonalizes suffering* by lumping oppressed persons in an abstract mass.

3. *It stereotypes the people* of diverse geographic and cultural backgrounds as one common herd, and diminishes the importance of unique differences.

4. *It blurs* the fact that *within these geographic areas there are disparities between rich and poor* as vast and critical as the global economic disparities between First World and Fourth World.

5. *It is degradation of language.* When used as an assessment of a nation's relative place in the world economic lineup, it totally obliterates the rich and important history inherent in the birth of the term Third World.

As originally used by Nehru, Third World meant a "third force" between the North Atlantic capitalist bloc (First World) and the Soviet-based communist bloc (Second World). As such, it connoted moral strength and had the proud bearing of peoples who aspired to determine their own destiny, apart from the power politics of cold-war confrontation. In popular use, the term has now been reduced to mean "not yet as well off" as the "First World" and "Second World."

It is important to the present discussion on Liberation and the National Security State that we recall some of the history surrounding the proud birth of the term Third World. In the height of the cold-war confrontation of the 1950s, Jawaharlal Nehru and his principal collaborators, Marshal Tito of Yugoslavia and President Nasser of Egypt, led a call for nonalignment. This call for nonalignment had two dimensions. The first was nonalignment with the "Great Powers." Its main element was a repudiation of the power politics of the Cold War. In an interview reported in *The Hindu*, Nehru asked: "Why should we inherit the hatred of others? It is bad enough to have our own burdens."[1]

A second, more positive thrust of the call for nonalignment was its focus on overcoming the powerlessness of three-fourths of the earth's people. As such, it followed the direction pioneered by Mahatma Gandhi during World War II. Gandhi had demanded Indian independence *before* the end of the war to assure India— as a spokesman of non-European peoples—of a voice in the shaping of the peace for the postwar world. The 1961 Belgrade Conference of Nonaligned Nations declared that it is "essential that nonaligned countries should participate in solving outstanding international issues concerning peace and security." The conference proceedings continued: "Nonaligned nations should provide encouragement and support to all people fighting for their independence and equality." Nehru told the conference: "We want to throw our weight, such as it is, in favor of peace."[2]

The weight of the nonaligned nations, however, proved to be ethereal. Their alliance lost its thrust after the 1964 Cairo Conference; it declined with Nehru's death. It had become clear that this effort to build a "third force," to have some countervailing influence on the power policies of the superpowers, had met a dead end. Nehru's vision of wielding moral power proved futile in the harsh imperatives of a balance-of-power world. The effort to "throw our weight" ended up proving that the nonaligned alliance had little weight in a world based on power politics. The "why" of this powerlessness is important. For it helps us understand the militancy of those liberation theorists and strategists who today are seeking to build a new kind of third force.

Five policy positions characterized the countries that participated in the nonaligned conferences in Bandung (1955), Belgrade (1961), and Cairo (1964). These nations:

1. were strongly anti-colonial;
2. belonged to the "less-developed" sector of the world, generally;
3. belonged to the non-Atlantic world;

4. embraced positions of peaceful coexistence;
5. were in favor of general and complete disarmament.

Despite these general characteristics, however,
there was little fundamental unity among the countries
who sought to forge an effective nonaligned bloc during
the decade that spanned the 1955 Bandung Conference
and the 1964 conference in Cairo. The nation-states involved were at different stages of economic development, with differing needs. They were often in competition with each other for aid and investment—bound up
with the Western development model of heavy industry
and vertical technology. Not a few remained dependent
upon their historical colonial connections for economic
viability. For the most part—with the exclusion of
Nehru's India—the nonaligned posture rested on an almost exclusive nation-state self-interest.

In addition to this lack of fundamental unity and
the powerlessness of a "moral voice" in the balance-of-
power arena, three other factors were responsible for
the limited impact of the nonaligned movement. The first
was the breakup of the tight bipolar construct that existed
when the Cold War began. Secondly, a new bipolar
system began to emerge, one which pitted the economically wealthy nations against the "have-nots." A third
was the vacuum of moral leadership after Nehru's
death. The Indian prime minister was the prime archi-
tect of the principle of nonalignment, based on a moral-
philosophical world view. Nehru's absence exposed the
fragile common ground of the nonaligned bloc.

THE LIBERATION MOVEMENT:
A NEW ALLIANCE

In the wake of this original Third World alliance has
risen a new force. It bears some resemblance to the earlier

effort. But significant differences make it a radically different creature. The most identifiable, and perhaps most
important, difference is that the new Liberation Movement
is just that: a movement. It is not a bloc of nation-
states, run by heads of government. It includes a large
grass-roots movement, the leaders of which are frequently
in strong opposition to their respective heads of government.
The starkness of this difference is evident in considering
the official title of the 1961 Belgrade Conference: "The
First Conference of *Heads of State and Government* of
Nonaligned Nations."

Another difference is that Latin Americans are
becoming strong and vocal leaders in liberation theory
and strategy. Latin America had little voice in Nehru's
alliance. In a book published in 1967 entitled *Politics of
the Third World*, for example, D. R. Miller excludes
Latin America from the Third World.[3] He reasoned
that its nations are older, are European in culture and
origin, and have relations with the United States. But
the politics of the Third World have changed this evaluation drastically since Miller wrote. In a peoples' movement struggling for local as well as global justice, the
age of one's nation-state becomes irrelevant. As does
the European culture of its ruling oligarchy—a culture
whose "benefits" and power the unempowered citizens
do not share. And the fact that most Latin elites have
close political, economic and military relations with the
United States actually provides a powerful rationale for
grass-roots justice and liberation movements in Latin
American nation-states.

A third difference is that whereas most leaders of
the nonaligned countries pursued goals that were almost entirely national and economic, the Liberation
Movement is increasingly united in a commitment to a

moral and philosophical vision of justice and human development. Latin Americans are making a special contribution in this regard, led by Christian leaders like Paulo Freire, with his educational strategy of conscientization; and Hugo Assman, a Brazilian priest, sociologist and theologian, whose faith energizes his commitment to a politics and theory of liberation. In a paper entitled "The Christian Contribution to the Liberation of Latin America," Father Assman says: "The God who raised up Jesus is not a God of the dead but of the living and . . . because life is the 'milieu' of God he wants it to be also the 'environment' of men."[4]

Most important of these three differences is the focus on *peoples* rather than on nation-states. The new bipolarity is seen not so much as a confrontation between "have" and "have-not" nations. Rather the emphasis is on "have" and "have-not" peoples—a distinction that refuses to be contained by boundaries of nation-states. This focus on the powerful and powerless people provides the basis for an alliance of oppressed, unempowered groups in "rich" and "poor" nations alike, an alliance that seeks to be global.

AN IMPORTANT CONTRIBUTION

The Liberation Movement is a force that could have an important bearing on the shape of a more human world order. Some of its important contributions include constructive criticism of traditional development goals; an insistence on social justice (not "aid") as a criterion for economic relationships between persons and nations; a philosophy of human development which outlines a revolution for *being* more (as opposed to the limitations of a revolution for *having* more), and a strategy or process focused on enabling the human person to be *subject* rather than object of development.

The Liberation Movement has already made a major contribution in its constructive criticism of some of the central assumptions upon which the development goals and strategies of the 1960s and 1970s were based. Liberation theorists have pointed out that these development goals and strategies failed to come to grips with a root cause of "underdevelopment," i.e., *dependency.*

Father Hugo Assman aptly described this problem thus: "Underdevelopment is not a primitive stage prior to developmental capitalism, but rather a direct consequence of it, a special kind of capitalism shaped by development itself: dependent capitalism."[5]

The Liberation Movement now argues that the agencies of "the development establishment" (the World Bank, regional banks like the Inter-American Development Bank, the U.N. Development Program, the International Monetary Fund, UNESCO, FAO, WHO, etc.) are instruments of this dependency when they limit the goal of development to solving the problem of technological "backwardness" as a means of overcoming poverty, but do not include plans to abolish or reorder the structures causing the dependency in the first place.

An important aspect of liberation theory, but one which makes many people uncomfortable, is the insistence on a total view of violence. As lamentable as "direct" forms of physical violence may be, they may not be as destructive as the "indirect" forms of structural violence, often inherent in established legal processes and social institutions that lock out millions of persons from access to the means of self-reliance and self-realization. Whether or not one agrees with some liberationists that violence may be a necessary historical component of the liberation of oppressed peoples, the contribution liberationists make in pricking the comfort and sensitizing their contemporaries to these forms of "indirect" violence is an important one.

Some liberation theorists, such as Paulo Freire, provide a potential corrective to "development for dependency" in their demands that the development *process itself* be consistent with humanizing goals. Traditional development scenarios have usually given priority to efficiency and order (thereby consciously or unconsciously reinforcing oppressive socio-political bondage to the status quo and placing decision-making power in the hands of a new technological elite). In contrast, Freire's process of "conscientization" was developed to engage persons in determining their own goals and change processes.[6]

Although there is no *one* model or philosophy of development among liberationists, the thinking of such persons as Gutierrez, Nyerere and Freire is important input in expanding the parameters of the development framework. As distinct from those who limit the criteria of development to economic growth, some liberation theorists view it as a *total social process*. This view does not contradict the need for economic well-being, but goes beyond that to also include social, political, cultural and spiritual dimensions of growth, stressing their interdependence. It is a view perhaps best summed up in the phrase used by Latin American liberationists such as Gustavo Lagos, who call for a "Revolution for *Being*."[7]

This holistic view of development implies for many liberation theorists an ethical dimension and a concern for human values as a criterion for economic decision making. Gustavo Gutierrez writes:

To view development as a total social process necessarily implies for some an ethical dimension which presupposes a concern for human values. The step toward an elaboration of a *humanistic perspective* of development is thus taken unconsciously and it prolongs the former point of view without contradicting it.[8]

The ethics of development are of concern not only to Latin American and other Third and Fourth World liberationists. Liberation advocates in the First World such as Denis Goulet,[9] building on the work of Louis-Joseph Lebret and others, continue to make significant inroads in questioning assumptions and exploring the moral landscape of development processes.

It is in the Liberation Movement, with its philosophy and ethics rooted in social justice and its central concern with the human person (as distinct from state or corporate goals), that the old breach between Marxists and Christians is beginning to be bridged. Through mutual involvement in the Liberation Movement, each is discovering that some of its most dearly held tenets are held in common, e.g., the dignity and value of the human person and the rightful role of the human person as "co-creator"/"subject" of history. The fact that the Liberation Movement has provided a meeting ground and basis for furthering such Marxist-Christian dialogue is in itself an important step in building a more viable human community. Continued efforts to develop a shared ethic and philosophic approach are of critical importance in laying the foundation for a more human world order.

Another important aspect of the Liberation Movement lies in its sense of hope and human possibility.

What was caused by human action can be changed by human action. Human oppression and powerlessness are not unalterable. Denis Goulet articulated this when he asserted that liberation vocabulary "enjoys high prescriptive value because it shows this powerlessness to be reversible; if domination is a human state of affairs caused and perpetuated by men, it can be overthrown by men."[10]

LIBERATION THEORY—IN NEED OF AN EXPANDED ANALYSIS

The liberation framework *can* be highly prescriptive, but to be so it must extend and deepen its analysis. Goulet contends that the new liberation vocabulary is empirically valid because it lays bare structures of dependence and domination at *all* levels.[11] But despite this claim, liberation advocates have to date failed to adequately take cognizance of the straitjacket that an obsolete world system and its oppressive principle of unlimited national sovereignty places on their humanistic goals. It is a weakness that is not incidental to the poor track record of liberation efforts and one that may result in the same limited impact as Nehru's "third force."

A widely held assumption in liberation theory is that human liberation is primarily a task of the people liberating themselves from oppressive domination by elites. An analysis of the National Security State modifies this assumption. Although not denying the stark and growing reality of oppressive elite rule, this analysis identifies a *new logic* for such rule. And in doing so, it broadens the task of human liberation to include the liberation of national *leaders* as well as the "people."

This broadened analysis and strategy moves us beyond demonology, beyond the syndrome that describes powerlessness of the people only in polarized "oppressor-oppressed" categories. For the problem of reversing powerlessness is more complex than simply engaging in power confrontation between the "haves" and "have-nots."

Liberation theory usually begins with *class conflict* at the core of its analysis. The oppressors are the "haves"; the oppressed are the "have-nots." What the oppressors have and the oppressed have not is *power*—economic, political, social and cultural.

Accordingly, the central task of liberation strategy is to enable the oppressed to share power, to participate effectively in the decisions that determine their personal lives. Stated in other terms, a prime goal of the liberation process is to break free from *alienation*, i.e., from the determination of one's life by forces external to one's person. As freedom from external determination is achieved, a person can then make progress toward the full human development that is the potential of all people; then a "revolution of Being" becomes possible in one's personal and social life.

Although liberation scenarios vary, they usually see people empowerment as being realized through one or more of three possible ways:

—by persuading the "oppressors" to share power (through a conversion of heart and/or through motivations of enlightened self-interest);

—by effective grass-roots political organizing so as to gain power through legitimate political processes;

—by seizing political power through force.

In the class-analysis approach, once the oppressed have been liberated by political empowerment, they will be able to construct a "New Society" in which class distinctions will no longer be important. The evils of corporate capitalism and the free-market economy will be replaced by decentralized, person-centered institutions which can operate according to criteria oriented toward full human development.

Liberation theorists usually assume that those presently in power—or those who would take power in the future—are or will be able to substantially eliminate oppressive policies and reconstruct social institutions if they make an *act of will* to do so. Another assumption is that once that act of will is made and implemented, then elites are free to distribute power (i.e., decision making) to local economic and political groups. A third assumption is that the reformed or new national decision makers will be free to use human-valued, life-respecting, person-centered values as the criteria for public policy.

These assumptions, however, do not square with the imperatives of today's world system. *More than change of hearts and acts of will are needed* to replace the aggregate power that politically sovereign nations require if they are to survive militarily, monetarily and economically. This requirement of aggregate power, which gives priority to security needs rather than human development needs, argues for a retention of many status-quo institutions and policies. This is as true for the Soviet Union's communist status quo as for the United States' status quo. It is also true for Castro's Cuba and other Third World revolutionary regimes.

After rejecting oppressive colonial and capitalist status-quo models of past and present, the liberation leadership itself is caught up in a "new," revolutionary status quo which is characterized by elite rule—often as harsh as its predecessor and employing similar national policies designed to guarantee military, monetary and resource survival. Despite some greater attention to citizen needs, the social agendas that would implement liberation goals of a new humanism are substantially subordinated to the exigencies of national survival.

Lacking a global security system that could provide

1. *security from military threat* (and thus limit the need for the third world's escalating arms purchases);
2. *access to foreign reserves* and assured trade preferences for their commodities (and thus permit greater expenditure on domestic needs like housing, health care, education and rural transportation which don't bring in foreign currency);
3. *access to scarce resources* at a fair price (and thus enable peoples to develop local industry and agriculture for their needs),

there is little choice for revolutionary Third World leaders but to become national security elites, preoccupied with managing a budding corporate society that is mobilized for and dominated by national security imperatives.

This is a most painful dilemma for persons such as Julius Nyerere of Tanzania, whose projections for "Self-Reliance"[12] were based in a philosophical commitment to a person-centered, participatory model building on traditional African socialism and the extended family. It is a liberation model that has inspired many liberation theorists and strategists the world over. Tanzania's efforts to develop "ujamma" villages of self-reliance remain very much truncated. Isolated by the world's development establishment, Nyerere's dilemma is that, given the present world system, Tanzania can only deal effectively with balance of payments, lack of development capital, inadequate foreign reserves, scarce resources and the danger of external subversion through a more centralized elite rule which seeks national corporate goals. Reluctant to place both feet on this centralized path, and yet having to take some steps in this direction, Nyerere is caught in the middle. The high hopes of his Arusha Declaration remain largely unrealized.

China's leaders are also constrained by the status quo of national security mobilization — a policy of constant revolution and periodic societal shake-up notwithstanding. The names and faces of top officials may change, some disappearing and reappearing. But *centralized* political, educational, economic and cultural decision making remains constant. Decentralization of decision making in China is limited, preoccupying people with local problems and quotas while leaving national decisions in the hands of isolated national elites—thereby (whether intentionally or not) serving to facilitate and consolidate, rather than undermine, centralized power at the national level. Hunger, poverty, disease and corruption have been largely wiped out. But the further stages of full human development and the conscious participation in shaping one's destiny envisioned by liberation theorists and strategists is not foreseeable in China as long as it remains a National Security State.

The syllogism that liberationists have not yet adequately dealt with is the following:

National survival in today's interdependent world system requires aggregate power.

Aggregate power requires corporate elite decision making.

National survival in today's interdependent world system requires corporate elite decision making.

Syllogisms related to the National Security State could also be made. Example:

Values and priorities which would undercut the mobilization needed for survival in today's interdependent world system must be precluded as central criteria for public policy.

The values and priorities of the liberation scenario (e.g., person-centered, self-determination) would significantly undercut such mobilization.

Therefore the values and priorities of the liberation scenario must be precluded as central criteria for public policy.

Unless liberation theorists extend their analysis beyond that of class conflict to include the straitjacket of national security mobilization, they will remain powerless to fashion strategies capable of achieving the "revolution of Being" that they seek.

A LIMITED TRACK RECORD

The challenge to expand beyond the "oppressed-oppressor" syndrome in liberation analysis, however, does not follow only from the National Security State analysis. Also challenging the limits of liberation analysis is the track record of the Liberation Movement.

This record is one of marginal gains—gains which are counterbalanced by drastic failures, frustration, unnecessary and perhaps unjust polarization, irrationality and widespread hostility.

Hard words, to be sure. But they are not meant as a put-down of the overall liberation framework. Rather, they are words of concern. It is a concern that human liberation is not being significantly achieved. It is a concern that the above negatives are unnecessarily discouraging or turning away people whose talents, energies and finances are essential in the cause of liberation.

Some of the negative aspects of the liberation track record stem from a near-exclusive focus on the powerlessness of "the people." This shortsightedness misses the other side of the powerlessness coin: the structural powerlessness of national leaders to radically reorder present corporate priorities. One reason for this incomplete analysis is a built-in bias that stems from the *class analysis*, a bias that immediately assumes that elite rule is only based upon some self-seeking motive of "haves" to preserve their power by preserving the status quo. It is a bias, of course, that is readily understandable, being built on wide historical evidence. For the class struggle is real—as widespread social injustice all over the world bears evidence—and cannot be downplayed.

Chile provides a dramatic example that national political sovereignty is not synonymous with human liberation—or with national security. If there ever was a scenario for proving the validity of liberation assumptions, Allende's electoral victory in 1970 should have been it. Years of careful and patient political conscientization had succeeded in producing an electoral victory in which Marxist and many Christian liberationists joined hands to work toward a national framework in which the people would be able to achieve control over their lives. Many of Allende's theoreticians had waxed eloquent about building a "New Chilean Society," one in which a new human person could emerge. The people were to be partners in building a new socialist social fibre.

But what happened? The preface to the answers consists of six words:

Lacking an effective world-order institution to assure access to foreign monetary reserves, Allende was straitjacketed by his country's chronic balance-of-payments deficits, unable to obtain the technologies needed to maintain, let alone expand, his transportation and production industries.

Lacking an effective world-order institution to provide additional capital, Chile was boycotted by the World Bank and other institutions of the development establishment and by capitalist countries, and thereby rendered powerless to implement Allende's socialist development plans.

Lacking an effective world-order institution to regulate multinational corporations, I.T.T. and other multinationals did everything possible to undercut the economic and political viability of Allende's government, including spending millions of dollars to foster unrest and strengthen his opposition.

Lacking an effective world-order institution to prohibit subversive disruption by another country, the United States was able to use the C.I.A. and other means at its disposal to weaken Allende's administration.

All of which points up the inadequacy of liberation movements if they remain conceived merely as *national* movements, concentrating on acquiring power only at *national* levels. This nationalist focus must extend itself to include institutional participation in the power that is being wielded at the *global* level. Building upon Paulo Freire's principle of conscientization, liberationists have assumed that if "the people" could be conscientized to identify the sources of their oppression (i.e., to identify their oppressors, whether they be institutions or people), a widely based grass-roots movement would eventually develop into a *national* liberation front that could effectively seize power over national institutions and, therefore, reconstruct society in the image of a humanistic "Revolution of Being." Hence, the letters "N" "F" "L"—referring to national liberation fronts—have appeared in different languages all over the world.

Karl Marx made the same assumption. His person-centered scenario of human liberation was based on a strategy of *national* liberation, of an ever-growing expansion of revolutionary socialist regimes around the world until, one by one, all the nations would be liberated. Then would come the cooperative, humanized world community in which the people would have significant power, i.e., sovereignty, over their personal lives and over their communities.

But as we saw in the last chapter, the Soviet revolution did not result in a human-valued, person-centered, participatory society. It became, instead, a National Security State dominated by centralized elite rule. This pattern is being repeated today in other states where socialist revolutions succeed in taking over. The rule of old elites is replaced by new elites, who today rule under the imperatives of national security.

To the degree that the new revolutionary elites have significant capital, foreign reserves, technology, technically trained people, natural resources and arable land, *some progress* in meeting the social justice needs of their people for food, housing, health care and education can be achieved. But this very qualification speaks for itself. Few of the economically poorer countries have these assets in quantity. Even those few "developing" nations that are blessed with the above assets are locked into limited gains. The escalating arms race among Third and Fourth World countries (they spend a higher proportion of their GNP on armaments than the United States) and mobilization for monetary and scarce resources are consuming precious capital, foreign reserves, trained peoples and natural resources which subsequently are not available for domestic development needs. Beyond these upside-down priorities resulting from national security mobilization, however, are other sources of leadership powerlessness. Rampant, unregulated global forces (such as inflation, monetary fluctuation and unstable commodity markets), as well as decisions made in the board rooms of multinational corporations and in the offices of international development agencies can uncut the most carefully designed development plans.

As long as present-day liberationists fail to include on the liberation agenda a world security system that can deal with these problems, the Liberation Movement will be limited to marginal gains. Even after strongly asserting that they reject the centralized, corporate model of the Soviet Union, that their liberation model is one of decentralized socialism which seeks a "Revolution of Being" rather than the Soviet's "Revolution of Having," *liberation theorists have yet to present a scenario in which an integral human development model has a realistic chance of succeeding.* The limited track record of the liberation movements is substantially due to the same obstacles that subverted the human liberation model of Karl Marx, namely, the principle of unlimited national sovereignty.

There is one difference, however, between the dilemma of Marx and that of today's human liberationists—a difference that is crucial. Marx had no alternative but to pursue his liberation goals in the frame of national sovereignty. The transnational infrastructure that could have provided a global security system did not exist in the nineteenth century. Global communication and transportation technology were not even envisioned, except perhaps in Jules Verne's science fiction. But much has changed in the intervening one hundred years. The global infrastructure for constructing a world security system of functional agencies operating at a global level to deal with those problems that individual nations cannot handle alone *do* exist now.

A second new factor also adds to the practical credibility of a world security system, i.e., the growing global consciousness that recognizes the interdependence of all peoples. This recognition, however, has not yet focused adequately on the straitjacket that the principle of unlimited sovereignty continues to place on efforts to deal with this interdependence.

A NEW INTERNATIONAL
ECONOMIC ORDER?

An example of this encouraging but limited recognition of human interdependence is the proposal for a New International Economic Order. Proposed by the U.N. General Assembly in April 1974, and then debated at the Assembly's Seventh Special Assembly in September 1975, the document was formulated as a preparatory step toward a *Charter of Economic Rights and Duties* of states that would codify basic principles of economic justice as part of international law. As such it could be a very important step toward a structural global framework guaranteeing poorer nations access to the means for economic development.

The proposal for a New International Economic Order builds upon the 1948 U.N. Declaration of Human Rights which, affirming the "equal and *inalienable* rights of all members of the human family," then goes on to apply the principle of inalienable rights to economic justice:

> Everyone has the right to a standard of living adequate for the health and well-being of himself and of his family, including *food, clothing, housing,* and *medical care* and necessary social services, and the right to security in the event of unemployment, sickness, disability, widowhood, old age and other lack of livelihood in circumstances beyond his control. (Article 25) (Emphasis added.)

A central flaw, however, exists in the design of the New International Economic Order. It is the same flaw that exists in the United Nations Charter and relates to the way it answers a critical question—Who owns the earth? Unfortunately, this question is once more answered by a reaffirmation of absolute national sovereignty.

The inherent weakness in perpetuating a policy of absolute national sovereignty is perhaps best seen from the perspective of *human rights*. Despite the U.N. Declaration of Human Rights (which was never universally ratified by the member nations), the world stands powerless before gross violations of these fundamental rights.

Case: Political prisoners who fill the prisons of many nations for no more than criticizing unjust policies of dictatorial regimes are often beaten, tortured, and die without ever having benefit of a trial or even being charged with violating a law. (Such arrests usually occur under the rationale of "national security.") In a system of absolute national sovereignty, political prisoners have no effective recourse to any higher law than that of the very government that imprisoned them.

Case: Soviet citizens are not free to leave or emigrate. Women in many countries do not have equal rights before the law. Racial minorities are in many areas of the world effectively locked out of decision-making positions.

Despite all the speeches decrying religious, racial or sexist discrimination, victims of such discrimination are at the mercy of the structures and laws of their own sovereign states, which are not accountable to any higher authority that is legally binding.

Case: Apartheid in South Africa is perhaps the most blatant example of the abuses that can follow from the principle of unlimited sovereignty. The South African government can claim national sovereignty in ignoring the ineffectual protests against its policies and warns would-be liberationist-supporters against external interference in its *"internal* affairs." White South Africans can rationalize that the Bantu population have their own homelands where they may exercise political power and enjoy land ownership, and that it is not the duty of South Africa to ensure these rights to "noncitizens" on her sovereign territory. What *legal* recourse do nonwhite South Africans have? There is presently no legally effective transnational authority to intervene on their behalf in defense of their rights.

The weakness of the existing U.N. Charter is that the U.N. may not intervene in human rights violations except at the request of the government involved. Will the present South African government make such a request?

What is of fundamental importance here is that unless the world develops an effective authority, legally empowered to safeguard the rights of *all* human persons, what recourse do those whose rights are violated by sovereign states have except terrorism and armed revolution? In cases such as South Africa, by reason of governmental controls and massive government firepower, such armed revolt from within is not likely to succeed.

In order to ensure the inalienable rights of all persons it is necessary to share some sovereignty in decision making.

It is precisely here—in its total embrace of the principle of absolute sovereignty—that we have difficulty with the New International Economic Order as it is now proposed. Our difficulty exists not only because the principle of absolute national sovereignty precludes the realization of the political and racial dimensions of social justice for millions of people. Absolute sovereignty also substantially limits the gains which the "developing" world can make in the *economic* dimensions of social justice. Without effective law, justice in any area is greatly truncated.

The underlying operating principles in the N.I.E.O. proposal are *power* and *confrontation*. Thanks to the recently acquired resources and financial power of OPEC nations, the Group of 77 (now composed of 110 Third and Fourth World nations) has been able to partially rectify the traditional balance-of-power configuration, hitherto dominated by the industrial nations of the earth. Some preliminary gains were made at the Seventh Special Session of the U.N. Assembly in the form of agreements on limited monetary reforms, international trade, transfer of resources and technology and other areas related to more equitable economic relations between the "haves" and "have-nots." But these gains are limited. And based on treaty rather than on law that can be enforced by effective transnational authority, even these limited gains are tenuous. Agreements and treaties are only as good as the will of both sides. Once such agreements seem to go counter to what one party believes to be its self-interest, they are easily disregarded. (This is actually written into the arms limitation agreements between the United States and Soviet Union.)

The assumption of N.I.E.O. is that all nations of the "developing" world will benefit from the "politics of resources." The facts refute this assumption. The greatest losers of the OPEC oil-price politics have been the people of Fourth World countries whose poverty, hunger and general powerlessness have escalated through the quintupling of oil prices. Their balance of payments deteriorated drastically, limiting their ability to import critically needed fertilizers and technology. The inflationary spirals that resulted from the oil-price rise—real and manipulated—meant that Fourth World countries were victims of higher prices for both basic commodities and manufactured goods.

Loudly heralded "Third World aid" plans were proclaimed as OPEC's response to this cause-and-effect powerlessness of many non-oil-producing countries. Already in February 1974, the Shah of Iran proposed a new $5 billion development fund, one billion of which was to be provided by Iran. This aid was to be in the form of *loans,* not outright grants; an immediately qualifying factor in light of the fact that many "developing" countries are already so overwhelmed by debts from capital borrowed in the past (and from interest on that capital) that often over 50% of present aid from the "developed" world and from development agencies must be used for debt repayment.

This development fund, however, soon shrank in size. After Venezuela joined Iran in 1975 in proposing that OPEC make $1 billion available in each of the next few years for "developing" countries hurt by higher oil prices, the finance ministers of the thirteen member states agreed in January of 1976 on a fund of $800 million. This is less than 1% of the $100 billion of total annual oil revenues received by the major exporters.

The $800 million represented only one-half of the *additional* $1.5 billion of annual oil bills that non-oil-producing countries of the "developing" world had to pay following an additional 10% price increase only four months earlier.

Which brings us back to our basic criticism of the New International Economic Order. Central to its various proposals is the unqualified affirmation of the *"full permanent sovereignty of every state over its natural resources."*

One can understand the concern and emotion of the peoples of Africa, Asia and Latin America that underlie this affirmation of "full permanent sovereignty." For too long they have experienced utter powerlessness vis-à-vis Western economic, monetary and military power. Now, even though a limited gain, the world's scarcity of natural resources is providing at least some leverage at the bargaining table over commodity prices and market preferences. But this new (and limited) leverage, in the long run, is at a serious cost. The principle of absolute sovereignty over geographic areas is incompatible with the concept of inalienable economic rights. It perpetuates the central weakness of the "old *national* economic order" which asserts that a single person or nation has a right to *absolute* ownership (spelled "sovereignty") to a particular parcel of the earth's surface and to whatever lies beneath it.

In other words, this principle undercuts a basic principle of N.I.E.O. It undercuts the moral argument that every individual has an inalienable right to the basic necessities of life, regardless of his or her ability to compete in the "market." It undercuts the moral basis for a fundamental principle of liberation—namely, *justice.* What is left is power and confrontation.

Besides undercutting the moral base of the N.I.E.O., the principle of absolute permanent sovereignty is counterproductive. Rather than achieving security, it leads to greater insecurity. Not only does it invite confrontation and possible economic/military breakdown, and even nuclear war, but the present "war" over resources is also a two-edged sword. Possessing a greater percentage of the world's exportable grain than the Arab nations possess of the world's exportable oil, the United States has already declared that its food surplus is a prime instrument of foreign policy. Just as Harry Truman, upon hearing of the successful explosion of the atom bomb, said that he "now had a hammer" on the Soviets, presidents of the United States can today say that they "have a hammer" on much of the rest of the world. The victims here are not the Arab oil giants, who have limited population. Rather, the victims will again be the Fourth World nations for whom a successful theory and strategy of liberation would have the greatest meaning.

MANIPULATION

The relationship between the National Security State and the difficulties which liberation movements have experienced in overcoming class differences, however, lies not only in the *logic* for corporate power, elite rule and a new type of class struggle (i.e., the struggle between national security elites and the people). Equally important is the *manipulation* of that logic. In the real world, the two cannot be separated.

Few banners in history have been so effectively waved to retain the status quo as the powerful, virtually irresistible banner of "national security." History is replete with examples of tyrannical rule, social injustice and dehumanization that were rationalized under this emotional banner. A main reason for its effectiveness is that—even before the advent of the National Security State with the new logic of a zero lead-time, interdependent world—there has always been a basic legitimate logic that was able to be manipulated by self-interested defenders of the status quo.

This more limited but nevertheless real logic for national security mobilization was operative even in the demobilization phase of the historic "feast or famine" cycles that prevailed prior to the post-World War II world. No doubt it was a logic manipulated by leaders of the Aryan and Mongol invasions, employed in shaping the rigid rules of Sparta, in imperial policies of Rome, in feudal baronic, medieval kingdoms and the European city-states, as well as the nation-states and totalitarian regimes of more recent history. People and humanistic priorities have always been vulnerable to the manipulation of the logic for national security mobilization. Together, the logic and its manipulation have played a considerable part in perpetuating the gap between "haves" and "have-nots" within the borders of sovereign units.

Some liberationists object to an analysis that includes a logic for aggregate power, elite rule and a new class conflict. It blurs the easy division of the world between "oppressed" and "oppressor." It also takes away some of the moral outrage that has proven an effective framework for organizing the powerless.

The advantages gained through a facile, easily grasped black-and-white scenario and an outrage based on demonology, however, are limited. More important, the analysis on which these advantages are based is incomplete. For it doesn't identify *all* the forces causing personal and social alienation. The strategies that flow from an incomplete analysis will also be defective.

CONCLUSION

Identifying the straitjacket that the National Security State imposes on leaders as well as on citizens does not minimize the significance of the class analysis or the grave reality of widespread social injustice. On the contrary. It helps us understand why corporate power remains so firmly entrenched in the modern state, and why such power becomes a goal even of those new liberation leaders whose revolutionary movements have been able to dislodge traditional capitalistic regimes. It helps us understand not only why the Soviet Union and the United States are ruled by a new class of elites, but also why Third and Fourth World nations have succumbed to their own new classes of elite decision makers. In helping us understand the greater circumference of the causes of powerlessness, the scope of liberation praxis (reflection-action) opens out toward greater long-range effectiveness.

8

Human/Religious Values Are "Subversive"

> . . . everywhere I go . . . I find minorities with the power for love and justice which could be likened to nuclear energy locked for millions of years in the smallest atoms and waiting to be released.
>
> Dom Helder Camara

With the foregoing chapters as a contextual background, we can now go more deeply into what is one of the central aspects of our analysis: *humanistic-religious values, if widely implemented as criteria for public policy, would undercut the ability of individual nations to survive the multiple balance-of-power competition of today's interdependent but lawless global arena.*

Values such as the primacy of individual conscience, the centrality of the human person and social justice for *all* persons would undermine the mobilization of national institutions, leadership, talent and resources needed to deal with unregulated global economic, monetary and military forces. Or, stated from a power perspective, such values would subvert the aggregate power that, in our existent world system, is essential to guarantee national societies viability in survival competition over balance of weapons, balance of payments and scarce resources.

Not that we are *recommending* such subordination of human values. Quite the contrary. But we are *recognizing* why such values are often logically considered a threat to national security. While there is frequent manipulation of national security logic, it is a mistake to prejudge as "devils" those national leaders who give priority to national security values.

This subordination of other human values to security needs is a central dilemma of the present world system. It is a dilemma that contributes to the ethical and structural lag that we will consider in this chapter.

In the title to this chapter "Human/Religious Values" is linked as one phrase because, although some people distinguish human values from religious values, we do not see them as exclusive of each other. The values of true religion are organically related to growth in human wholeness. Thus we use the terms human values and religious values interchangeably.

The relationship of religion and humanism to the development of alternative world systems and strategies has already been alluded to and will be discussed more fully in a later chapter. It is important, however, to emphasize here that the development of a more human world order is not a task of external, structural change alone. It is a task that also critically involves values change and the development of a human ethic commensurate with the human need for survival and for meaning. Intrinsic vision and growth are also integral to a new human order. For the question is not whether there *will* be a world order. We already have one, an unjust and dehumanizing order based on unregulated power;

an order that is on its way to becoming entrenched. The question, rather, is what kind of world order would we prefer and which values do we want to inform that preferred world order.

AN ETHICAL LAG

Many thinkers have been articulating concern about the future of the human species and the erosion of values that have traditionally provided for human survival. This moral erosion has commonly been attributed to the rise of technology—once humanity's servant, now its new religion. For those who hold this view, first God, then human beings were displaced from their once revered position at the center of the universe —a position now held by technology.

Another view is that this ethical lag is the result of a structural lag, which changes the perspective from which one views technology. The argument here is that "structures of violence" are at the center; and that technology is the servant of those structures. Let us examine the relationship between an ethical and structural lag.

An ethical lag theory has been articulated for some time by thinkers such as Jacques Ellul[1] who warned us that technology is divorced from human values, that it is driven by its own imperatives and that it is running out of control; by M. Bertrand de Jouvenel, who found "no correlation between the priorities of human needs and the priorities of research";[2] and even earlier by Nietzsche who tried to make us aware of technology's reversal of the means-end relationship—that "man was no longer *the* end-in-itself of religion and philosophy but had become the material substratum of the industrial machinery."[3]

Arthur Koestler described it as the disparity between the "growth curves of technological achievement and ethical behavior."[4] Ethical evolution, he says, has not kept pace with technological evolution. In this ethical lag, technology has operated in a moral vacuum. Scientists and technologists have pursued progress with no responsibility for the results of that progress, nor has an awestruck public held them accountable. Penicillin and the H-bomb were equally acceptable, with little public reaction.

There appears to be a strong case for the ethical lag theory. The symptoms of such a lag seem apparent in physical evidence everywhere around us: nuclear stockpiling and potential genocide; ecological waste and destruction; urban decay and congestion; unprecedented crime and violence; erosion of family life; and "progress" and "development" measured in concrete, GNP and missiles rather than increased humanization. Perhaps the most painful effect of the misplaced belief that technology in itself could lead us to the Promised Land has been the philosophy of *meaninglessness*. When technology (which had already displaced God and the human person at the center of the universe) failed to fulfill its promise there was left only the sense of a great void and emptiness. The resulting widespread anguish and alienation was aptly summed up by David Reisman when he wrote: "What we dare not face is not total extinction, but total meaninglessness."[5]

Has this spiritual/ethical lag in modern human evolution done permanent damage? Is the present suicidal course we are on irreversible as some believe? Not so long as we are still able to imagine alternatives and make intentional decisions to set off in another direction.

Some of the most acutely aware and concerned persons of our time have felt with anthropologist Colin Turnbull that humankind can yet "make a conscious decision in favor of the values we still describe as human."[6] Behaviorialist B. F. Skinner,[7] economist Robert Heilbroner,[8] and anthropologist Alexander Alland[9] are among others who have called for conscious and intentional subscription to human values and a moral code favorable to human survival. They urge that survival, both in the physical sense and in the sense of retaining our humanness, demands that we use our capacity to *choose;* that we are not genetically determined and we do not have to and we must not submit to the destructive direction humanity is presently tracked on; that it is possible to select, live, teach, reinforce among ourselves those specific values and life styles most supportive of human survival and human wholeness.

In the past decade, humanists representing many disciplines have been calling for such a new consciousness and intentionality about values for human survival and a meaningful future. Usually the first step they outline is a recognition of our present demise. The next step is to break through the limitations of outmoded paradigms of reality, to develop a new perception of the universe within which ethical considerations must be applied. They compare the effect of such a new perception to the Copernican Revolution which, in changing notions about the physical universe, brought about a social revolution. The new paradigm most frequently substituted is spaceship earth. This image of our earth as a fragile vessel, itself but part of a subsystem of a vast universe, carries with it a heightened awareness of our place in time and space; a consciousness of our planet as a shared habitat, with limits and possibilities for sustaining life; a sense of our ties to each other as cohabitants, of our *mutual responsibility* for each other's well-being; and a renewed confidence in our power as human beings to make a real difference for good or ill.

Such a new consciousness, it is presumed, would provide the basis for developing the new ethic and life-styles needed for our survival. But a third step is also necessary if the new perception and ethic is not to remain theoretical abstraction. That step is to overcome today's critical structural lag.

THE STRUCTURAL LAG

The dehumanizing symptoms cited above—which are commonly attributed to the disproportion between technological and ethical development—are as much related to a structural lag as to an ethical lag.

Global institutional change has simply not kept pace or been commensurate with growing global inter-dependencies and competition. Technology is not inherently a negative force. It is the social *goals* and *application* of technology that determine whether it has a positive or negative effect on the environment and human personality. In this regard a spiritual/ethical lag and the structural lag are integrally related. Lacking a highly developed sense of moral direction in a suddenly expanded, planetary world, and spurred on by survival competition in a global arena lacking effective structures to insure each nation's security, the new technologies were harnessed more in the cause of immediate security competition than on behalf of universal human development goals.

Despite whatever truth there may be in the ethical

lag theory, our crises today are not due primarily to a lack of values or to lack of an inherent moral sense. Nor are they due primarily to apathy about human survival and the quality of human future. (It is anxiety over these that is at the heart of so much conscious or unconscious despair.) What is crippling human action on behalf of our survival and humanness is not that we do not know we need a new ethic—or even what the scope of that new ethic may be. But we have not yet seen that our *personal* changes in values and life-styles will make much difference when we seem *institutionally* locked in.

There has been considerable values ferment. Although the ethical lag is still in evidence, there has never before in history been so much activity in the attempt to articulate and foster a new humanism, a new sense of human, moral direction. It is drawing from Eastern philosophy as well as from the Western heritage of Greek, Judaic-Christian, Medieval, Renaissance and Enlightenment thought. It is drawing from the sciences, from biology, psychology and anthropology. It is drawing from religious experience of East and West in a great exchange of thought and insight. It is seeking, inside and outside of traditional religious structures, to rediscover a spiritual rootedness through such experiential forms as transcendental meditation and prayer groups. It is experimenting with alternative life-styles and community living. It is exploring ways to implement the human development theories of people like Dewey, Maslow and Carl Rogers or researching, like Lawrence Kohlberg, the area of moral development.

Educational leaders, concerned about rising violence as well as the broader aims of humanistic education in a future-shock world, are beginning to reexamine their previous biases against value teaching in the schools as they realize that values are always being taught, consciously or unconsciously. Now they are asking whether values for life in the approaching twenty-first century shouldn't be a conscious part of education and considering which values should be given emphasis for a future of human wholeness as against increasing violence and potential annihilation. (Just beginning to ask, but nevertheless asking.)

Scientists, too, are beginning to question the uses to which their own research and discoveries are put. And the emergence of groups such as the Institute of Society, Ethics and the Life Sciences, which probe such areas as the ethical ramifications of new knowledge in genetic engineering, are indicative that the lag, while still a problem, is not an unbridgeable chasm. Likewise, the rise of increasing numbers of environmental protection, consumer protection and social justice lobbying groups is evidence that people are not apathetic about questions of their survival and well-being nor shy about ethical considerations.

All this ferment suggests that we *know* we need a new ethic, or at least need to see new applications of traditional ethics. Increasingly we even have a broad outline of the scope and content of that ethic. Although expressed in different terminology, according to pet in-house phrasing of a given group, there is some consensus that the new humanism be rooted in *reverence*: a deep reverence for life—all life, a reverence for Being rather than having, a reverence for the centrality of the human person. The new humanist would consciously strive toward *wholeness*: wholeness of self, wholeness of the community, wholeness of the planet. The new humanist would be a communal person, i.e., living "in communion with" fellow persons, aware of our mutual dependence and concerned for the common good. Meaning would be sought not so much in material goods and success but more in the sense of destiny beyond self and beyond immediate history. Responsibility would not be seen only in terms of self, but also in terms of the whole community and the environment on which all depend.

Very important to the new humanism would be a de-emphasis both individually and nationally of such values as "individualism," "doing your own thing," and "competition," which may have served in the past decade to counter mass conformity, but whose overemphasis in national life in the past twenty-five years has led to many of our present crises, and worked against the common good. In Skinnerian terms, we would have to learn to defer some of our own personal gratification for longer-range goals and the good of the species. *Cooperation,* or "harambee," the Swahili concept of pulling together, would be given emphasis over competition against other individuals, groups or nations to be Number One. Simpler living would be essential for some so that others would have enough. Power, as a personal or corporate resource with potential for negative or constructive uses, would have to have those uses evaluated not only in terms of short-range benefits to "me," "my" group or "my" nation, but how it would affect others, now and long-range, in the total human community. *Social justice, economic well-being, nonviolence, ecological stewardship, participation in decision making,* for all peoples, would be words of key value.

It is not our purpose here to explore in great detail

the ethic and values needed to sustain our global village, although they are of deep concern. Suffice it to say that, to be of global effect, such an intentional value system needs to be developed and nourished in transcultural dialogue and experience. Our purpose here is to point out that even though the ethical lag has been recognized, named and explored from numerous directions, and even though there is increasingly a consciousness of the need to reexamine values and lifestyles and some sincere starts in this direction, *still* there is relatively little true progress in the direction of a new humanism and new moral order evidenced in major national decisions being made in the world today.

The question is, *Why*? A major reason is the one with which we began this chapter: *human-religious values are "subversive."* If widely implemented as criteria for public policy, they would subvert the ability of individual nations to survive the multiple balance-of-power competition in today's interdependent but lawless global arena.

But there is a "so long as" clause that accompanies this statement. Human/religious values are subversive *so long as* the structural lag that causes these values to be subversive continues. Such values are subversive *so long as* we continue to tolerate the obsolete principle of unlimited national sovereignty. Much of the ethical lag will continue *so long as* we fail to develop just and effective world order structures. Technology will continue to serve structures of violence *so long as* we do not commit ourselves to construct alternative structures.

Because of this structural lag, most of the energy expended in fostering a new humanism is principally from isolated individuals and groups who are removed from major decision-making power. Publishers may show good profits or develop a good reputation for serious, value-centered publishing lists. But few such books enter the board rooms or oval offices around the world where the corporate decisions that determine the policies and institutions of National Security States are made. Few men or women who are deeply committed to basic human development or to a new humanism enter such rooms or offices. Their values and goals are logically locked out from such power centers—*so long as* humanists and religionists remain on the sidelines of the movement for effective world order institutions.

The following paragraphs examine some obvious areas of leadership to assess why the ethics of a new humanism is not being more widely adopted.

POLITICAL LEADERSHIP

In the existent system of competing nation-states, the creative leadership for applying a new humanism to the goals of public policy is unlikely to come from political leadership. This is so because the application of an ethical humanism by one state, without its universal application, could undermine that nation's ability to survive inter-nation competition.

The following statement made by General Matthew B. Ridgway is an articulation of the line of thought that dominates national governments:

"Grave as are the domestic issues which confront us—inflation, the poverty level, drug

abuse, crime and the erosion of moral principles—they are of *lesser importance than the
potential menace of a foreign state* which sees
us as the only major barrier to the expansion
of its power, and once this barrier is demol-
ished or neutralized, a clear open path to the
seizure of the riches of this, the most affluent
people on earth.

In this savage, brutal, amoral world we must,
if we value our independent national existence
and our fundamental principles, insure that
our armed forces are adequate for our security against the most dangerous challenge any
foreign power is today capable of presenting."[10] (Italics added.)

One value generating such a philosophy is obviously the protection of American economic privilege. But
an even more fundamental value, given the perception
of a "brutal, amoral world," is that of independent, national survival.

What Ridgway says on the shores of the world's
most affluent nation is increasingly also said on the
shores of the world's less affluent and even destitute nations. As shown in previous chapters, the United States
is not alone among nations in its central fixation on national security values. It is part and parcel of the present system that the political leadership of all nation-
states must give priority value to national security, defined in terms of economic, monetary and military
power.

It is not that national leaders are without values.
As is evident from Ridgway's concerns and from the

national security concerns of other national leaders, there are plenty of values at the basis of government decision making. It is a question of *what* those values are and what values are given priority and whether those values that may serve a particular nation's immediate and pragmatic interests will serve the broader, more universal interests of the human species. It is a question of the dehumanizing, alienating character of those values and the illusion that the policies and institutions from which they spring preserve "our fundamental principles."

The values crisis in the world's national leadership is not so much personal as it is structural. Because of the nature of its tasks and objectives, values of the National Security State are often in opposition to individual (and universal) values or morality. Individuals may be morally opposed to killing. The nation-state sees killing (of the "enemy" as currently defined) as a necessary evil for national survival. Persons may hold that needless ecological destruction is morally wrong. Nations hold that it is "strategically necessary in order to contain and limit the enemy." People may hold that lying and stealing, spying, and knowingly misleading others by manipulating the truth are morally wrong. Nations hold that this behavior is sometimes "strategically" necessary and even commendable when it serves the "national interest."

"Saints can be pure, but statesmen, alas, must be responsible," wrote Arthur Schlesinger Jr. in defense of the "necessary amorality" of the nation-state in foreign affairs. "A nation that rejects national interest as the mainspring of its policy cannot survive." Asking the question whether overt moral principles should decide issues of foreign policy, Schlesinger answered, "as little as possible."[11]

Schlesinger's argument points up the reality that, in our present world system, the nation has become more important than the person who is the citizen. The nation must survive, but citizens are *expendable*. As is morality.

The "national interest" has come to mean retaining, or aspiring to attain, the *Number One* position in the world. And being Number One in our competitive nation-state system has come to mean being a nation of Might rather than a People of Greatness.

Being Number One has meant, as Ridgway urged, valuing above all else military power as the guarantor of our economic power. And economic power has meant continued economic growth and production, which in turn has meant a continuing emphasis on aggregate goals where persons are valued for their consumption and production potential rather than their dignity as human beings.

Being Number One has come to mean escalatory technological growth as necessary to corporate, military, monetary and economic power. Such a national security technology, driven by the imperatives of weapons, monetary and resource competition rather than human development needs, will continue to erode, rather than support human values and social cohesion.

ECONOMIC LEADERSHIP

Today there is one interdependent world economic fibre. But lacking effective global structures for long-range economic planning and regulation in the best interests of the world community, this global economic fibre has become a chaos of private and corporate interests all competing against each other for resources, labor and markets. Multinational corporations, not subject to effective world law, are able to shift location or capital when local laws or conditions are not favorable to their goals. Giant conglomerates are able to gain de facto monopolies in some areas of production. And nation-states, left to their own resources to protect their national economies, are increasingly engaged in economic warfare in which changing strategies, alliances and sudden unilateral decisions can tear dangerously at the threads of world economic well-being.

In this structural lag the goal of national economic planning is not being directed primarily toward human well-being and basic needs such as food, shelter and environmental protection. (For economics, like technology, does not establish its own directives and uses but is directed by individual and societal objectives.) Increasingly, for lack of global regulation, national economic goals are determined by the security imperatives of global competition.

Here again we see the relationship between the ethical lag and the structural lag. Personalist and humanist economic scenarios have not been lacking since the advent of the National Security State. An example is E. F. Schumacher's *Small is Beautiful*[12] proposals for decentralized economic development. His book has gotten widespread consideration. But not by those who are responsible for the corporate economic goals required for military, monetary and resource survival in the present world system. Nor by those who manipulate the logic behind those corporate goals to preserve their own power and privilege.

Even apart from the national security logic for such corporate economic processes and institutions, there is a second reason for the ethical lag—again quite directly related to the structural lag. It is the reality that, in today's interdependent global economy, it is extremely difficult for nations already enmeshed in global economic institutions to radically transform their economic priorities or institutions. Few, if any, can successfully opt out from the corporate processes that are globally operative, processes that tend to ossify economic institutions in the status quo. It makes little difference what ideology that status quo represents. The balance of viability—vis-a-vis balance-of-payments deficits, for example—is for many countries extremely fragile. To *unilaterally* attempt substantial economic and social reconstruction—especially if it is toward more decentralized and personalized production units— is extremely risky. But, within a world security system in which a significant portion of the world community would be free and secure enough to take similar steps, the risk would be greatly reduced.

Whatever the fine humanist goals or dreams of people favoring one economic system over another, these goals—with few exceptions—have not affected public policy. For, as described in previous chapters, the central focus of economic planning in capitalist, socialist or communist nations alike has necessarily drifted toward corporate power and aggregate economic growth to ensure national survival.

In the context of genuine national security concerns, as well as of the illegitimate manipulation of national security as a means of keeping power, those persons or groups who seriously espouse a radical departure from the dehumanizing aggregate economic goals of today are labeled subversive and considered a threat to the state. Depending upon the degree to which they appear to threaten these security goals, they will either be ignored or imprisoned. It is in this anomaly that the ethic of a new humanism in economics is trapped.

EDUCATIONAL LEADERSHIP
What about educational leadership? Many have

looked to education as the only hope in implanting a new ethic and humanism sufficient to effect meaningful human survival. There has even been talk of the need for an *ethical quotient* of commensurate importance to the intelligence quotient.

An assessment of the capacity of education to nurture the development of a broadly based humanism must be looked at from the broader environmental context in which learning takes place as well as from the context of formal educational structures. From both perspectives, the total cultural context and the "schooling" context of education, effective humanistic education is very difficult.

Informal Education

The total impact of a culture on human development cannot be offset by a few hours a day in a classroom, which is only one aspect, and probably a less consequential one, of the total learning process. In the United States, isolated parents or even small clusters of parents working together on educational alternatives are up against one of the most powerful educational forces in the world: Madison Avenue. Using all manner of appeals and motivation, business and industry are successfully using public relations firms to "educate" millions of viewers and readers in a consumer identity and values. To *have* more is of more importance than to *be* more. Whether or not such "education" works for the best long-range interests of the human species is not questioned.

With the dispersion of American films and TV shows throughout the noncommunist world, there is a growing emulation of behavioral violence and materialism. Indicative of the disproportionate influence of

U.S. communications (unfortunately we do not even send the best we have to offer) is the fact that the offerings in the U.S. of media presentations produced in other areas of the world is negligible.

Mass media communications could be a major educational vehicle for people throughout the world to explore together the development of a more human future, drawing and sharing from the historical, esthetic heritage of our various past and present experience. We do not lack the technological capacity for such humanistic and extremely revelant education. With instant satellite communications we do have the technological ability. Nor do we lack skilled technicians. Nor do we lack people who combine human and moral vision with esthetic talent. *What we do lack are the global structures that would facilitate the use of media for human development goals;* structures not tied to national biases or to a market system or restrained by national security exigencies from open pursuit of truth.

What is, of course, implied here is the overall educational effect of national goals, which, though less visible than the picture tube, is more significant because it affects the uses of an otherwise neutral technology. Directly or indirectly, national goals significantly affect the ends to which communications are used. In the competitive atmosphere in which national goals focus on accumulating ever greater national power—military, monetary and economic—there is emerging a world culture which, in its *external* manifestations, is characterized by mass (not necessarily humanizing) similarities throughout the world. But the *inner* space of our deeply shared but hidden human potential and the riches from our unique, personal and cultural experiences, have yet to be significantly developed.

In this area of *human inner space* lies humanity's

greatest potential learning adventure and its greatest educational challenge. But, in the face of other mass educational preoccupations and priorities, it is an area that remains grossly underdeveloped.

Formal Education

Within formal education circles there has been considerable thought and discussion, as well as some innovative experimentation, related to humanistic and affective learning. This activity has been generated both by a concern about various forms of violence in schools (the educational process itself as a form of violence as well as racial and overt physical violence) and a desire to enhance the learning potential and facilitate holistic growth of students.

There has also been growing interest in the relationship of the classroom to human issues such as racial and ethnic identity, sex-role stereotyping, ecological balance, world hunger, population, social justice, world peace, etc. Some pioneer work in related curriculum development and teacher education has been undertaken independently and collaboratively in several areas of the world.

Although still at an early stage, this growing interest of education in world community issues made it possible for the World Council on Curriculum and Instruction to focus its world gathering at Keele, England in 1974, on Peace Education. At this conference, educators from around the world shared developments in their own homelands and explored the further development of transnational educational approaches to the question of war prevention. The Consortium on Peace Research and Educational Development (COPRED) is an affiliation of more than 100 university, public and private educational organizations all engaged in peace research and related educational activity. In 1976, the bicentennial focus of the U.S. National Education Association (N.E.A.) celebrated the past by looking to the future. With the theme "A Declaration of Interdependence: Education For A Global Community," it gathered peace education materials from all over the world, engaged in transnational educational dialogue by satellite, and presented the outlines for a forward-thinking program of education for life in a whole earth community.

Throughout the world, professional *international* education networks, such as the Association of World Colleges and Universities, the Association for Childhood Education International, the International Schools Association, the World Future Studies Federation, the International Federation of Catholic Universities, the International Studies Association, to name just a few, are a global fibre that can be effectively utilized to foster the type of educational activity vital to human survival and well-being. The advent of the United Nations University in Japan is also a positive development toward transnational approaches to education that is relevant to the needs of the world community.

Although such efforts are still in a pioneering stage, they are evidence of both the growing concern and the possibilities within formal education for responding to issues of global survival and well-being. But how widespread are such efforts? And to what degree can they be forwarded without a commensurate advance in global structures?

Since the inception of formal education, there has been a tension concerning its true purpose and objectives. That tension was well articulated in debates between different schools of thinking in Greek society, including the followers of Sophocles, Socrates and Isocrates. Socrates and Isocrates saw education both as a means toward self-realization and service to the common good. It was a vision of education for *Becoming and Being.* It was a process of personal growth in truth, beauty, goodness and love and, simultaneousiy, it was a process leading out from private concerns and interests to active, responsible participation as a *citizen.* The "idiots" were those who looked only to their own good.

Without a holistic approach that preserves in delicate balance both these aspects, education can degenerate into a dehumanizing activity. Lacking a public philosophy the followers of Sophocles reduced self-realization goals of education to *self-serving* goals. Education for the sophists was a means to personal status and position in the community. Educational sophistry is a problem still very much with us today.

The "citizen" ends of education have likewise been historically usurped, making education a *tool* of the state for mass domination and control. The abuse of education on this side came into ascendancy with the rise of the nation-state.

Napoleon was quick to seize on the egalitarian goal of the French Revolution for popular education as a means to further his personal ambitions. He wanted a strong, powerful state, with a united citizenry loyal to his one-man rule. He also needed a trained and loyal bureaucracy to efficiently manage affairs of state and pursue expansionist goals. In line with these national goals, the First Consul under Napoleon launched a strong, centralized, nationalist scheme of education under control of the state. All teachers were to be trained in the National University to ensure wide-spread permeation of the new nationalism. The Catholic Church was permitted to continue its own schools, but in all, public and private, national patriotism had to be inculcated.

As Napoleonic despotism grew and dominated other European states, a reactionary wind set in which fanned the flames of counter nationalist movements. The insecurity, humiliation and defeat they had experienced led to cries throughout Europe for national sovereignty. Nationalist leaders, quick to learn from France's example, seized upon education as the vehicle for the new gospel of nationalism. There followed throughout the European states the founding of strong, centralized, national universities and educational systems enlisted in the service of the state. Each had as its end the instilling of a strong sense of national identity and unity and the training of people in skills and attitudes that would serve national needs of economic and military survival.

Nowhere was this usurpation of education for nationalist goals so strongly and universally developed as in Prussia. By 1871 there was what H. G. Wells described as a "systematic exploitation and control of school and college, literature and press, in the interests of the Hohenzollern dynasty"[13] that was to have a tremendous impact on citizen psychology among the Prussian people and on the history of the world.

"A teacher, a professor, who did not teach and preach, in and out of season, the racial, moral, intellectual, and physical superiority of the Germans to all other peoples, their extraordinary devotion to war and their dynasty, and their inevitable destiny under that dynasty to lead the world, was a marked man, doomed to failure and obscurity. German historical teaching became an immense systematic falsification of the human past, with a view of the Hohenzollern future. All other nations were represented as incompetent and decadent; the Prussians were the leaders and regenerators of mankind.

The young German read this in his schoolbooks, heard it in church, found it in his literature, had it poured into him with passionate conviction by his professor. It was poured into him by all his professors; lectures in biology or mathematics would break off from their proper subject to indulge in long passages of patriotic rant. Only minds of extraordinary toughness and originality could resist such a torrent of suggestion. Insensibly there was built up in the German mind a conception of Germany and its emperor as of something splendid and predominant as nothing else had ever been before, a godlike nation in "shining armour" brandishing the "good German sword" in a world of inferior—and badly disposed—peoples."[14]

The human hostilities engendered and reinforced by such blatantly militaristic uses of education in Prussia and later in Hitler's Germany, as well as the nationalist biases being instilled throughout the rest of Europe, were a major contributing force leading to eruption in two world wars.

In the post-World War II era there was significant reform of overt nationalist biases in German and other European schools, but education remains integrally related to national goals.

The pattern of nationalist-oriented education did not stop with Europe. In the aftermath of their revolutions, the universal education introduced in both the Soviet Union and China was directed at building a strong national identity and unity and skills essential to national goals of economic and military survival in a world of competing states. Recent attempts by some Soviet educators to introduce humanistic educational perspectives were squelched by a government dictate that all schools must return to a strong nationalist emphasis.

The colonized countries of Asia and Africa inherited European national education systems. Post-independence revisionism has not been so much aimed at changes that humanize the content and methodology as at simply substituting a different nationalist bias. Besides expanding clan and tribal loyalties into new national identity and cohesion, education is a vehicle for "national development" and "modernization" so that these new nations will be able to compete and survive in the world marketplace.

In the United States, which has prided itself in the notion that its education was free of government controls, and was not a vehicle to propagandize or brainwash children in political ideologies, there has nevertheless been a great deal of curricular time, energy and religiosity consciously or unconsciously put into the formation of young people in "citizenship" values that have, in effect, contributed to American ethnocentrism. With great areas of ommission in global historical and literary heritage, the educational content has stressed American heroes and history, flag rituals and a "my country first" patriotism that has fed a sense of superiority and prejudice.

As in other National Security States, public and private school curricula in the U.S. were adapted to enable the nation to adequately compete and to retain its Number One position in Cold War competition. When the Soviets sent up Sputnik in 1957, the call went forth to get rid of the "fripperies" in American education and to stress the subjects that counted—science and technology. One result was the National Defense Education Act, which funded research and scholarships that were judged to relate to "national security." Educational priorities were determined accordingly. In the 1960s student protests in the United States began to reveal the degree to which universities (which profess to be *universal* in vision) had succumbed to large grants and contracts from government and national security related industries. Higher education had quietly but effectively been enlisted as a research and education partner in national security mobilization. These grants were primarily being given not to humanities or scientific research related to human services such as health care, nor to develop a science of peace or a science to overcome hunger and poverty or other pressing human issues on the global agenda, but to a science and technology that would enable the nation to compete militarily and economically.

The subordination of humanistic educational goals to national security needs has not been confined to research and development projects on the university level. From kindergarten on, flag rituals and citizenship training is a way of inculcating in young Americans that their country and flag are superior to others and that (as our daughter reported after kindergarten, one day) "war is what you have to do for your flag."

At a time when human survival is threatened by nuclear proliferation and ecocide, education should be leading us out from the "idiocy" of limited national self-interest to a new perception of global citizenship. Instead, education throughout the world is still widely psychologically attached to nationalism and heavily affected by national security goals in our present nation-state system.

With World Peace Day, World Ecology Day or United Nations Day given only an annual mention against the everyday indoctrination in national flag worship, it is unlikely that the world's education systems, dominated by the national security values of their respective nation states, can pave the way in reinforcing the values of a new humanism. In the present nation-state structure, to *effectively* lead students out toward universal love and to have students really seek the truth in studies of history and comparative government, to have them explore a universal application of a human ethic, to have them truly seek solutions to problems that will work to the common good of humankind rather than the immediate benefit of their own nation, would be labeled subversive.

Teachers cannot expect to be successful in teaching an ecological ethic when they must defend or remain silent about the massive ecological destruction rendered in the name of national security by their nation against another in "foreign" and "enemy" lands. Teachers cannot expect to be effective in teaching brotherhood or sisterhood when they must defend or be silent about their nation's war policies, armaments sales and expenditures, and injustices perpetrated against brothers and sisters in other nations in the name of "national interest."

Not that educators cannot try to nurture the ethic of a new humanism or to reinforce reverence for life and being on a universal scale. Some are. And more could and should be done, even within the existent National Security State framework. But only when educators (whether in the total cultural context of education or within formal educational settings) are freed from the psychological, political or community pressures which make such teaching a "subversive" activity will they be able to truly approach holistic educational goals.

We spoke of the delicate balance between personal and communal goals of education. Further enabling educators to put their full talents to the development of educational approaches that are both integral to personal human realization and simultaneously relevant to the needs and common good of the human community as a whole, is related to the development of just and effective world-order structures.

Such world-order structures would help to humanize educational goals from two perspectives. The first is the tremendous effect that national goals consciously or unconsciously have on education. When nations are freed from the security concerns that now subordinate human development aspirations there will be a parallel liberating effect on educational goals. The second is the tremendous psychological constraint posed in a system that forces on the human psyche an artificial identity system and an artificial dichotomy between loyalty to one's nation and loyalty to the human community as a whole. The development of a human world order in which this dichotomy is removed would open the psychological space of educational activity. This would have a liberating and humanizing effect on teaching and on the learning process as a pursuit of truth and human realization.

RELIGIOUS LEADERSHIP

There is every evidence that the mass exodus from organized religion in our century has not been due primarily to a loss of belief in a spiritual force informing and encompassing all life. A more frequent cause has been the impotency of organized religion in the face of the struggles and crises—both personal and global— that humankind confronted in the twentieth century. What was being demanded of humankind seemed more than could be met within traditional religious structures. Many were taken up in awe of a new supernatural—technology—and its seeming promise of personal fulfillment and human salvation. The hungry would be fed, the thirsty given drink, the homeless sheltered, the ill made well, the tired laborer given leisure— more by the power of machines than by power of religion. Religion steadily lost its power to affect human behavior or provide meaning.

Nor was it able to provide social cohesion or cultural security in the face of the threats, conflicts and power struggles between nations of the world. People sought security more in the new technology (which would provide for their physical and economic needs) and in the nation-state (which would provide for their physical safety from the "enemy," the "outsider," the "evil ones") than they did in religion.

But such security has proven illusory. The eventual and inevitable disillusionment with the ability of either technology or nationalism to provide meaning or security has led to a resurgence of spiritual search. Inside and outside of formal religious structures people are seeking some kind of spiritual, ethical or humanistic salvation from the effects of a world that seems bent on extinction. Empty, searching for self, for meaning, and for alternatives, persons have joined alternative communities, meditation classes, charismatic and pentecostal movements. But even though finding reinforcement in communal settings, most of these efforts are aimed at *personal* salvation or growth at a time when the crises are global and communal as well. With this personalized focus they are largely considered harmless to society and not very consequential beyond an affect on relatively few individual persons.

But what if religious institutions and movements were to become effective in nurturing those values, common to all the world's major religions, that go beyond personal salvation and fulfillment? What if religious institutions, on a massive scale commensurate with the *global* nature of the crises we face, became *effective* in reinforcing a lived ethic related to love of the enemy and a truth-seeking reverence for life (*all* people's lives and environments)? What if religions should really begin to *effectively* reinforce and universalize the commandments "Thou shalt not kill" (including an "enemy"); "Thou shalt not take thy neighbor's goods" (including the wealth and labor of the poorer nations); "Thou shalt not bear false witness against thy neighbor" (including the people of thy neighbor nations)?

If religion could really effect a perception of the world in which the "enemy" became a person, a friend, and his "alien" land became the sacred and shared heritage for which we are mutually responsible, then religion, *in our present system of competing nation-states,* would become the enemy of the state, and the followers of religion, like the conscientious objectors, would be suspect and the prisons would be filled beyond capacity.

For true religious values are "subversive." The deepest spiritual values of most major religions, if promulgated and lived, would subvert the ability of independent sovereign states to survive the multiple competition in the present lawless global arena. The love of neighbor, in practice, the search for truth in practice could rock the foundations of today's national security structures.

To allow the free and full implementation of fundamental human/religious values such as the primacy of individual conscience, or the centrality and inviolability of the individual person, would subvert the "logical" mobilization for national security values. The subversion power of other religious values is also clear. What if the people, spurred on by their religious faith and spiritual growth, insisted that national leaders design policies that would embrace the solidarity of all humankind; or the responsibility *in justice* to every member of the human family; or a commitment to embrace truth whatever and wherever it may be, even when embarrassing to the government? What would happen? The answer is quite simple: the nation-state, as presently constituted, could not survive. Its economic and monetary institutions would collapse. Chaos would reign. Thus, today's national security elites have little choice but to utilize rhetoric, political harassment and national security ideologies to silence vocal advocates of such values.

But, if religious values are subversive to the National Security State, national security values are also subversive to true religion. It is a two-edged sword. In the past, religious people have sinned in silence while their global neighbors were being killed or dehumanized, not wanting to apply the moral code for individuals to affairs of the nation-state for fear of being condemned as "unpatriotic," "disloyal," "un-American," "un-German," "communist," "capitalist," "traitorous," "treasonous." The denunciations carry greater weight than sacrilege. But in the very failure to respond and speak out against human injustices, true religious values are successfully subverted by the values of national self-interest. To condone, or silently abide, lying, stealing, false pride, hate, murder, violence or injustice on the part of the state (regardless of the national security rationale being used), while condemning it in individuals, is to feed a cancer that will eat away at the flesh and soul of spiritual life till there are but dead bones and emptiness—a spiritual vacuum impotent to inspire faith in God or to motivate human behavior on the side of life and humanization.

It is not only the traditional institutions of organized religion whose silence has been a factor in social deterioration and dehumanization. We suggested above that the new religious movements have been largely *considered* harmless and inconsequential to society as a whole. But they are *not* inconsequential. And, while they may appear harmless, followers of the new spiritual groups, if they do not make a deliberate effort otherwise, may actually be capable of wreaking great harm on the course of history and the future of humankind.

Rollo May has written about power and innocence[15]—something that concerns us here. When persons withdraw from society, rejecting the "evils of this world" as disassociated from themselves, fixing the source of evil on external devils—human or otherwise—and seeking only their personal salvation and exemption from guilt, they feign an innocence and powerlessness that contributes to the perpetuation of those evils and are perhaps as dangerous as the more overt destructive decision making and behavior they reject. Instead of seeing power as an energy resource that is neuter and capable of being used for good or ill, many think of power, and people who exercise power, as inherently evil. To avoid guilt they relinquish their own power and responsibility for shaping human destiny and thereby allow it to be shaped around them. Then they claim innocence of the resulting destruction.

"We are all part of the tragic event," writes Rollo May, "we are all involved. Without a radical surrender of consciousness no one today can draw his moral skirts around him and claim immunity from such tragic situations."[16] Many persons fleeing the problems in society and seeking salvation in religious movements run the risk, if they do not consciously and responsibly exercise their own power, of drawing their "moral skirts" around them and "claiming immunity" from the destruction and guilt of the world. It is one of the dangers we see in the embracing of an apocalyptic vision by those who believe the end of history is in sight and, instead of using the personal and communal power available to them to change the situation, bring about the fulfillment of their own prophecy by behaving as if they were powerless victims. With a vision of themselves as members of God's faithful remnant who will enjoy eternal bliss when this world passes away, they scrutinize their personal lives to make sure they are ready for the end. And thereby they contribute to the resulting destruction by failing to take any positive initiative on behalf of the world and humankind.

In a failure of vision and a failure to *use* their powers creatively, religious institutions and movements may be failing to respond to what is being asked of them by their Lord of history: to throw in their lot with the human community and be a *leaven* for a new shape, height and fullness to human existence on the planet—a shape reflecting the glory of the Lord of their belief; a shape freeing them to more fully implement the values of true religion.

There is a responsibility flowing from authentic religion to be true to one's faith commitment on all levels of activity in the world—on a personal level and an institutional level. There has been much effort given within organized religion to the science and technology of individual spiritual development. Can we now move more fully beyond the sphere of individual growth to full human development of the whole earth community and develop a science and technology of that? One aspect of this larger sphere of activity is the development of a more human world order.

SCIENTIFIC LEADERSHIP

It has become common practice to attribute the ills of our contemporary world to the technological society outlined by Ellul and others. Grave concern is expressed about technology's enslavement of the human person. The concern is well founded. But the error is to blame technology. This is to forget that technology is neutral. Nothing inherently dehumanizing has been discovered in its use. It has the potential of lifting many of the burdens and conflicts that have blocked true human development in past history. The problem lies not in technology itself, but in the *goals* for which science and technology are used and the runaway escalation that those goals generate. The national security imperatives of our present world system prevent the calm and flexibility to use technology to *conserve* human values and to respond adequately to today's personal and social breakdown. Only in the development of a world order that minimizes national security concerns can we begin to apply technology to more positive, humanizing goals.

In his book *Future Shock*, Alvin Toffler asserts that the *rate* of change is more important than its *direction*. Toffler warns of a massive adaptational breakdown if the rate of change is not controlled. The result of the speed, turmoil and impermanence in society is a psycho-biological disease that is rooted in the ephemeralization of a person's links with his or her environment. Effects of this disease include identity confusion, noninvolvement and social violence.[17]

One reason that Toffler's valuable book was so popular was that it affirmed and organized the experiences of the amateur and professional observer alike. It identified what we feel as a loss of control over our lives, a loss that we tend to attribute to some person, group, or institutional demon. Toffler describes this sense of losing control with a quote from Ralph E. Lapp's book *The New Priesthood:*

> We are aboard a train which is gathering speed, racing down a track on which there are an unknown number of switches leading to unknown destinations. No single scientist is in the engine cab and there may be demons at the switch. Most of society is in the caboose looking backward.[18]

Here we have an effective image of the forces in which national societies are caught. Lapp complains that no single *scientist* is at the controls. His focus on the role of scientists, however, blurs the full import of his image. For even if his complaint were answered by the election of a scientist as head of state, who in turn appointed scientists with a uniform future scenario as cabinet heads, and whose administration was reinforced by a congress of similarly like-minded scientists, all acting in unison, the runaway train could still not be brought under control. For new, scientific heads of state would still be caught up in the escalating competition of an interdependent global arena. National societies, in which technology remains a tool of competition, cannot unilaterally disembark. The runaway train can only be slowed down and given direction within a global juridical order which minimizes the "need" to use technology for security imperatives.

Failing to adequately identify the national security imperatives which are a root cause of a dehumanizing application of technology, as well as its escalatory rate of growth, Toffler's analysis of our future-shock world stands incomplete. Because of this incomplete analysis, Toffler's truly remarkable book fails to come up with a practical, viable strategy to develop the "change regulators" which he says are necessary if we are to avoid massive personal and institutional breakdown.

In Toffler's analysis, the prime *engine* of the escalatory change that is causing the disease of future shock is technology. We can agree that this is a major engine of change (although, as mentioned before, technology is not in itself harmful). But then, speaking about the "knowledge explosion," Toffler identifies knowledge as being the *fuel* of that engine. Here we must dissent. For knowledge, like technology, has no inner imperative in itself. How many library shelves are decked with Ph.D. theses and heavy Brookings Institute type of in-depth research books that stand gathering dust? It is the *goals* of a society that largely determine what knowledge on those shelves is chosen to become operative. And in today's National Security State, the central goals are largely determined by the imperatives of nation-state competition.

Thus, rather than the knowledge explosion being the fuel that energizes the engine (technology) of escalatory change, the major fuel is *competition among totally independent sovereignties.* But even accepting Toffler's premise that the knowledge explosion is, at least partially, the fuel of an escalating technology, the problem still remains the same. Where has much of the research and development money that has generated the knowledge explosion of the past generation come from? And for what purpose? The answer is clear. Hundreds of billions of dollars since World War II have come from federal government offices to seek that type of knowledge that would develop the technologies needed, not for human liberation and development, but rather for survival in the global arena. The contemporary knowledge explosion did not come without an exorbitant price to pay.

An explosion of knowledge, however, need not trigger escalatory change at the dizzy level that we are experiencing today. A society freed from the straitjacket of national security mobilization could afford investment in a different type of research and development. It could be a search for knowledge aimed at, first of all, understanding better the "Science of the Human Person." It could be a search for the kind of integral community and regional planning that would respond to alienation and individual identity needs. An example: such planning could seek to stabilize neighborhoods and coordinate transportation and employment opportunities, thereby cutting down on the destructive impermanence of jobs, relationships, and other identity signposts of which Toffler speaks.

Toffler's description of the "disease of change" includes the impermanence of a culture in which the guideposts upon which we depend for a continuity of identity disappear. A central area of this impermanence is that of *value* change. As much as anything else, it is the instability of values that underlies the near universal crisis of self-identity. A stable identity depends on *meaning*. But without an internal stability built on core values, meaning is elusive, if possible at all.

The problem of values is two-fold. One is the type of values that dominate a culture. Our present National Security State system institutionalizes impersonal and often dehumanizing values which preclude the person-centered and transcendent values that permit an individual to weather social change with his/her identity intact. The second problem is the instability of values in a society of escalatory change.

Our main concern right here is the second problem of value instability. This is not to argue for a conservative, static society in which nothing changes. Our concern is rooted in the paradox we see in our times, i.e., that in the world of escalatory change, things are not fundamentally changing. Yet, precisely because of the lack of institutional change, *everything* is changing.

In seeking institutions to regulate change, we are not seeking to hold back history. We place ourselves on the side of change. We argue for both institutional and value change. The change we pursue is fundamentally conservative: a change that will *conserve* those person-centered values that are being wiped out in the national security culture that encircles this planet. The key to this change lies in the transformation of our static, obsolete National Security State system that is at the center of our paradox. For the present world system is both the obstacle to a movement toward human-centered institutions and values, and a major cause of unstable institutions and values.

This question of values helps focus on the pregnancy of our times. The Chinese characters for *crisis* convey a double meaning. They depict a crisis as having a potential for great catastrophe or for great positive breakthroughs. This aptly describes our times, in which human history faces a catastrophe and/or an unprecedented breakthrough. The crisis of values is illustrative of this double dimension. Traditional values are being challenged and subverted on every side. Some of those values are the human-centered ones that preserve personal individuality, primacy of conscience, and social justice. Fortunately, however, they are not the only values being challenged. Also being challenged are some traditional values that have been dehumanizing and oppressive. A major tension of the past decade was between proponents of "establishment" culture and proponents of "counterculture." Emotions were high, and the pain was intense all around. Caught in the straitjacket of an outmoded world system, we were all denied the institutional and political flexibility to place the search for stable human values in an environment that would permit the pregnancy of new value insight and experience to bear fruit.

The past decade produced countless books and articles reevaluating the contemporary model of industrial-technological progress. There was a literal renaissance in this regard—at least in analysis and commentary. But the renaissance remained primarily a literary phenomenon. The domination of national security institutions precluded such analysis from affecting actual planning. The highly paid consultants of the Rand Corporation and the Hudson Institute knew (and know) that the national security managers who contracted them would not—more accurately, *could* not—tolerate scenarios that would integrate the alternative concepts of human-centered progress spawned by the new renaissance. The future scenarios that these consultants proffered, therefore, were mainly within the general framework of unlimited growth.

There is no way that the "change regulators" advocated by Toffler can be effectively installed as long as the world continues to worship around the obsolete altar of unlimited national sovereignty. The only way that today's rampant global economic, monetary and military forces can be effectively regulated is through transnational agencies to which nations relinquish some sovereignty in order that those forces and crises which nations cannot handle individually may be managed collectively.

Until we begin the journey on the road to such a world order—one fashioned according to the values of person centrality and universal justice—the escalatory change that is breeding our future-shock world will continue.

NOT A DEAD END

Some thinkers have become very cynical. They consider this period of despair as the great and *final* despair. They see no chance for survival in the long run, feeling things have gone too far and people are too unchangeable.

But others see this as a period of great possibility. They see the void all around us as a *sacred* void; a void in which we are being asked to reexamine some of our cherished assumptions; a void in which we are being called to utilize our personal and corporate powers to create and energize the new structures that will support a new stage in human evolution; a void in which it is being demanded of us that we choose, that we be intentional, that we assert ourselves as cocreators of our own reality.

But hope, to be sustained, must be rooted in a future of concrete possibility. For us, hope is not an opium dream. It is rooted in the perception of a concrete, viable alternative—the creation of a world juridical order whose vision and powers go beyond the limits of the National Security State. The condition upon which we base our hope is the condition of eliminating the major obstacle to the creation of a more human order. That obstacle is the absolute sovereignty of individual states in our present system—a system in which nations vie *against* one another in the protection of their own interests and, thereby, threaten human survival and obstruct human fulfillment.

Religious, educational, scientific, governmental and economic institutions all could, if they worked *with* each other, holding each other mutually accountable, be energizers in the development of a new humanism and a new era of human greatness. Participation in that task requires that they lend their talents, resources and insight to the development of world order structures capable of supporting a new humanism.

The next chapters will discuss various conceptions of alternative world systems based on human/religious values, systems that build on existing trends. They will also explore strategies for developing the structures necessary to permit and foster the new humanism.

Involvement in the further development of such alternatives and strategies is not related only to the ideals of a new humanism. It is also related to a new pragmatism. It is a bedrock pragmatism that in true self-interest examines alternatives and initiates strategies toward human survival and future well-being. Where once people who spoke of global systemic change were considered unrealistic idealists, the world order movement is increasingly looked at by scientists and nonprofessionals alike as presenting the only realistic alternative humanity has.

9

On Conceiving a New World Order

> The actual future of a civilization—vigor and growth, or decline and breakdown—is prefigured in the shared images of the future possessed by its people in the present. . . . In this sense the future is a prologue to all history.
>
> Robert Bundy

The central focus of previous chapters has been on the *WHY* of world order. We have outlined three basic arguments: to overcome the powerlessness of the people; to overcome the powerlessness of national leaders to reorder and humanize priorities; and to resolve the critical survival questions that confront humankind.

It is now time to examine the *WHAT* of world order. We will consider what forms a global security system based on basic human values might take and then make recommendations on the several possibilities.

In the following chapters we will discuss the *HOW* of world order, exploring concrete strategies and timetables for developing an effective global security system.

All the questions—Why, What, How—must be answered if the world-order movement is to have the credibility it deserves. If the WHY is not powerful, i.e., if the cost/*benefit* ratio is not compelling, the WHAT and HOW will receive only passing interest. Similarly with the other questions. Without credible models, strategies for world order would lack positive direction. And without credible strategies, a rationale and models for world order would be academic exercises with little practical possibility of realization.

There are *eight premises* underlying our approach to the WHAT of a more human world order. Some of these will be explored more fully in this chapter, but we wish to state them briefly at the outset.

1. *We can choose a preferred world.* Human persons have the capacity to imagine, assess and choose from a variety of alternative courses of action. We therefore have the capacity to explore and initiate action toward the realization of a *preferred* future.

2. *Human values, related to inherent needs, affect the invention and development of social structures and institutions.* Physical survival and security, while basic, are not the only needs and values that will or should be operative in the development of a preferred future. Social justice, ecological balance and participation in decision making, among others, are integral to human survival and future well-being.

3. *A more human world order will be built upon foundations already existent in the present.* The development of a preferred future will be a gradual process utilizing the infrastructure already available in its initial stages. It is more likely to capitalize on the machinery of existing organizations and strategies, such as specialized U.N. agencies, than to develop totally new structures.

4. *A nonideological, problem-solving framework* within which to develop world-order structures is more likely to succeed in the immediate future than a world

federation. A problem-solving framework would be one in which *functional agencies* (such as a world monetary authority, law of the seas, world food authority, world environmental agency, disarmament agency, etc.) would be established and given adequate means and the authority of effective law to manage problems beyond the ability of individual nation-states. World structures and unities built around the management and resolution of problems of common concern are more likely to succeed initially because they do not hinge on the condition of overcoming psychological attachment to ideological differences.

5. *The principle of subsidiarity* should be a central principle in developing a *world legal framework* and authority lines for the management of problems. Subsidiarity begins with the proposition that decision making should be made at the lowest possible level. Only when problems cannot be managed and justice cannot be achieved at the local municipal, provincial or national levels are effective juridical institutions necessary at the global level. A world order based on functional institutions and established to function according to the principle of subsidiarity is not a quantum jump into the unknown. It is, rather, the next logical step in social evolution.

6. *Some sovereignty would necessarily be shared with transnational authorities.* This does not mean that national states would cease to exist or lose all autonomy. (In fact one result of an effective world order would be that nations could achieve greater *true* sovereignty as they regain power to place domestic priorities at the top of their agendas.) But it does mean that, in those specific mutually agreed-upon areas where nations acting alone are not able to effectively manage

problems because they are global in scope, some authority would be invested in functional global authorities for their management.

7. *The actors involved in the shaping and administrating of a more human world order should include more than political representatives of nation-states.* One reason is that many existing governments are not truly representative of the people they govern and are ill-equipped or disposed to represent the best interests of all their own citizens, much less the common good of the whole earth community. Secondly, the needs and problems of the world community are complex and multifaceted and need a more interdisciplinary approach than can be nourished by nation-state actors alone. The world has grown interdependent in multiple ways and needs the input and participation of the world's scientific, educational, economic, cultural and religious organizations. A third reason is that the task of formulating a preferred world future should not be undertaken apart from the participation of the people most concerned, especially as a primary aim of a new world order must be people empowerment and participation in shaping one's own destiny.

8. Finally, *the participatory development of a new world order must be undertaken as a transnational and transcultural process.* It cannot be a Western model handed to the rest of the world for acceptance.

FUNCTIONAL AGENCIES

We have stressed that the task of imaging and creating the future is not one of squeezing history into a predetermined mold, but rather one of building upon basic trends and developments of our times. But this does not assume that these trends and developments carry with them the values and person-centered orientation that we seek, and that all we need do is clear away obstructions in the path of their further advancement. Nor does it mean that these embryonic forms have within themselves the inherent capacity to adequately cope with the multiple problems and challenges that confront humankind.

None of the preferred models that we will present are considered—by us or by their designers—as definitive. But all have value in today's critical dialogue on what kind of future humankind needs and wants (or might want). The task before us here is not merely to promulgate the preferred futures of the "experts," meekly transmitting them through the communication channels of our constituency networks. Our role as "the people" is not limited to one of being the objects *for* whom world order is developed. We must also be the subjects *by* whom it is conceived and shaped. In collaboration with our respective colleagues we must become actors in the formulation of what we would like our future to be.

In this collaborative effort to develop a human and just world order, it is important to stress that there is no "one single way." There are a variety of approaches to achieving a global security system.

The persons and institutions involved in developing world-order scenarios are growing in number. Their approaches vary. Some put major stress on functional institutions that would have effective authority to deal with the global crises and the rampant global forces with which national societies cannot cope by themselves. Others begin with a more drastic reconstruction of existing institutions, including a radical diminishing of the role of the nation-state. But even these latter scenarios give significant place to the principle of functionalism.

For reasons outlined in point four above, our own preference is one that begins with functional agencies as providing the basic structure for a world security system.

Regardless of where one puts his or her primary emphasis, a world security system cannot be developed in a vacuum. The future must build upon the present. Fortunately, we need not begin from scratch, desperately searching for building blocks. Strategic foundations already exist.

These foundations include the general global infrastructure spawned since World War II by the communication and transportation technologies which also spawned today's monetary and economic interdependence. They also include the specialized agencies of the United Nations that have been developing a global fibre of cooperating institutions, organizations and experts for more than thirty years. More recent—and perhaps more strategic as providing embryonic infrastructure for the functional agencies of a global security system—are the world conferences sponsored by the United Nations since 1972:

Stockholm	World Conference on The Human Environment (1972)
Bucharest	World Conference on Population (1974)
Rome	World Food Conference (1974)
Caracas *Geneva* *New York*	World Conference on the Law of the Sea (1974-78)

Mexico   World Conference on International
              Woman's Year (1975)

Vancouver   World Conference on Human
              Settlements: HABITAT (1976)

Geneva   World Conference on Employment
              (1976)

Mar del Plata   World Water Conference (1977)

Each of these conferences concentrated on a crucial issue of global concern. Although the official actors were representatives of national states, most of the conferences had parallel assemblies called tribunals that were conducted by nongovernmental actors.

Representing action-oriented groups from around the world, these tribunals frequently wielded significant influence on the political representatives. More important, they conscientized participating leaders from educational, professional, religious and issue-oriented networks to the global dimensions of their specific issue. Equally significant were the intercultural insights and experiences, the personal friendships and the collaborative alliances between participating groups—all of which have prepared people around the world who share a commitment to a common issue to become actors in strategies to construct the specific functional agencies of a world-order system that would enable them to find solutions to that specific issue.

World Order Models Project

One of the most far reaching and comprehensive approaches to formulating preferred world-order futures is the World Order Models Project (W.O.M.P.). A project of the Institute for World Order, W.O.M.P.

has brought together scholars from every major area of the world in a transnational and multicultural effort.

Eight teams have been working closely together in a coordinated effort since 1967. The teams are from Latin America, Japan, India, Africa, North America, Europe, the Soviet Union and a transterritorial team in Scandinavia.

These W.O.M.P. teams began with several common parameters:

1. The time frame in which their respective models would be realized would be the final quarter of this century.
2. The criteria for formulating the models would be certain fundamental "world-order values." The values all teams agreed upon were war prevention, economic equity and social justice.
3. The models were to speak to the problem of transitional steps, i.e., to the practical steps through which to move from where we are today to their preferred world.
4. Each team would implement the above three parameters within the context of their respective regional and cultural perspectives.

In the process of developing their respective models, the leaders of these teams have met regularly in different parts of the world to share their research and insights. One result of this W.O.M.P. effort was the publication of their models simultaneously in the country of origin and in the U.S.[1] Besides these individual volumes there is a valuable book entitled *On the Creation of a Just World Order*.[2] Edited by Saul Mendlovitz, this book contains essays written by various directors of the W.O.M.P. teams which summarize their respective models. Also included is an essay that presents a Chinese perspective for considering world order.

The wide scope of the W.O.M.P. models makes it difficult to categorize the overall W.O.M.P. project. Most models stress the need for certain *functional* institutions at the global level. But several place the emphasis elsewhere. An example is the African model which places its major focus on *cultural* criteria for constructing a new world order, a dimension which the Japanese model also touches in its stress on the changing symbols of identification.

The Latin American model described in more detail below illustrates some specific formulations of functional agencies of a world security system. The Latin American team was headed by Gustavo Lagos and the formulations were published under the title *The Revolution of Being.* The Latin model focuses on full human development as a central goal—a goal articulated in Lagos' distinction between a "revolution of being" and a "revolution of having."

Seven functional agencies are listed. When considering them, the reader can keep in mind that these agencies would largely build upon the global infrastructure to which we referred above—an infrastructure already in place and developing.

1. *World Agency for the Seabed*
   Objective: Exploiting those seabed resources which lie outside the limits of the jurisdiction of the States and Regional Economic Communities. Establishing a system of research, investment and exploitation which will permit the rapid development of the physical, chemical, geological and biological resources of the seabed for the common benefit of humankind.

2. *World Agency for Science and Technology*
   Objective: Administering the rights to the use of all

scientific discoveries and/or technological innovations, taking special care
to promote development of the relatively
less developed regional economic communities and nation-states.

3. *World Agency for Global Mass
   Communications Media*
   Objective: Owning and administering the world system of mass communications in such a
   way as to guarantee the regional economic communities and states members
   access to the use of the system, to provide constant and factual information on
   world events, and to ensure real plural-
   ism so that the Agency's programs will
   represent the various ideologies and political and cultural currents of the world's
   people.

4. *World Agency for Outer Space*
   Objective: Establishing norms for the exploration
   and utilization of outer space and the celestial bodies for the benefit of all countries and regions, whatever their degree
   of economic and scientific development.
   All areas of the celestial bodies will be
   freely accessible, and freedom of scientific research therein will be guaranteed
   under the principles and norms of the
   U.N.

5. *World Agency for Ecological Balance*
   Objective: Achieving an increasing balance between
   the life-sustaining systems of the earth

and the demands—industrial, agricultural and technological—which its inhabitants make on it.

Organizing, sharing and deploying knowledge and expertise, identifying the priority problems and coordinating national measures within an effective global framework.

The Agency will be empowered to establish world standard and compulsory norms for the conservation of the environment and will be endowed with the appropriate means to police and enforce its decisions.

6. *World Agency for Planning and Financing for Development*
Objectives:

PLANNING:
Establishing an indicative plan for world development in close collaboration with the agencies for ecological balance, the seabed, science and technology and outer space.

The Plan will contemplate a) an equitable division of labor in order to secure the harmonious and balanced development of the national and regional economies and of the world economy; b) an equitable distribution of the benefits resulting from the integration of the regional economies and of the world economy.

MONETARY SYSTEM AND FINANCING:

Establishing a monetary system which will afford sufficient liquidity for international payments. Special drawing rights will be allowed mainly to economically less developed regions and countries.

Providing: 1) long term credits at low rates of interest for the financing of specific projects or development programs; 2) grants for the purposes specified above, 3) provision of technical assistance of every kind (in close collaboration with the Agency for Science and Technology).

7. *World Agency for the Control of Transnational Corporations*

Objective: Establishing a code of good conduct for the operations of transnational corporations, with the appropriate means to police and enforce its decisions.[3]

In Lagos's models, we have examples of a "preferred" future explicitly constructed according to basic moral values. Most evident is concern with the value of social justice as a primary criterion of world-order institutions. The result is that the limited "international law" of present treaties and other bilateral and multilateral agreements is not only extended and institutionalized with global authority; in these models, world law goes beyond the traditional *legal* justice as determined by custom and by the powerful. It seeks, according to moral principles commonly shared, to achieve what is *just* in future relations and to correct what is unjust in current relations.

"World Communities"

A second valuable effort to formulate models of functional world-order institutions is Elizabeth Mann Borgese's work on what she calls "World Communities." A senior fellow at the Center for the Study of Democratic Institutions at Santa Barbara, California, Ms. Borgese played a pioneering role in U.N. conferences for a "Law of the Seas." Her model of a world "Ocean Regime" provided a strategic conceptual framework for these conferences, and her personal leadership at these conferences was an important factor in achieving the first limited steps toward such a regime.

Borgese proposes several transnational functional institutions in addition to an Ocean Regime. Each of these institutions—often paralleling the global agencies of the Lagos's W.O.M.P. model—would constitute a functional world community, granted a limited global authority and power to manage certain problems whose global dimensions surpass the capabilities of individual nation-states.

Of special interest is her assumption that sovereignty no longer implies possession of territory, but rather means autonomy and participation in decision making:

> The adoption of some new forms of transnational representation offers the only way out of the dilemma posed by the drafters of the

documents now before the United Nations: i.e., shall the new organization be dominated by the few big powers, by the many small ones, by the rich, or by the poor. The division of nations into first- and second-class participants in decision-making is unacceptable to the vast majority of the nations. True, the one-state-one-vote system has become dysfunctional. But patching it up only makes it worse. Unless we take an entirely new approach, this problem will bog us down for years to come.[4]

Ms. Borgese then presents a tentative model as an example of an alternative type of representation, one which combines *nations*, *regions* and *transnational functional interests* as world order actors. An overall *World Charter* would associate together the individual charters of each world community. Working on the assumption that nations, i.e., governments, must still play a decisive role in an international organization—at least in the foreseeable future—she places the ultimate control function of each of her world communities in a *Commission*, where nation-states are represented on the basis of equal sovereignty. This control provides a safeguard for national interest. But because decisions in the various functional areas affect people as individuals and deal with issues that transcend the competence of political territory, the Commission is denied a monopoly on policy formation by a *bicameral assembly* structure.

Borgese projects six world communities (which on a regional level have a preliminary archetype in the European Coal and Steel Community). These include:

1. *Ocean Regime*

Its function would be to regulate the use and resources of the seas according to the universal common good. Its responsibility is for *ocean space* which is seen as an indivisible whole: "Geological structures extend, currents and waves move, species migrate across the high seas and the ocean floor regardless of political boundaries."

2. *World University System*

Operating as the science and technology "world community," it would be a research/development organization under world aegis. It would provide a vehicle for a nonpolitical transfer and share of technology. It would also provide a forum for respected voices to freely speak to *world* interest and *world* justice. This system would leave existing national and private universities autonomous.

3. *Management of Atmosphere*

The function here would be pollution control and regulation (i.e., restraint) of weather control and modification. As example of such concern: The weather of Minneapolis is already forming over Siberia and could thus be drastically influenced by interference there. Or cloud-seed elsewhere can diminish monsoons in South Asia, thereby destroying grain crops in India.

4. *Communications and Transportation*

Not only the negatives of controlling terrorism and drug trafficking is involved. Social justice is very much involved as well, for control of decisions and policies within global communications and transportation systems deeply influence economic and social development.

5. *Energy Production and Management*

Limited supplies of present energy resources make this area one of immediate urgency. Energy consumption has been increasing exponentially since World War II, with world consumption doubling about every 13 years. It is estimated that as much oil will have been used by the end of this decade as in all of history before 1970.

6. *Earth Resource Management*

The underlying principle here is that the physical resources of the earth constitute the common property of the human race and thus must be conserved and utilized accordingly, i.e., according to norms of universal social justice rather than economic or any other type of power.[5]

Borgese does not place much emphasis on war prevention or on enforcing disarmament, and thereby lists no "world community" for these goals. For her, "war will not be abolished in the present nation-state system. It will be abolished if we *change the system*."[6] Frank Tannenbaum tended to agree: "The threat to the security of the nation-state must first become meaningless before the present danger of atomic weapons can come to seem irrelevant to the needs of mankind."[7]

Borgese argues that a peace-keeping agency would not be necessary if social justice was provided for through other transnational agencies:

> With the internationalization of energy and resources, the national production of weapons of mass destruction would not make any sense. The five interlocking communities, embracing practically all human activities of world-wide scope, create a peace system in which war simply has no place. War between nations would be as unlikely as war between

"the six" in the European community. War
between the communities is an absurdity since
everybody belongs to every community (war
between continents might have been a possibility).[8]

Our own opinion is that the several functional
world communities that Ms. Borgese envisions would
move ahead more quickly if a "Disarmament and
Peace-Keeping Community" were also emerging. Without such a world-order agency, no nation can be sure
that a transfer of limited sovereignty to an agency for
managing scarce resources, for example, would not
jeopardize its national security. As long as other nations could take advantage of such development by use
of strong military power, few national leaders will risk
a joint collaborative effort to guarantee an equitable
distribution of the earth's vital resources. Whereas they
would be open to such a joint effort if they saw a gradual process toward disarmament and the development of
a peace-keeping force to parallel transitional steps toward other functional agencies related to national security.

Clark-Sohn Plan

The value of the Clark-Sohn plan is that it has
given considerable thought to how such a global peace-
keeping agency might be concretely constituted and
function as a "World Security Authority." This plan is
comparable to the world-order framework envisioned
by many World Federalists who are committed to a
reconstructed and strengthened United Nations.

Recognizing the present structural inadequacies of
the United Nations, Grenville Clark and Louis Sohn

published, in 1958, a comprehensive and detailed plan for a world structurally ordered for maintaining peace. The fruit of nine years of preparation, their *World Peace Through World Law*,[9] has been translated into French, German, Spanish, Dutch, Norwegian and Swedish. Their introduction—summarizing the major features of their plan—has been translated also into Arabic, Chinese, Danish, Italian, Japanese, Polish and Russian.

In the authors' words, "the purpose is to contribute material for the world wide discussions which must precede the adoption of universal and complete disarmament and the establishment of truly effective institutions for the prevention of war."[10]

The Clark-Sohn plan calls for total disarmament by stages with strict inspection. It would establish such legislative, executive and juridical institutions as are necessary to maintain world order. These would include a *world police force*, an *Outer Space Agency*, a *Nuclear Energy Authority*, a *World Development Authority* for economic assistance to "developing" countries, a *United Nations revenue system* and a *Bill of Rights*. Although cast in the form of detailed proposals for revision of the United Nations Charter, the plan could also be implemented through a wholly new world organization.

Constitution for the Federation of Earth

The "Constitution for the Federation of Earth" is a model being promoted by the World Constitution and Parliament Association. It was adopted by regional delegates to their 1977 conference in Innsbruck. It outlines a World Parliament — consisting of a House of Peoples, a House of Nations and a House of Counsellors for particular purposes — and a World Executive responsible to this Parliament. Democratic procedures for world elections and world administration are based upon not more than 1000 "World and Administrative Districts." The constitution is developed around the following functions: disarmament; human rights; social justice; environmental protection; economic and social development; and the regulation of international processes such as trade, transportation and communication.

Club of Rome

Supplementing the institutional models presented above is a study commissioned by the Club of Rome, entitled *Reshaping the International Order*.[12] It is the work of twenty scholars and businessmen from "developed" and "developing" nations, working under the direction of economist Jan Tinbergen, Nobel Laureate from the Netherlands.

This study follows by three years the Club of Rome's original *Limits to Growth*[13] document which sold over two million copies around the world. Based upon computer projections by a team from the Massachusetts Institute of Technology (M.I.T.), *Limits to Growth* challenged the principle of unlimited economic growth. It warned of ecological and structural breakdown if present trends of population growth, pollution and consumption of nonrenewable resources continue unchecked.

The "limits to growth" theory was strongly challenged by many people from Africa, Asia and Latin America who saw little evidence of concern about justice for the "developing" world by the Club of Rome— an international group of 100 scholars and businessmen, mainly from Western industrial nations. These critics pointed out that the M.I.T. team had made little distinction between areas of the world in their advocacy of the limited growth scenario.

A second report was commissioned by the Club of

Rome entitled *Mankind at the Turning Point*.[14] It provided a corrective to the unsegmented construct of the original study, breaking down its analysis of social and economic processes into regions. From one aspect, this was an improvement. For the focus no longer was on an aggregate, no-growth scenario. From another aspect, however, by dividing the world into ten regions —a breakdown capable of being further broken down into smaller units, even into single nations—a framework was provided that could be used for a policy of triage, i.e., of affluent parts of the world cutting themselves off from those Fourth World countries that they might judge to be "nonviable." The problem was that this division of the world was not accompanied by a strong enough focus on strategies that stressed *differentiated* growth by which affluent countries would accept limited growth while promoting policies that would stimulate economic growth in the impoverished world through a transfer of capital, resources and technology not dependent solely on the natural processes of market forces. (Even less was said about inalienable rights of every human being to adequate food, shelter and health care.)

The new third study, *Reshaping the International Order,* takes some tentative steps toward addressing this central question of *social* justice. The scope of this study was first revealed at an international conference of scholars and businessmen in Philadelphia in April 1976.

Speaking at this conference, the founder of the Club of Rome, Aurelio Peccei, said that while the M.I.T. study had "punctured the myth of exponential growth," it was now necessary to seek strategies and institutions capable of resolving the problems that the first study had outlined. In order to do so, a second myth would have to be punctured: "the myth of *national* competence."[15]

One of the objectives of the above conference was to outline the ten major areas in which the Tinbergen team would present concrete proposals. These areas, as outlined in this preliminary report, provide a context for understanding better the principles and goals of the functional agencies of the world security system that we have been discussing.

1. *The international monetary system:* The report is expected to call for additional creation of monetary reserves for the purpose of financing more rapid development of the Third World.

2. *Income redistribution and the financing of development:* The report will probably call for substantial increases in transfer payments to Third World countries, especially the poorest, with particular attention on the use of these resources for directly addressing the poverty problem. The Tinbergen report will openly endorse the principle of greater equity for the poor nations, which it regards as an essential principle for the achievement of world peace.

3. *Industrialization, trade and international division of labor:* The report is expected to call for closer collaboration among regional blocs and for more "multilaterality" rather than bilateral relations in trade. It will also call for reduction of import impediments to industrial products from the Third World.

4. *Food production and distribution:* The report favors implementation of decisions made at the World Food Conference in Rome for adequate stockpiling, to be furthered by the pressure of agricultural organizations on the governments of industrialized countries.

5. *Energy, ores and minerals:* The report favors extra efforts for research on fusion, nuclear, solar and

geothermal energy, possibly to be coordinated by a World Energy Research Authority.

6. *Environmental programs and ocean management:* The report favors preparation of a 1977 conference on the law of the sea by a group of experts, with concentration on building a federation of international organizations.

7. *Transnational enterprises:* Mr. Peccei favors the internationalization of multinational corporations. He recognizes that this may be difficult to do in the short run, but he feels that it is urgent to separate multinational corporations from the national governments of their home countries.

8. *Scientific research and technology:* The report favors a system of subsidizing the prices at which technological expertise is made available to Third World countries.

9. *Arms reduction:* The Tinbergen study will call for reinforcement of the United Nations peace force and the exertion of pressures on the superpowers (the United States and the Soviet Union) to redirect military expenditures toward development since "underdevelopment constitutes a more serious threat to world peace than the other superpowers."

10. *A general category that includes increasing the efficiency of the United Nations.*[16]

A central premise of the new Club of Rome document is the need for *international economic planning.* It argues that such planning must be substituted for the uncontrolled play of market forces. Peccei suggested that this global planning would be accomplished by utilizing regional and industrial groups such as the European Common Market, the Andean Pact and the

Organization of Petroleum Exporting Countries.

Commenting on this premise was John R. Bunting, Chariman of the First Pennsylvania Corporation:

> The market, essential as it is, is myopic; it is good for dealing with problems that lie only five or seven or possibly 10 years ahead, but our most serious problems are long-range problems.[17]

In an interdependent world, such long-range planning cannot take place except in a world order system. Today, long-range problem solving and goal realization —at national and international levels alike—require effective global authority that is capable of dealing with those unregulated economic, ecological, military and political forces that are making mockery of national boundaries—and, therefore, of national plans.

A Tentative Overview

The overall form of a world security system has to undergo much further exploration and development in transcultural dialogue. A general outline of basic structure, however, can be suggested. In agreement with most models is what Richard Falk calls a "central guidance system." A principle task of this guidance system would be to coordinate the work of the *functional agencies*. At the core of such a system would be a *global charter* that would establish basic principles by which decisions would be made in these functional agencies. It would be this charter—most probably formulated in a restructured United Nations granted by its member nations limited world sovereignty (a limited "global social contract")—that would give appropriate authority to the various functional agencies.

A *World Court* would interpret the implementation of this global charter, make decisions in the case of conflicts over its interpretation, rule on infractions of those laws which cannot be settled in local or regional courts, and arbitrate conflicts between the global agencies.

Also needed is a *World Representative Body* duly constituted by some system of representation (either elected or delegated according to regional, national and/or local districts). Such a body—which most models envision as a strengthened and revamped United Nations Assembly—would facilitate the drafting and approval of a global charter, the coordination of the separately functioning agencies, the approval of major appointments to functional agencies and other legislative roles as defined in a global charter.

A tentative diagram of a World Security System is outlined in the chart opposite.

A final observation that serves as a transition to the next section of this chapter is the decentralized nature of this system—as evident in the lack of any strong executive structure with centralizing powers.

Not all the proposed world-order agencies will develop evenly. Some will develop more quickly because of the urgency of their functional concerns. Others will develop according to the degree of transnational infrastructure already existing. Here it is well to point out that in most of the areas covered in the above models, significant international organizational structures are already in place and functioning, and could provide important infrastructural foundations for the respective global agencies. Thus it is not a question of starting

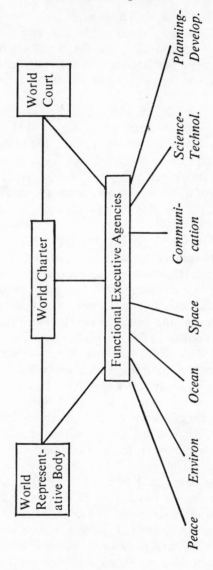

from scratch with sterile theoretical projections. Important building blocks are already in place. The problem is to expand the framework and authority of existing global organizations that are substantially crippled by obsolete devotion to the principle of unlimited national sovereignty.

As we have already stressed, a global security system is not to be achieved suddenly by some global constitutional assembly in the future. Rather, it will be a gradual, organic process—a process that, in itself, constitutes "world order" all along the way. Every step forward will have its own value and concrete ramifications for justice, peace and human well-being.

NO GLOBAL BIG BROTHER

Rather than seen as first steps toward a centralized world government, the functional institutions of a world security system would foster *decentralization* through regional and local decision-making by turning down the national security motor which presently energizes a centralization of power on the national level.

Domination by the "National Security State" would be radically diminished. For individual nations would no longer be solely responsible for their military, monetary and resource security. Orwell's 1984 scenario, based on a premise of a world divided into three regional National Security States, would no longer be relevant. In a new world order, the nation-state would remain a basic political unit. But in the more distant future, once the basic institutions of a global security system would have emerged and stabilized, it is possible that present nation-state units would be adjusted to smaller or larger size. Especially important here would be adjustments to bring national boundaries into greater conformity with more natural cultural, economic and geographic factors.

Biologist René Dubos speaks of the need for smaller organic societies, constructed according to common interests and social identity systems.[18]

Others, like Rajni Kothari, director of the Institute for World Order's WOMP team in India, propose a world of fewer regional states (suggesting twenty-four of relatively equal population and geographic size) to ensure against world domination by a few superpowers.[19] Such a reorganization would also prevent another type of domination by a majority of smaller nations representing fewer of the earth's people. Kothari's grouping of twenty-four regions would still be internally open to groups of smaller, organic societies, as advocated by Dubos.

The twenty-four regional constituent units of the world association proposed by the India world-order team is envisioned as the result of a gradual but guided evolutionary process, one not "left merely to the pressure of local factors." Looking at several regions where such groupings are already subjects for discussion (e.g., South Asia, West Africa, South Pacific, Southeast Asia, the Andean South America), the Indian team sees possibilities of a chain sequence which may "in the not too distant future bring about a quite differently structured world than is the case today."[20]

Members of the WOMP teams see important initiative toward a reordered world coming from the nations of Latin America, Africa and Asia. They see the world not simply divided between large, rich and powerful countries on one side confronting small, poor and powerless countries on the other. Intermediate nations —in respect to size, economic development and political and military power—in the Third World can be important actors in this process of regional reorganization.

This type of input and initiative points up a special

strength and value of the WOMP project. The dialogue created by the various cultural teams around the world overcomes a weakness of the other models which are creations of Western thought, culture and experience. WOMP provides complementary and sometimes corrective viewpoints from non-Western peoples, correctives that are necessary not only for achieving the most workable model but also for arriving at a world consensus.

Now that the W.O.M.P. models are available for use around the world, the Institute for World Order is working to develop what they call a "Transition Model." Its focus is to develop strategies and policies through which the human community can move through the next twenty years to a "just world polity." The Institute has begun to put together a transnational group of persons from all walks of life (projected as numbering between 500 and 1,000 members) to work on this transition model.

Designed to be completed by 1980, this global document will be an amalgam of diagnosis and prognosis that will suggest guidelines and strategies for transition steps for getting from where we are now to a preferred human future based on world-order values.

WORLD-ORDER VALUES

What the above world-order models have in common is a commitment to basic human values as fundamental criteria of world order. They begin with specific problems and then formulate functional institutions to cope with those problems according to conscious value criteria.

It is here that the preceding chapter on values achieves its full significance. For underlying the rationale for transnational institutions is the fact that, in today's nation-state competition, those values that conflict with national security goals have little chance to become operative on any significant scale.

Traditional political science—particularly as applied to international relations—accepts this dominance of national security values as the "nature" of world politics. Political scientists often speak of the need for practical realism. They speak with pride of their "hard realism" as compared with the impractical utopian idealism of those who insist on beginning with "altruistic" values. Herman Kahn is an example. Affirming a *value-free* framework as the basis for the Hudson Institute which he directs, he identifies himself as part of the "responsible center" maintaining the barricades against the "humanist left."

Such a framework assumes that there is a dichotomy between "humanism" (i.e., a values approach) and responsible, practical problem solving. We recognize no such dichotomy. Quite the contrary! It appears to us that a human-centered values approach, in the long run, is the only adequate and responsible approach to world problem solving of any lasting quality. What is ironic is that Kahn's alleged "value-free" framework is not value free at all, but replete with the values that are operative in the various national-security-related institutions that fund the research of the Hudson Institute. The paradox here is that this "value-free" national-security-oriented approach is neither effectively nor responsibly resolving the problems faced by the human community in our times.

"Hard realism" today means facing the incontrovertible fact of moral and social deterioration, and that what is at stake is the future survival and well-being of a species. A viable future for humankind is dependent upon a strong moral fibre rooted in strongly operative and life-centered values.

As we have indicated earlier, an example of a values focus in developing an alternative world-order scenario is the approach of the *Institute for World Order*. The starting points for each of its WOMP teams are *nonviolence, economic well-being* and *social justice.* These values are considered by all the WOMP teams as moral imperatives as well as preconditions for human survival. A fourth value is articulated by the Institute as basic to a viable world order, namely, *ecological balance.* Some WOMP teams speak of a fifth value: *participation in decision making*, a value which others see as inherent in the value of social justice.

The evolution of WOMP's basic "world-order values" as the criteria for its models is interesting. The project was begun under the direction of two U.S. citizens, Saul Mendlovitz and Harry Hollins, with the overriding objective of war prevention, thus reflecting a dominant concern of North Americans. But almost from the very beginning of the project, WOMP's value base was expanded to include economic well-being and social justice—thanks to the insistence of participating Latin American, Indian and African scholars.

A pivotal question related to using humanistic values as criteria for developing world-order institutions is how to get the necessary agreement on common values. Throughout history conflict has resulted over differing values. Some commentators speak of a vast gulf existing between values that predominate in different cultures and ideologies, concluding that any significant value consensus is still in the distant future.

The world-order values that we are discussing here, however, are not foreign to any major culture or ideology. They are increasingly recognized as basic for survival in an interdependent planet. The slow and painful road toward the practical implementation of each value, however, is substantially obstructed by the present nation-state system.

It is not the purpose or scope of this book to give a detailed description of all the various alternative models that are being or could be proffered. (Even if it were, it would be too premature to suggest definitive forms. Much more global dialogue and exchange is called for before formal configurations are concretized and solidified.) What is clear is that we need a global security system. The above models were briefly described as an indication of the general forms such a system could take. They are also an indication that competent work on conceptualization is already underway. Rather than duplicate this work, we refer you to the works mentioned above and in the supplementary reading list at the end of the book.

Our main objective in this book has been the elaboration of WHY such world-order formulations are necessary and how, rather than being abstract exercises, they are vitally relevant to human self-interest, to national interest and to the resolution of local problems.

The *linkages* between local and global problems—which constitute a primary WHY of world order—have, to date, been largely overlooked by those scholars involved in world-order formulations. Also largely overlooked or only vaguely touched on have been ways in which people could be involved in the processes of conceptualizing and realizing world-order alternatives.

WORLD-ORDER ACTORS

Traditional international affairs considers the nation-state as the sole actor on the world stage. The world-order movement, however, considers a wide range of actors. World-order actors can be subnational, national, regional, international, transnational or global. They may be social, economic, political, cultural or religious. They may be individual persons or they may be movements, organizations or institutions.

Each of these various actors can participate in the making of contemporary world history. Each can have some impact on the goals outlined by the world-order movement. Much depends upon whether or not the above persons, movements, organizations and institutions *believe* that they can be shapers of history, and upon how much they grasp the profound self-interest involved in initiatives toward a future in which humanizing values can prevail.

The next two chapters will outline the role of nongovernmental actors in constructing the functional agencies of a world security system. A key aspect in the development of a more human world order is the involvement and preparedness of grass-roots constituencies. The present bottleneck of unlimited national sovereignty cannot be broken until national leaders either get a mandate from their people to work to transcend this obsolete principle, or, recognizing a growing movement and viable strategies toward such a mandate, they provide leadership to help promote such a mandate.

THE ROLE OF THE PEOPLE

Concrete world-order scenarios—when presented with a rationale (WHY) and strategy (HOW) that speaks to particularized grass-roots needs—have pragmatic value in effecting a mandate for a more human world order. Such scenarios provide a catalytic effect that is important for the development of a grass-roots movement. Saul Mendlovitz, President of the Institute for World Order and Director of WOMP, says that we have "underestimated the extent to which the presentation of a vivid and compelling image of a future world order, capable of dealing with a set of interrelated problems, is itself part of the transition process."[21]

Ian Baldwin concurs: "The creation of a large and vociferous community of world-minded educated men and women schooled in visioning the future will naturally generate pressures for planetary social change."[22]

The danger is that the task of imaging world-order futures is being left to intellectuals and political elites. One of the tasks of the multi-issue coalition for world order that we will be discussing in the next chapter is that of getting citizen groups involved as actors in the world-order movement.

There are two pragmatic reasons why citizen groups must become involved.

The first reason is that the input of local grassroots experience and of the citizen's natural savvy of human relations and practical wisdom provides a vital dimension of reality that is essential if any world-order system is to work. These elements complement the knowledge and experience of the "experts."

The second reason is strategic. A more human world-order system will not materialize without the understanding and assent of the citizens. It will not happen if it is not the will of the people.

Woodrow Wilson's failure illustrates this second point. His design for the League of Nations began with the presumption of elite support. He depended upon congressional elites to share his vision. But without having first created a national forum for raising the

consciousness of the voters, Wilson saw his statesmanship torpedoed in a Congress that, sensing little
grass-roots support, could claim the people were "not
ready." Today's world-order movement must avoid this
mistake. In the following chapter on "Strategies Toward World Order," we will show that people have
come a long way since 1919. Many more persons are
now open to, or actively seeking, alternatives.

Although more people will be involved in the consciousness-raising phase of the world-order movement
than in the conceptualization and implementation
phases, the *general* forms of these agencies are discern-
ible for most people. Depending upon the openness of
the political processes in the respective countries, they
will be able to let their will on the essential dimensions
of such agencies be known.

The danger is that the value of "average" citizens'
input is too easily, and unjustly, denigrated. Yet it
could easily spell the difference between a workable
system—at least a workable democratic system—and
continuation of the status quo. The more that people
have a personal voice from the very beginning, the
more they will have a sense of "ownership" about the
future and persevere in active participation in the
world-order movement. Their early input also guarantees that their local and personal needs are duly considered.

THE PATRIOTISM QUESTION

In discussing world-order alternatives, the question
inevitably arises as to whether people can transcend
deeply instilled feelings of attachment to their nation-
states and extend their loyalties to the human community as a whole.

It should be clear that to advocate world order is not the same as advocating an abolition of national sovereignty. We do not seek to eradicate the nation-states. What is needed is a transfer of *some* of the sovereign legal power presently located on national regional levels to a world level—a transfer limited to the several areas in which problems are so transnationally interlocked that they can only be resolved by transnational approaches based upon effective global institutions.

This sharing of sovereignty with certain world order agencies should not be seen as a *loss* of national sovereignty. Quite the opposite. Such a sharing would result in an *increase* of true sovereignty. For a world security system that could control rampant global forces would increase the ability of national leaders to reorder priorities and resolve domestic problems.

There is no dichotomy between love of one's homeland and concern for the well-being of the human community as a whole. The two are not only mutually compatible but integrally related to each other. Cardinal John J. Wright spoke about the relationship of national and global patriotism in his book, *National Patriotism in Papal Teaching.* He stressed the "patriotic obligation to promote a world order within which the fatherland can achieve in peace and security its own national good, and thus fulfill its own purpose: the *development and service of individual* personality."[23]

Cardinal Wright then spoke of the *destiny* of a nation. What is of special significance is how he linked together the destinies of the individual person, the nation-state and the total human community:

> The destiny of a nation is that of the individuals who comprise it, and the national work of

the individuals who comprise a nation is the service of humanity according to their special endowments as sons of the several nations. Through them, the nation achieves its destiny rather than through the nation do they achieve theirs. But in either case, the relation of any national destiny to the general good of the human race proves that the function of the nation is subordinate to the ends of the general human community, and that it cannot, therefore, legitimately separate a people from the human community they share with all men.[24]

Patriotism, like the concepts of family and sovereignty, has historically been abused to avoid responsibility to the larger human community. Moral arguments to overcome such limited application of patriotism have largely received limited response. For to date we have lacked a sufficiently compelling argument of "self-interest" to complement—or even precede—moral arguments for justice and love. We have also lacked sufficiently credible models and viable strategies for world order. Fortunately, in the final quarter of this century, all three once-missing elements are available.

Thus the artificial dichotomy between *national* patriotism and *world* patriotism can be transcended as we see that true national patriotism—i.e., a commitment to national interest and security—compels its realization not at the expense of, but within the larger context of the whole human family.

10
Strategies for a Just World Order

Part I: Multi-Issue Coalitions

> The question is not one of "surrendering" national sovereignty. The problem is not negative and does not involve giving up something we already have. The problem is positive —creating something we lack, but that we imperatively need.
>
> Emery Reves

Regardless of how compelling the reasons for a world security system, they have little practical meaning if not accompanied by viable strategies.

The following pages outline strategies which flow organically from the analysis of the National Security State. They

—include transitional steps with a general timetable;

—relate to the concerns and experiences of a broad range of institutions and constituencies;

—place emphasis on building an informal *citizens' coalition* of special-issue constituencies;

—utilize existing networks and channels of communication.

THREE STRATEGY PHASES

The time frame in which these strategies are placed is the final quarter of the twentieth century. This time span is realistic. It does not expect instant solutions. Yet it is not so far in the future that it has no meaning for present problems and programing. The urban deterioration of Newark or Bombay, for example, will not be substantially reversed in two years. But significant progress could be realized through transitional steps over the next generation if. . . . The big IF is if national priorities can be reordered so that urban renewal can become a top agenda item. And, in the case of India, if the world community accepts its responsibility in enabling Indians to have access to the capital, monetary reserves, primary resources and technologies needed to resolve the multiple national problems that underly the urban deterioration of Bombay. In both ifs, the precondition is a world security system.

Within this time frame, three phases are generally projected as marking progressive development toward world order: consciousness raising, politicization and transformation.[1] A general strategy progression can be seen in relationship to these phases:

I. *Consciousness Raising*

The main strategy objective in this first phase is to develop widespread public consciousness about the WHY, WHAT and HOW of world order. The major effort is to enable citizens and leaders to see that true *national* interest and security and true *personal* interest and security lie in a world security system. A central focus is on the straitjacket of the present National Security State system and the powerlessness it engenders. Also included, however, is an awareness of alternative world-order scenarios, such as those outlined in Chapter Nine, and the practical dimensions of multi-issue coalition strategies that we will be examining in this and the next chapter.

II. *Politicization*

In this phase the question of world order moves into the sphere of politics as *a public issue of true national interest and security.* Building on the general consciousness raised in the first phase, the main strategy effort here is to mobilize grass-roots coalitions into effective movements for political change. When possible, the focus is on catalyzing "the people" as agents of change. In democratically closed societies, however, the actors would be the New Class of managers and technical elites.

The political task is a double one: to demonstrate to political leaders that "the people" are ready for world order; and to have "the people" declare ownership in the world-order movement by contributing their own insights and preferences in the conceptualization of the functional agencies of a world-order system.

III. *Transformation*

This is the period in which the various components of the world-order system take concrete form. A major focus here is to develop the functional agencies of a world-order system and delegate effective global authority needed by these agencies to accomplish their functions.

Obviously these three phases are not mutually exclusive. The processes of consciousness raising, politicization and transformation, to varying degrees, are all already in evidence and will continue to be operative throughout the next twenty to twenty-five years. It is a question of emphasis. Consciousness raising about the WHY, WHAT and HOW of world order—already begun in many countries—will be predominant in the late 70s and early 80s but continue through the late 80s and 90s. Similarly, the *politicization* processes, evidenced now in limited form, will strengthen in the 80s and continue into the 90s. *Transformation* of the present world system is also a process that will be operative throughout the next decades. Indeed, as evidenced in the Law of the Seas Conference and other institutional developments at the global level, signs of such transformation are all around us, even if only in embryonic forms.

The main *immediate* need, however, is to strengthen and broaden the base of support and involvement in a widespread world-order movement. Thus, while some people will be involved now in political and transformational processes, the major effort in the next five to ten years must be to bring the need for world order into the consciousness of the world's peoples and to enlist their active involvement. The strategies which follow are thus directed primarily toward this proximate goal as an intermediary step toward political transformation.

It is important to stress that consciousness raising *is action.* Indeed, it is perhaps the most critical of all action. For the latter two phases build upon it.

Identifying Linkages

The key to developing a world-order readiness is to relate the need for world-order institutions to people's particular concerns and preoccupations. Each of us *hurts* in a number of profoundly personal ways. Much of this pain relates to a sense of personal powerlessness.

This is why we began in Chapter One with a discussion of the "powerlessness of the people."

Our hurt may be that we are ill-housed, or malnourished, or suffer from inadequate health care. We may be elderly, considered a nonproductive burden in a society mobilized for national security productivity. Our hurt may lie in the fear of walking the streets alone. Or it may be the alienation of living in a dehumanized society without meaning, a society in which humanizing values are logically excluded as criteria for public policy. It may be the fear of facing a future that seems closed—or a future-shock world with no change regulators. Our concern may be the inexorable deterioration of the local environment and of the earth's fragile life-support system. We may be women, frustrated because we are locked out of decision-making positions that are statistically and strategically mobilized and determined by "masculine" values. Or our concern may lie in the realization that nuclear proliferation makes a nuclear confrontation more likely each year.

It is relating the need for world order to each person's personal and specific sense of powerlessness that is the basis for mobilizing "the people" as actors in a world-order movement. Consciousness raising begins with specifics. It articulates the *linkages* between a person's or group's particular area of powerlessness and the straitjacket of the National Security State system.

The starting point is to assist constituency leaders to analyze the connection between the insolubility of their issue and the straitjacket of constant mobilization for national security.

This recognition of linkages can be fostered through general articles, books, media presentations, seminars, conferences, etc. Also helpful would be particular articles prepared for journals and newsletters of the issue organizations to which these leaders belong.

Of special strategic value for involving leaders of issue constituencies in personal dialogue on world order is the researching and preparation of the special issue monographs which we will discuss later in this chapter.

CATALYZING A WIDE BASE OF SUPPORT

A principle goal of the multi-issue coalition strategies which we will outline is to catalyze sufficient grassroots support *to make world order a public issue of true national interest and true national security.*

It is a goal to be accomplished in a majority of the world's countries. Once the majority of nations perceive world order as an issue of self-interest—recognizing the straitjacket from which much of their powerlessness to reorder priorities stems—they will be in a position to exert enormous leverage upon the remaining reluctant nations whose destinies are so intertwined in today's interdependent world. There is, therefore, a need for *simultaneous initiatives around the world.* No single group of countries can carry the burden of the world-order movement by themselves. Leadership must come from the "developed" and "developing" world alike.

It is important that at least one of the superpowers be among this vanguard. No substantial movement toward world-order institutions with effective global authority is possible unless one of the superpowers explicitly embraces world order as one of its policy objectives. Once, however, such superpower seriousness is established—and the motivation for it is seen by the rest of the world as a legitimate self-interest that does not preclude the similar self-interest of other nations—then world order will gain a new credibility with world leaders and with people of other countries.

Our strategy assumes that the superpower to first opt for a global security system will be the United States. At the present time, the people of the United States have greater freedom to develop a grass-roots, multi-issue coalition than the people of the Soviet Union or China. We do not, however, rule out initiatives from leaders of either country. For indications are that they also recognize that national security is increasingly fragile in the present lawless global arena; and that many unmet domestic needs remain subordinate to security goals. The more probable scenario, however, is one in which Soviet and Chinese leaders respond to a movement in the United States, a movement catalyzed by a multi-issue coalition that will make world order an important public issue of true national interest and security by the early 1980s.

The "developing" world has already made a significant contribution to the world-order movement by its initiatives on behalf of a New International Economic Order. One of the major contributions of the N.I.E.O. documents and debate lies in the fact that they are making the concept of world order a household word around the world.

The importance of this simultaneous approach to constructing multi-issue coalitions for world order in many countries was affirmed by Rajni Kothari, director of the Indian WOMP team and of the Center for the Study of Developing Societies in New Delhi. During a consultation on world order that we conducted in New Delhi in December 1975, we expressed appreciation for the leadership that the Indian team was providing in the movement for world order. We stressed that parallel efforts in India, Africa, Latin America, China, the USSR, etc., will increase its credibility in the United States. Kothari replied that the reverse was also true:

credibility in India and other "developing" countries depends upon whether people of the United States and Europe will be able to mobilize public opinion in favor of a world-order system based on justice.

But people of other countries are not waiting around to see if the multi-issue coalitions in the United States will successfully mobilize U.S. public opinion in favor of a global security system by the early 1980s. The World Order Models Project (WOMP) of the Institute for World Order is an example of regional initiatives. With most of the models from the eight regional WOMP teams now in print, WOMP is entering a second stage. It is developing working networks of scholars and institutions to build upon the research and model building of its teams in Africa, India, Japan, Latin America, Europe, the Soviet Union, the United States and its transterritorial team in Oslo.

It is possible to outline *four steps in constructing an effective multi-issue coalition to catalyze grass-roots support*. Although the outline will be presented here in the context of coalition building in the United States, the four steps are generally applicable in other countries as well.

1. *Conscientizing Constituency Leaders*

The concept of conscientization[2] includes more than raising one's consciousness on a particular issue. It also means a *personal* commitment to that issue: a personal commitment to *act* upon the basis of raised consciousness.

The major emphasis in the early effort of coalition building will be placed on the involvement of creative persons who represent constituents of various networks, i.e., issue networks, religious networks, educational networks and professional networks. (We will discuss these four networks in the next chapter.)

As the constituency leaders of these networks become involved in developing an analysis relevant to their issue concern and the National Security State system, they will more fully comprehend how the attainment of their respective goals is increasingly dependent upon building world-order agencies. They can then translate this understanding into the appropriate context for their constituents. This is a pivotal step. A great deal depends upon *who* endorses world order, and *how, where* and *when*.

The following seventeen issues (outlined earlier in Chapter Four) illustrate the type of constituencies that are represented by these leaders.

—Hunger	—Care of the Aged
—Housing	—Racial Justice
—Health Care	—Women's Rights
—Education	—Religious Freedom
—Employment	—Penal Reform
—Environment	—Urban Planning
—War Prevention	—Population
—Crime Prevention	—Democratic Participation
—Prevention of Alienation and Addiction	

There are a number of organizational networks—local, national and international—that, directly or indirectly, are concerned about each of these issues. It is with the constituents of these networks that the constituency leaders are/will be working in their consciousness raising and politicization efforts.

2. *Constituency Leaders Catalyze Their Respective Networks*

Constituency leaders will facilitate a conscientization process among their respective networks, enabling their constituents to recognize the linkages between the straitjacket of the National Security State and their powerlessness to significantly resolve the problems or achieve the goals related to their respective concerns.

Some of this constituency education is already being facilitated through talks and papers given at conferences and workshops. Articles written for trade journals and in-house organs are also important. Of special strategic importance in catalyzing network constituents is the development of issue monographs (described below)—some of which are already being prepared—which will relate specific issues to the security straitjacket and the need for world order. The whole process will be boosted by the media involvement in stage three.

Much of the formulation of the multi-issue coalition strategy has resulted from an eight-year dialogue with grass-roots people as well as with leaders of the different issue groups. An encouraging experience in this dialogue was that the natural wisdom and experience of local citizens sometimes proved more capable of embracing world order as relating to true personal interest and security than some intellectuals whose peripheral data tended to take them off on tangents. Encouraging as this preliminary dialogue has been, however, the best response comes when it is the natural constituency leaders who relate world order to the particular issues of "their people." Such leadership knows not only the grass-roots concerns, predispositions and prejudices of their constituents, but also the priorities and politics of their organizations.

3. *Response from Public Opinion Media*

As initiatives by natural constituency leaders move

forward, the growing grass-roots interest in world order can be expected to attract the attention of media people. Journalists, editors, T.V. and radio commentators will begin to include a world-order dimension in their coverage of the various issues. As the emerging multi-issue coalition adds credibility to world order, artists and filmmakers, especially of documentaries, can also be expected to respond. Articles and books covering particular issues will begin to include the world-order perspective in their analysis of causes and solutions.

This stage of media participation will provide important, complementary input into the educational initiatives already taken with the various constituencies in step two. A cultural awareness that makes world order a responsible and urgent issue in the public forum will greatly assist the efforts of constituency leaders with their grass-roots people. Thus the interplay between the media and the constituency education efforts can be expected to result in a mutual escalatory feedback.

4. *Developing a Political Commitment*

The explicit goal of this step is to build upon growing public consciousness and develop a grass-roots political movement that will make world order a respected and urgent public issue on the national scene. As general consciousness grows, a transition can be made into the politicization phase of strategy development.

The various groups and networks that are committed to the issues outlined above and have been conscientized to seek world-order alternatives will join in this politicization process. Seeing the connection between world order and the resolution of their respective issues, they can be expected to actively support those public officials who will initiate and promote legislation that moves national policy toward the construction of transnational institutions with global authority.

Significantly, an encouraging number of Congress-men and women are already close to the movement for world order. Witness the organization called "Members of Congress for Peace through Law" which has about 170 members. Although these legislators endorse the concept of world order, the present limited voter interest in world order results in a reluctance on their part to make it a practical priority in their personal political agendas. Also lacking are concrete handles with which to grab hold of world order as a viable voter issue. But with the multi-issue rationale and coalition strategy, a number of personalized concrete handles become available—especially as the peoples' coalition begins to gain momentum and develop grass-roots support. And, of course, media support will play an important part in encouraging initiative among members of Congress—men and women who are always ready to respond to opportunities for public support.

The number of senators and representatives belonging to Members of Congress for Peace through Law can help us illustrate concretely how the goal of the multi-issue coalition strategy—namely, to make world order a public issue of true national interest and security—can be realized in the United States by the early 1980s. The political goal here is to have at least 51% of Congress take a public stand in favor of strengthening global institutions with real functional authority.

With 535 members of Congress, the 51% goal is 268. With approximately 170 already formally affiliated with Members of Congress for Peace through Law and perhaps another 25 already sympathetic to global strategies that would strengthen present global institutions (thanks to the pressures and crises from the new global interdependencies), the political gap to overcome within the next half decade is less than 75—a number that, when placed in the context of the four steps we have enumerated which seek to mobilize grass-roots constituents of members of Congress, is not unrealistic.

Once the 268 figure is approximated, advocates of an alternative to the balance-of-power policies championed by the Achesons, Dulleses and Kissingers will finally have an alternative scenario going for them.

A second result of reaching this 268 figure is that once world order becomes a public issue in the United States, it will take on heightened credibility around the world.

A good many members of Congress, however, will already have become active even before this fourth step of pulling the coalition together as an effective force to move the country toward a world-order position in practical policies. Members of Congress have been active in ranks of each of the seventeen issues for a long time. But the linkages between unsolved local issues and unregulated global forces have not yet been adequately identified.

As world order becomes an issue with public support, men and women running for public office will have to declare how they stand in relation to world order, and will accordingly be supported or opposed by world-order coalitions and constituencies. For the past several years, a number of self-identified "world order Democrats" and "world order Republicans" have run for office. Some public issue groups are promoting the election of candidates who will initiate and support legislation that fosters the evolution of transnational institutions and common world policies to meet crises in ecology, peace-keeping, trade and monetary matters that cannot be met by individual nations alone. As the relationship of other more local problems are also seen to be relegated to the bottom of national agendas because of the logical, structural mobilization for national security, such efforts can be expected to multiply.

This political action stage, therefore, has already begun. Pulling the coalition together as an effective force on the national scene, however, will continue as an ongoing process during the last two decades of this century.

MULTI-ISSUE COALITIONS

Coalitions begin with a common concern. Sharing a common interest, a variety of organizations, institutions and/or individuals join hands to achieve certain goals relating to that interest.

The various actors who come together in coalitions for world order may be homogeneous, all committed to the same issue. Or they may have quite different commitments; but each recognizes that the coalition relates to one's own issue. The common concern around which they come together is powerlessness, i.e., the powerlessness of national societies and leaders to substantially reorder priorities.

The multi-issue coalition that would create public support at the national level would consist of constituencies of the seventeen issues listed earlier—and possibly more, for our list is an arbitrary one.

The individual issue coalitions that join hands in the multi-issue coalition are not single corporate entities. It is not a question, for example, of going out and recruiting all the local, state and national organizations working on drug abuse into one large superorganization. What is involved is an intentional effort to raise consciousness about:

1. the national security straitjacket,
2. world order alternatives, and,
3. the peoples' coalition strategy.

The members of the general public not belonging to any formal group, but still concerned about a particular issue, will be reached through media coverage of activities of the various coalition groups and by articles and media commentators who begin to take the world order question seriously as the coalition builds. As consciousness and a new vision take hold, artists can be expected to give expression to it in art forms such as films, literature, etc., furthering and deepening a more universal and human vision of life.

Because of the obvious overlap of people and organizations interested in more than one issue, collaboration and particular strategies will emerge quite naturally without a formal umbrella organization. A catalytic team, however, may eventually form, providing full-time people to take collaborative initiatives, providing leaders of the constituencies with concrete data, contacts and legwork. Members of such a team would be people who come from the ranks of the particular issue-grouping with whom they would be primarily working. Such a team could greatly facilitate collaboration between the various constituencies.

Although the multi-issue coalition is important for a number of strategic reasons, one reason needs to be made explicit. Consciousness of being part of an ongoing coalition strategy should be stressed right from the beginning. For most people know that a *single* issue—as clear as its relationship to the national security straitjacket may be—is not enough to move the majority of the public to take world order seriously. (Witness the limited response to the "Bomb" issue.) So they are reluctant to invest much of their time and finances in world order efforts if everything seems to hinge upon their single issue. But when people deeply concerned about "their" issue see that persons and constituent networks equally concerned about the other issues are also identifying a common straitjacket, and the alternative of world order and the coalition strategy, then world order receives a radically enhanced credibility. As this credibility grows, people will increasingly commit their energies and financial help toward promoting world order within their specific constituencies. The momentum will increase as they become conscious of being part of a growing, dynamic *global* movement.

Important in the development of this global movement will be the return of tens of thousands of international students presently studying in North America and Europe. Add to this number the many thousands of nonstudents who visit these two continents each year. These long- and short-term international visitors have a unique opportunity to develop an intercultural, transnational perspective by contact with people from all over the globe.

International visitor participation in coalition-building strategies in the United States and Europe is doubly valuable. Not only is their input of great value to the consciousness-raising dialogue among various issue constituencies, especially in helping to interpret the insights from the Third World teams of the Institute of International Order's WOMP project. But the participating international students and visitors prepare themselves for parallel multi-issue coalition building upon return to their respective countries.

This adds to the significance of the groundwork presently being laid by the WOMP teams in India, Japan, East Africa, South America, Europe and the

Soviet Union. The use of WOMP manuscripts in the United States will prepare many international students and visitors to become involved in world-order coalition building upon return to their homelands.

The *immediate* focus of the multi-issue strategies is on developing a variety of coalitions built around special issues at local, regional and national levels. And as these special-issue coalitions develop, more informal *international* coalitions will also develop around a particular issue.

Indeed, coalitions on some of these issues already exist at all of the above levels. But most of them are not operating out of a world-order context. Each seeks to solve its problems and achieve its issue goals within a national framework. Most of these coalitions have not yet identified the full nature of the National Security State and the structural logic that renders leaders as well as citizens powerless to reorder priorities. The *linkage* between the powerlessness of their particular issue constituency and the straitjacket of the National Security State thus is only vaguely discerned, if at all.

Special Issue Monographs

These monographs will examine the linkages between issues such as housing, alienation, technology or social justice and the constant mobilization within the National Security State system.

Each monograph would be designed as a strategic tool for catalyzing the local and national constituents of a particular issue concern as actors in the world-order movement. The monographs would place an issue within the *macro* framework of global interdependence, examining all the forces that impinge upon that issue: local, regional, national and global.

The monographs are and will be developing out of working sessions that bring together people active in the particular issue constituencies. The participants assess the unregulated economic, monetary and political forces that are devastating domestic priorities—forces with which national institutions cannot cope by themselves. Building upon this assessment, the working sessions then concentrate on the WHY, WHAT and HOW of world order. The tasks would be:

1. to identify the *linkages* that exist between the powerlessness of the constituents of the particular issue being examined and the straitjacket of the National Security State system.
2. to examine and formulate *alternative scenarios* in which the rampant global forces could be regulated and the straitjacket loosened.
3. to explore concrete *strategies* for conscientizing the issue constituents about global interdependence and world order.

Preliminary papers for these working sessions are prepared by a task force of scholars and actionists from the particular issue constituency. Their working papers are read and *critiqued* by workshop participants before coming, enabling them to contribute at the workshop their own insights into the relationship between their issue and global interdependence, and to propose related action strategies. This sharing of knowledge and insight and the brainstorming of action strategies involves people in the formulation processes and gives them ownership in the world-order movement. Moreover, it provides valuable content for the development of the issue monographs which are used in the next stages of consciousness raising.

The monographs resulting from these leadership workshops are then printed for widespread use with local, regional and national networks concerned with the particular issues—as an aid in conscientizing and mobilizing their constituents regarding world order.

A task of the issue leaders (whether scholars or grass-roots community actionists) is to "translate" the analysis into the mind-set and language of their constituents. This mind-set and language could be, on one hand, the idiom of "street people" or of the middle-class citizen. On the other hand, it could be the sophisticated language of professional and technological specialists.

This translation process is not passive. Rather than simply transferring data, it actively responds to the analysis of global interdependence and the straitjacket of inadequate structures from the particularized context of one's own person and concerns. Similarly, in dealing with the projections of "preferred world order futures," the translation includes new and creative input into future designing. And, finally, the translation includes particularized action strategies by which grass-roots people, middle-class citizens or specialists can become actors in the world-order movement.

Preliminary working papers on most of the above seventeen issues have been prepared by the staff and consultants of Global Education Associates. A number of issue symposia based on these working papers have already been held.

Obviously, there are no "final" monographs for any of the issue networks. The relationships between world order and each issue are complex—as complex as global interdependence itself. The monographs are seen as means, not ends. There probably will be several for each issue, speaking to the multiple dimensions and to various approaches, some of which will differ.

Each area of the world can be expected to develop

its own issue monographs, taking into consideration the particular social, cultural, economic and political realities that are unique to it. But this does not mean that each country or area will have to start from point zero. Many of the basic characteristics of the National Security State are similar all over the world. Thus, basic working papers and monographs developed in one country—particularly if prepared by transnational and transcultural task forces—will have many common touch points for other areas of the world.

One outcome of the team effort to develop issue monographs is the conscientization of those involved. Even more strategically, the working documents that result from this effort provide a tool to be used by constituency leaders for consciousness raising and politicization among their constituents.

Networking

Major vehicles for conscientization are two kinds of networks. One is the *issue* network, i.e., the national organizations committed to a particular issue. An example would be organizations committed to environmental responsibility. Each one of the issues we have listed has local and national organizational networks. But most are seeking their issue goals within the limited framework of national boundaries, not placing their respective issue in the macro context of global interdependence—and, therefore, not identifying the straitjacket of the National Security State that is a major factor in their powerlessness.

A second type of network would be more *general*, e.g., religious, educational and professional networks. Such organizational networks are internally linked by bonds that transcend particular issues. Their membership, therefore, is concerned about more than a single issue.

As we will discuss in the next chapter, there is a *geometric*, rather than arithmetical, response that is possible from such networking—especially through religion-oriented networks. Indeed, such response is not just a theoretical possibility, for significant progress toward world order programing through networks has already been made.

11

Strategies for a Just World Order

Part II: Network Programming

> It is a mysterious characteristic of human nature that we are prepared to spend anything, to sacrifice everything, to give all we have and are when we wage war, and that we are never prepared to take more than a "first beginning," adopt more than "minimum measures" when we seek to organize peace. When will our religions, our poets and our national leaders give up the lie that death is more heroic than life?
>
> Emery Reves

Having outlined an overall multi-issue coalition for world order, we will now explore how such consciousness-raising and coalition-building efforts can be—and in some instances already are—implemented through existent channels of four types of networks:

1. Issue networks
2. Religion networks
3. Educational networks
4. Professional networks

Each of these networks has its own momentum which, in varying degrees, transmits ideas and promotes action initiatives through its respective constituents. Some networks have only individual members as constituents. Others have institutional and organizational constituents. Indeed, some are "networks of networks." And many networks from each of the above categories are *global*.

There is an overlap among the above networks. Each has constituents who are also members of the other three. Rather than being problematic, this overlap has strategic ramifications. For it multiplies whatever initiatives are taken in any one of the several areas.

An example of such overlap would be a world-order consciousness-raising program initiated within the area of the *housing* issue. Utilizing a monograph on "Housing and World Order," a person might organize a symposium on the subject for people living in Midwestern United States. Participants attending this symposium would likely include some clergy, religious sisters and lay people from a number of religion networks. They would presumably include educators who are teaching in the social sciences or urban affairs, or who may be interested in housing issues in their extra-professional life. And they may well include social workers, community organizers or urban planners, each of whom is affiliated with networks of particular professions.

As these various participants are assisted by their workshop participation to identify the national security straitjacket on housing and other domestic priorities, they would come away with a framework for promoting this consciousness among the constituents of their respective religious, educational and professional networks.

This raised consciousness will not move everyone toward political action, or personal formulation of world-order models, or direct involvement in the construction or administration of a global functional agency. But widespread consciousness has strategic value in itself. Without a grass-roots understanding that world order is an issue of *personal* and *national* self-interest and security, the actual transformation of present structures will not take place.

Experience to date, however, indicates that many will become personally involved. Some of those conscientized (either directly through participation or indirectly through network initiatives taken by someone who participated in such a consciousness-raising event) can be expected to become personally involved in one or more of several ways. Some may spend time—conceivably even full-time—to further expand consciousness about the national security straitjacket and the need for a world juridical order. (Especially important here are persons who can work full-time to catalyze their respective network toward world order consciousness and action.) Others may commit themselves to contributing reflection and research and world-order model conceptions related to some aspect of the global functional agency that would deal with their particular issues. And some—admittedly a relative, but strategic few—may choose to pursue a career related to one of the budding global institutions.

Some concrete initiatives can be suggested:

1. Giving or arranging a talk on some aspect of world order.
2. Utilizing a world-order monograph as a basis for organizing a workshop that places a par-

ticular issue in the context of global interdependence and world order.

3. Writing articles for newsletters or journals of one of the four networks, showing the linkages between its issue and world order.
4. Developing media presentations on such linkages.
5. Bringing together colleagues to informally explore the ramifications of the National Security State system and world-order alternatives for their work.

ISSUE NETWORKS

By "issue network" we primarily mean an organization that concentrates on a *single* issue. The issue may be housing, environmental protection, education, health care, alcoholism, or hunger, etc.

One can take any important issue in most countries and find at least one national organization devoted to it. Frequently, there are several. These single issue networks play a special role in a multi-issue coalition for world order for two reasons: they usually have the power to influence national dialogue and programing related to their issue; and they have the experience and competence to be able to generate new insights and new initiatives.

This is true not only in countries where democratic processes permit the citizens to have a voice in public policy. It is also true in those more closed societies in which isolated elites and their New Class technocrats largely determine policy. These elites—also confronted with national security priorities and unmet domestic needs—have their own issue networks with corresponding journals, newsletters and conferences.

There also are *transnational* issue networks. Some of these are formal organizations, with active members attending international conferences and contributing to related international journals in which scholarly or action-oriented papers are exchanged and published. Other issue networks may simply be comprised of the readers of an international journal. Sometimes a transnational issue network will be largely an association of national affiliates which periodically have a regional or international conference and an international newsletter.

The nongovernmental organizations (NGO's) that are affiliated with the United Nations are transnational issue networks that merit special attention. They operate with organic relations to the center of world community activities. Plugged into the center of world affairs, they have solid roots with local and national grass-roots issue constituencies around the world.

These NGO issue networks provide a bridge for communications between the people of the world and the policy makers at the world and national levels. Article 71 of the United Nation's Charter invites input from the NGO's and their experts. Admittedly such input is only marginally effective at this time. But as the world-order movement expands through multi-issue coalitions and initiatives through the four networks we will be discussing, such influence can be expected to increase.

Having special significance for each other are these issue networks and the issue *monographs* (described in the previous chapter). Monographs examining the relationship between the environment and world order, for example, are strategic instruments for getting environmental network constituents involved in the three interlocking world-order stages outlined earlier: consciousness raising, politicization and transformation.

But the converse is equally strategic. For among the prime writers of preliminary working papers and monographs will be members, officials, or staff consultants from the various special interest groups.

Persons deeply committed to a particular issue have a general readiness to become involved in the world-order movement. Such persons are usually quick to recognize that such involvement is not extracurricular. It is not something that distracts them from their primary commitment or hurt. Quite the contrary. They see their involvement in a multi-issue world-order movement as an occasion for expanding their own competence.

Most members belonging to single issue organizations are aware of their own powerlessness. They are also somewhat aware of global interdependence. But they seldom see the connection between the two. What they presently lack is a framework for making the linkage.

Rather than their involvement in the world-order movement being a distraction from a primary responsibility or interest, it provides a timely opportunity to make their issue-related activities more efficacious.

RELIGION NETWORKS

Religion networks, church-related organizations and religious institutions that encircle the earth, constitute a unique global social fibre. They can be major actors in the construction of a more human world order.

Despite the historical reality of human destructiveness in the name of religion, true religion professes the values fundamental to a viable world order. These include the solidarity of the human family, reverence for life, love, compassion, justice, human well-being, primacy of conscience, etc. A widespread reordering of priorities is taking place among men and women of faith. Along with this reexamination of the implications of one's faith commitment in the contemporary world is a diminishing of culture-bound condescensions of the past, replaced by an awareness of the richness and truths that can become interchangeable in a global society.

Already active as an important vehicle in the people's coalition, these networks are unique in more ways than just their size and extensiveness. Several special characteristics give them extraordinary potential for providing the creative leadership needed for new direction, hope and integration in our planetary world:

1. Many people are already *committed to universal religious values* which parallel the "world order values" that the Institute for World Order lists as peace, social justice, economic equity, ecological balance and participation in decision making.

2. The explicit profession of universal values, upon which religion-related networks are built, provides a basis for members to hold each other *accountable for acting upon these values.*

3. The universal values of religion provide a unique *common ground* uniting various faith networks in a way unmatched by secular organizations and institutions. The lack of such common ground is a major reason why most organizations operate mainly with an arithmetical rather than a *geometric* rate of program progression. (An arithmetical progression moves slow-

ly, adding up individuals one by one, i.e., 1,2,3,4,5,6,7, etc. A geometric progression moves 2,4,8,16,32,64, etc. in a multiplier effect as whole groups join a movement.)

Let us not be misunderstood. Certainly many "nonreligious" humanists would be among those with the highest quality and deepest intensity of concern and commitment to human values and to the hotal human family. And the shallow character of the human concern of many church leaders and members is equally evident. But having said that, one can point to many thousands of clergy, religious and laity whose very identity is rooted in religious values that are also world order values. And these people are further strengthened and empowered by reason of being bound together in interlocking networks that are uniquely defined by a special quality and intensity of human concern.

Religion-related networks, therefore, provide a unique global fibre for developing the people's coalition for world order. Not only do they constitute a special constituency connected to one of the issues (i.e., concern about human/religious values), but each religion-related network, through its membership, is in touch with grass-roots people *representing all of the other issue constituencies*—an "in-touchness" that is growing as many men and women relate themselves full-time to one or more of these issues.

One can cite particular religion-related programs dealing with every one of the issues listed in previous chapters. And because a large percentage of these people are also active in parallel secular organizations and networks, the spin-offs from these religion-related efforts can be enormous.

Strategically important, the groups and individuals who are related to their own issue network within most countries also have liaison, to varying degrees, with a wider global network of institutions related to the same issue. Thus a concentration on religion-related networks provides a geometric entree to hundreds of organizations and tens of thousands of creative and initiative-taking men and women dealing with the major issues with which humankind must deal in the final quarter of the twentieth century.

At this point it would be worthwhile to consider in greater detail examples of several religious networks that combine an increasing commitment to world-order values with global channels or organizational and network communications.

1. *Pontifical Commission for Justice and Peace*

With affiliates in many countries around the world, the Pontifical Commission provides a strategic global forum for consciousness raising about all three aspects of world order: the WHY, WHAT and HOW of world order. Besides these affiliated national Offices of Justice and Peace, each of which has regional affiliates within the country, the Commission works closely with two network organizations based in Rome: the Union of Superiors General (USG) and the International Union of Superiors General (UISG).

The USG is a union of 95 international organizations of priests and brothers which coordinates 250,000 men working in a wide variety of educational, religious and social action programs and institutions around the world. The UISG is a union of 220 international organizations of religious women which services some 900,000 sisters working in similar efforts.

With the Catholic Church putting increased emphasis on social justice and on full human development (as affected by social structures), the Pontifical Commission has been an effective catalyst for increased global awareness among church networks around the world. One of its top agenda items is the New International Economic Order. Twice in 1975 the Commission arranged workshops on "Religion and World Order" which the authors conducted for superiors and representatives of the USG and the UISG.

An example of the Commission's power for catalyzing a consciousness of world-order priorities is evident in the size and structure of the religious orders and congregations that it serves. The Jesuits, with some 29,000 men around the world, most of whom administer or teach in hundreds of Jesuit universities, colleges, high schools and institutes, are but one of these orders.

Meriting special mention, however, are the networks of religious women. Analysts of the contemporary Catholic Church in the United States affirm that religious sisters are one of its most dynamic elements. Their growing initiative in social justice and global concerns is both an expression of the potential power of their faith commitment and the potential power of liberated women to provide leadership in the future. The educational formation of American nuns over the past twenty years has focused on contemporary issues and professional competence. Spurred on to bold new initiatives by awareness of the growing influence of women, many are beginning to grapple with the planetary dimensions of contemporary problems. Within the United States, for example, sisters administrate and teach in about 200 Catholic colleges, nearly 3,000 high schools and thousands of primary schools. Many are venturing out in full or part-time adult education, public service and social action projects.

Some 520 heads of different religious congregations, each of whom is in charge of a separate network of persons and institutions, constitute a national network of networks as members of the *Leadership Conference of Women Religious*. Recognizing the planetary dimensions of today's world, the LCWR established a "Justice and Peace Commission" as a step toward raising the consciousness of the 130,000 women they represent. LCWR officials are active in many international programs, including Vatican-based operations—a strategic position from which to influence also the thinking of other church networks around the world.

Also meriting special mention is a membership association of progressive women, the *National Assembly of Women Religious*. NAWR is very much issue oriented, searching for ultimate roots of present problems and for strategies for resolving them.

These multiple networks of religious sisters present a number of concrete areas for world-order programing. Most obvious is the incorporation of world order as an integrating framework for school and college curricula through the educational institutions which sisters administrate around the world. A natural vehicle for this formal educational approach to world order in the United States is the *National Catholic Educational Association*, a professional association of individual educators teaching in 14,000 Catholic educational institutions. Most of these members are sisters. The NCEA launched a "Peace Education" program in 1972 which seeks to develop a global consciousness among its member educators, thus laying the basis for developing a planetary framework for integrated curricula development.

2. *The World Council of Churches*

The World Council of Churches has been in the

vanguard of the movement for world justice and peace. Like its regional national council affiliates around the world, it has consistently spoken to the social issues of our times.

The 1975 gathering in Nairobi of some 2,300 participants from around the world for the WCC's Fifth World Assembly bore witness to this growing emphasis on social issues of global concern. The Assembly put great emphasis on human liberation and global social justice and gave a strong endorsement to the New International Economic Order.

The scope of the World Council of Churches network—a network of networks—can be seen through an examination of its structure. Its highest authority, the General Assembly, meets every seven years. Members of the Assembly are official representatives of the groups of churches that are WCC affiliates. The Assembly is responsible for the World Council's policy, and appoints the Central Committee that is responsible for implementing the Assembly's policies.

Six presidents and 130 Central Committee members were elected at the Nairobi Assembly. The international nature of the presidents and the committee members illustrates the WCC's global and multicultural character. The area breakdown of these officials is as follows:

Africa	17
Asia	19
Australasia & Pacific	7
West Europe	28
East Europe	21
Middle East	9
Latin America	4
North America	28

The various departments of the World Council of Churches serve different functions of service and con-scientization for its network membership. They give special emphasis for dialogue and collaboration with its national affiliates.

One department that has special significance is the WCC's Commission on the Church's Participation in Development. Working closely with local leaders in-volved in socio-economic development projects around the world, CCPD staff are in close touch with grass-roots needs, aspirations and initiatives. Ongoing educa-tional programs as well as community development programs not only have meaning for local development goals; they also provide an exchange of insights and ex-perience for network affiliates around the world.

With the reality of global interdependence now clearly being felt by local development programs, an awareness is growing among WCC staff and national affiliates that more than the class analysis (which has sometimes been too simply used to diagnose roots of social injustice) is needed.

In talking with many religious leaders at the Nairobi Assembly about the relationship between reli-gion and world order, we found considerable interest among them in participating in the development of a "Theology of World Order" as applicable to their re-gional and cultural contexts. Such a theology could help bridge the chasm between advocates of the social gospel and advocates of the spiritual gospel. And it could provide a framework for "Liberationists" and "Evangelists" to come together on some common ground.

This interest in world order is being strengthened by the growing perception of the interrelatedness of

domestic and *global* issues that many church leaders
have traditionally approached as if they were separated
issues. This old dichotomy is best illustrated in the traditional separation between domestic and overseas
"mission." A result of this separation was that, instead
of providing a global fibre for a world community
based on social justice and human priorities, church-
related networks reinforced the paternalism and imperial domination of the West. But as we will see, things
are beginning to change.

3. *"Mission" Organizations*

The Christian concept of "world mission" is un-
dergoing radical reevaluation. The traditional identification of Christianity with Western culture is fading,
as is a too-exclusive preoccupation with proselytizing.
A new emphasis includes greater focus on developing
social institutions that will permit all persons to live in
dignity in accord with their own cultural heritage.
Some missiologists are beginning to understand that
rather than the unity of humankind being the *result* of
lived religious values, such unity may well be the
precondition for the living of those values. The analysis
of the National Security State as a straitjacket on true
religion helps make this point. Thus, "world mission"
becomes a mission to build the global unities that will
enable values of love, justice and freedom of conscience
to be operative.

Giving way is the traditional distinction between
"home lands" and "mission lands." The new vision is
one of peer consciousness among equal churches united
in global networks of local communities and institutions.

A world-order framework has special relevance

here. For it provides a basis for a mutual dialogue between church men and women of North America and Europe and those of the "developing" world. A grave crisis of identity exists among traditional mission organizations who now find their "missionary" personnel unwelcome in Africa, Asia and Latin America. The result is paralysis of initiative. (A similar problem exists in secular development groups whose own "mission" is challenged by Third and Fourth World peoples.)

A world-order perspective provides a basis for overcoming this identity crisis and paralysis. For it is no longer a question of one group coming with the "answers" for the other. Rather, people from various faiths and nations work together as equals in all areas of the world to deal with global interdependence and its many ramifications for human and religious values. One of their common tasks is to become actors in the creation of a more human world order.

The World Order Models Project is an example of such transnational and transcultural collaboration. Asian, African, European, North American and Latin American scholars all participated in the development of scenarios of a preferred world order offering the insight and experience from their own cultural viewpoints.

Most major Protestant denominations in the United States and Europe have an equivalent of an overseas mission division. These offices promote and coordinate a variety of overseas religious, educational and socio-economic programs that sometimes emanate directly from the national office, but more often are initiated and sustained by local congregations around the country. Some denominations, however, have already replaced their separate office for *overseas* ministry with an office for *global* ministries. An example is the *United Methodist Board of Global Ministries*, which attempts to deal with its various programs overseas and at home in an integrated way. One of its current projects is to build, in collaboration with other groups, a global educational model, designed by a transnational team, for adaptation all over the world.

The Catholic Church also has several global networks of "mission" organizations. One grouping is of *regional* congregations, with headquarters in North America and Europe, which send members to overseas assignments in Third and Fourth World countries—similar to overseas mission programs of Protestant organizations. A second type are *global* congregations that coordinate regional provinces, often quite autonomous, through a "generalate office" usually located in Rome. The Jesuit Order (Society of Jesus) is such a global congregation. A third type of network includes issue-oriented commissions such as the Pontifical Commission for World Justice and Peace, which has national affiliate offices in most countries. And the Vatican itself provides a national communications network that can have significant influence in promoting world-order goals.

Examples of this latter influence are papal documents that have already provided a rationale for world order. Pope Pius XII repeatedly insisted that a "supranational juridical community" was a prerequisite for world peace. Pope John XXIII saw the global dimension of today's problems as demanding "a public authority, having worldwide power and endowed with the proper means for the efficacious pursuit of . . . the universal good." Paul VI called for a "world authority,

capable of acting effectively in the juridical and political sectors." And Vatican II advocated the "establishment of some universal public authority . . . endowed
with the power to safeguard on the behalf of all, security, regard for justice, and respect for rights." A major
reason that church leaders on national levels have not
taken such documents seriously was the lack of a grass-
roots rationale and a strategy to give world order im-
mediacy and credibility. Both of these now exist.

4. *The World Conference on Religion and Peace*

The above church-related networks, united by
world-order values that are inherent in the Christian
religion, provide an existent global fibre that stands un-
paralleled. A constant flow of people, information and
ideas provides an exceptional opportunity for advancing
people's coalitions for world order around the globe.
This flow, however, must take place in a more broadly
ecumenical context—one that joins hands with Judaism,
Islam, Buddhism, Hinduism, Shintoism, indigenous African religions and other living faiths, each having their
own networks.

A global network that has played a pioneering role
in such global ecumenism is the *World Conference on
Religion and Peace.*

A long-standing hope has been that world religions
would work for world peace and justice, and that organized religions not be a source of intolerance and war.
This hope was expressed concretely in the World Parliament of Religion held in Chicago in 1893, which
outlined a common platform for all world religions on
the basis of equality. This effort was continued in the
1930s through the World Conference for International
Peace Through Religion, but World War II broke out
before its world conference could be held. After the

bombing of Hiroshima and Nagasaki, religious groups in Japan met to explore the role that religion could play in preventing a nuclear war. In 1966 religious groups in the United States convened a National Inter-Religious Conference on Peace. One result of this was the 1968 International Inter-Religious Symposium on Peace at New Delhi, sponsored in part by the Gandhi Peace Foundation. Then Japanese, Indian and U.S. religious leaders pooled their concerns to convene the first World Conference on Religion and Peace (WCRP I) in Kyoto in 1970.

The Kyoto Conference brought together almost 500 leaders from the world religions—Buddhism, Christianity, Confucianism, Hinduism, Islam, Jainism, Judaism, Shintoism, Sikhism and Zoroastrianism—to discuss, not theology, but the "U.N. agenda for human survival: disarmament, development and human rights." Using their religious and ethical insights, the delegates adopted the Kyoto Message (printed below). WCRP I voted to establish an *ongoing World Conference on Religion and Peace*, with headquarters near the UN in New York City. The organization soon acquired consultative status with the United Nations' Economic and Social Council.

A second world conference (WCRP II) was held at Louvain, Belgium, in late August 1974. Leaders of the world's religions added environment to the three agenda items of the 1970 Kyoto conference.

The *Kyoto Message* outlines the common ground that exists for representatives and institutions of world religions to join hands in the task of building a human world order:

As we sat down together facing the overriding issues of peace we discovered that the things which unite us are more important than the things which divide us. We found that we share:

A conviction of the fundamental unity of the human family, and the equality and dignity of all human beings;

A sense of the sacredness of the individual person and his conscience;

A sense of the value of human community;

A realization that might is not right; that human power is not self-sufficient and absolute;

A belief that love, compassion, selflessness, and the force of inner truthfulness and of the spirit have ultimately greater power than hate, enmity, and self-interest;

A sense of obligation to stand on the side of the poor and the oppressed as against the rich and the oppressors; and

A profound hope that good will finally prevail.

Because of these convictions that we hold in common, we believe that a special charge has been given to all men and women of religion to be concerned with all their hearts and minds with peace and peace-making, to be the servants of peace. As men and women of religion we confess in humility and penitence that we have very often betrayed our religious ideals and our commitment to peace. It is not religion that has failed the cause of peace, but religious people. This betrayal of religion can and must be corrected.

From the Message of WCRP I.

The World Order Models Project, described earlier in Chapter IX, provides an opportune springboard from which to launch ecumenical, intercultural and interdisciplinary initiative related to the development of world-order institutions. The "world-order values" which provided the common ground for the nine WOMP teams around the world to develop their world-order models resonate with inherent values of Buddhism, Hinduism, Islam, Judaism and Christianity.

Bold initiatives by world religious leaders and institutions could make a difference in the further development and realization of such scenarios. Our religious values call on us to put explicit focus on the construction of societal institutions that will sustain human dignity and *personal* sovereignty. If real local autonomy is to be guaranteed in today's interdependent world, some of these institutions must be transnational. Representatives and institutions of the world's major religions are in a unique position to provide leadership related to the development of such global institutions.

EDUCATIONAL NETWORKS
Although this section overlaps both the religion-

related networks above and the professional networks below, education merits its own section. No other institution so explicitly sets out to form attitudes toward the institutions and world around us.

The question of global consciousness and world order cuts to the core of relevant education. We are not dealing with extracurricular issues. Our concern is with preparing citizens for the real world of escalating interdependencies. It is a question of *justice*—for the students who have a right to demand a refund of tuition if they are not prepared to handle such a world. It is also a question of *security*—for the nation whose human priorities and future security depend upon citizens prepared to build the transnational institutions commensurate to an interdependent planet. Today, relevant education means curriculum approaches designed within a global framework. It means the commensurate preparation of educators to effectively deal with such an expanded framework.

There are several types of educational networks that are at various stages of progress related to global perspectives in education. Some are organizations with individual, group or institutional membership. Others are held together by a particular institute which sponsors periodic national or world conferences, or provides particular services related to international education. Also contributing to transnational dialogue are educational journals that reach an international pool of readers.

Some examples of *national* networks in the United States that are involved in this process toward a global educational framework are the National Educational Association, the National Catholic Educational Association, the National Council for the Social Studies, the

Association for Supervisors and Curriculum Development, and the Consortium on Peace Research, Education and Development. Similar networks exist in other countries.

Examples of *international* networks are the World Council for Curriculum and Instruction, the International Council for Educational Development, the International Institute for Educational Planning, and the International Peace Research Association.

We have already spoken of the role of international students and educators in building world-order institutions. They can be an important resource in the global consciousness-raising process. Strategic recruitment of international professors and students by U.S. and European schools and universities, for example, can assist curriculum development and teacher training, as well as providing personalized interest and insight for Western students. And a globalized educational framework would enable international students to return to their respective countries to provide a broader, transnational perspective to the institutions and professions there.

Richard Falk speaks of the role of formal education in consciousness raising. Part of this task is

> . . . to gain greater access to conventional educational resources by penetrating school activities at all levels with materials and courses that are more realistically related to the world order situation and more enlightened about lines of response. The Institute for World Order has been pioneering along these lines, but its efforts have been largely confined to achieving *mechanical penetration* of exist-

ing curricula rather than aiming at the *organic reorientation* of the educational program, which is what would enable students to develop an understanding of what is needed, what is desirable, and what can be done.[1]

He then spells out a central challenge which world order presents to all persons and institutions engaged in education, whether that be classroom, community or constituency education:

By *organic reorientation* we mean more than new materials for old courses, or even curriculum revision; we mean, in essence, changing implicit symbol and belief systems that underlie the whole way citizenship, national goals, and even personal fulfillment are approached in the educational system.[2]

A special word must be said on "Peace Education," a concept replete with professional authority but describing only a part of the whole. The *whole* would be the overall curriculum that—in the framework of global interdependence—sees all subjects approached in the framework of responsible citizenship on planet Earth. Whereas a *part*, i.e., Peace Studies, would be a formal study of the various dimensions of "peace-making." Sometimes called "Irenology," it is becoming a new academic major.

An example is Manhattan College's Peace Studies Program which offers a peace studies major that yields a Bachelor of Arts degree taken in conjunction with a second related major such as English, History or some other discipline. Its multidisciplinary nature is evident in the courses offered to the peace studies major during the academic year 1972-73:

> Biology of Human Behavior (Anthropology)
> The Social Psychology of Social Problems (Psychology)
> The Anatomy of Peace (History)
> World Economic Geography (Economics)
> International Relations (Government)
> International Organization (Government)
> The Literature of Peace and War (World Literature)
> Philosophies of War and Peace (Philosophy)
> Religious Dimensions of Peace (Religious Studies)

The number of colleges that offer peace education courses is estimated to be nearly 500. Indicative of the rising interest in peace education is the Consortium on Peace Research, Education and Development (COPRED). Its purposes are to stimulate and support peace research and education activities, and to perform a variety of clearinghouse, synthesis and contact services for all people in the growing field.

A pioneer in world-order education is the Institute for World Order. It has labored since 1961 to train educators and produce educational materials relative to world order. The Institute describes the problem that its educational program is concerned with as follows: "the nonviolent transformation of the World System to a new system directed to the Maximization of Warlessness, Economic Welfare, Social Justice and Ecological Balance." Worthy of special note is the Institute's statement on the difference between International Relations and World Order Studies:

International Relations	*World Order Studies*
1) Value-free objective study	1) Value-oriented— aimed at clarification and realization
2) Focuses on present and past	2) Focuses on future and present
3) Nation-state primary actor	3) Includes a range of actors from individuals to world organizations
4) Policies based on national interest	4) Policies emphasize consideration of world interest
5) Violence legitimate tool of nation-state and may be used	5) Inquires into alternatives to violence
6) Descriptive	6) Prescriptive[3]

The basis for world-order education is well stated by the Institute of World Order's Chairman, C. Douglas Dillon:

1. The present international system, while it worked reasonably well in the pre-atomic age, is not only inadequate to provide nations with security but will ultimately end, if not changed, in a major world catastrophe. Furthermore, there is no reasonable chance of reducing the current world armament expenditures so long as this system prevails.
2. Governments are not equipped to deal with long-range problems of this nature in their initial stages. The burden and responsibility for the initial steps in bringing about major social changes rests, in a democracy, with private citizens.

3. The first essential step is a sustained educational program. The Institute for World Order has established itself as the leading organization concerned with the difficult task of producing the instructional resources required for the introduction of the subject of world order into the academic world.

4. The method adopted by the Institute for World Order to promote such a study is eminently sound in that it does not recommend any particular resolutions but sets forth in a responsible way the dimensions of the problem, suggests various alternative resolutions and asks the student to determine what changes are required and how they suggest we proceed from where we are to a preferred international system.[4]

PROFESSIONAL NETWORKS

An important group of actors in the world order movement are national associations of "professional" persons, i.e., engineers, educators, medical personnel, physical or social scientists, etc. These networks within national boundaries provide opportunities for multiplier communications with thousands of persons who share a common concern about particular issues. Most of them also have some type of connection with parallel associations in other countries.

Members of professional networks have a built-in answer to their question, "How can *I* get involved?" For every profession has at least one major professional membership association that carries on a continual dialogue through conferences, workshops and publications on problems, methods and strategies related to achieving the common goals that bind its membership together.

An example would be the various associations of *engineers*. Each discipline within the overall field of engineering has its own society. Thus we have the American Society of Civil Engineers. Similar societies exist for chemical, electrical, mechanical, agricultural, systems and other types of engineers. There are also problem-oriented engineering associations, of which engineers from several of the above disciplines are members, e.g., the Air Pollution Control Association. A third type is exemplified by the Engineers Joint Council, whose membership is organizational and serves as a coordinating and servicing vehicle for thirty-six particular member engineering associations. The interrelated character of these various entities is concretized in the United Engineering Center located in New York City, in which most engineering societies have offices. The Center's location at U.N. Plaza symbolizes the further relationships with parallel engineering associations in other countries.

The Engineers Joint Council illustrates the type of transnational dialogue that is an ongoing reality among engineers of different nations. As the largest federation of engineering societies in the United States, the Council takes pride in what it considers its substantial international responsibility. EJC represents U.S. engineering in the Pan American Federation of Engineering Societies (UPADI). Through its U.S. National Committee for UPADI, a delegation of thirty-six attended the XII Convention of UPADI in Lima, Peru in October of 1972 and presented several important papers.

UPADI offers one of the few channels through which the exchange of information and ideas among engineers of the Western Hemisphere can take place in a *nonpolitical* atmosphere. The significance of this organization to the development of Latin America is seen in the titles of the four main conference themes: 1) fishing for human consumption; 2) peaceful uses of nuclear energy; 3) environmental engineering; 4) agricultural realities in Latin America.

EJC also serves as the secretariat for the U.S. National Committee of the World Energy Conference. This worldwide organization's purpose is to exchange technical information on the generation and distribution of energy in all its forms. The last three international meetings were held in Moscow, Bucharest and Detroit, with over 5,000 attendees from nations throughout the world.

Through its Commission on International Relations, EJC aids in the coordination of the activities of the various national committees with the activities of overseas engineering groups. The Commission now includes representatives of the U.S. National Committee of UPADI, the World Energy Conference, the Committee on Large Dams, UNESCO, the World Federation of Engineering Operations, and works in liaison with the international interest of the National Academy of Engineering.

Because of the relatively high level of engineering sophistication in the United States, American engineering societies, not surprisingly, play a key role in these organizations and in this global dialogue. Formal international engineering associations also exist to tie in national networks of local county and state chapters with counterpart networks around the world. Three examples are the International Material Management Society, the International Commission on Irrigation, Drainage and Flood Control, and the International Association for Exchange of Students for Technical Experience.

Staying with the field of engineering a moment

longer, we can see a practical example of the goal-set, problem-solving orientation evident in the very concept of engineering, i.e., "a science by which the properties of matter and sources of energy are made useful to man." But an increasing number of engineers are management oriented. This is not to say that such persons are all moving into business management, though a considerable number are accepting management positions in large corporations. The point is that many engineers are moving beyond an individual task orientation to an orientation of *responsibility to the larger community*. This direction is due in part to Ralph Nader's dialogue on social responsibility, which raised the question regarding the degree to which engineers have become slaves of technological and corporate goals. An example of this social concern is the agenda of the New Jersey State Society of Engineers, whose 1973 conference agenda scheduled almost no technical meetings, focusing instead on topics relating to human and social behavior.

We need not spend more space elaborating on particulars. The basic rationale and strategy of working through national and global networks should be clear. One can list each of the issues we have identified and find several professional networks that include a major commitment to the resolution of each issue. Sometimes the commitment to a single issue may be the explicit reason for an organization's existence. An example would be the Society of Public Health Educators. In other organizations this commitment to particular issues is multiple. An example would be the National Association of Social Workers, whose concern is not with just a single issue but many of the issues on our coalition list as they relate to the social problems with which its members are dealing. A third type of society is that which, though not defined by a particular profession, has a membership that is predominantly made up of professional men and women. An example here is the World Future Society, whose members are very much concerned about systemic change as related to particular problem solving.

As the connection between resolving particular problems and a new system of world order is seen, these various networks become natural vehicles for bringing their constituencies into the coalition-building process. And as professional people are reached through networks of professional associations, they, *as individual members of other nonprofessional organizations*—e.g. the Wilderness Association, the National Association for the Advancement of Colored People, the War Resisters League, the National Organization of Women, and the American Association of Retired Persons—will also take initiative to relate world order to these special interest organizations.

CONCLUSION

These four types of networks provide the central vehicles of the multi-issue coalition for world order. Each has its own momentum that carries ideas and action initiatives through its respective institutions and organizations to particular constituencies. As the coalition moves forward—always explicating the triple conceptualization of the rationale, models and strategy for world order so that each issue constituency is aware of the momentum of a widely based movement—the growing credibility of world order will make it an increasingly urgent agenda item within these networks.

As made clear in previous chapters, we are not

talking about a strategy that prepares the people of the world for some *sudden* systems change by a single constitutional act. What is involved is a systems change through gradual evolution of transnational structures—an evolution already in process on many levels. Systems planners are reluctant to follow any plan that seems to presume a dismantling of a system and a subsequent reconstruction. Rather than such dismantling in favor of a completely new design, a systems approach seeks change in those pivotal areas in a system that will permit and energize movement that is presently stagnated.

This basic principle of systems change underlies our approach to world order. The National Security State system *runs itself*, with a national security logic and dynamic over which national leaders do not have direct control. The pivotal key to loosening human-centered movement in the system is an adjustment of the principle of *absolute* national sovereignty. The multi-issue coalition does not seek to abolish national sovereignty, but to transform it within a world juridical framework that assures national security in all its dimensions of peace, justice and personal sovereignty.

This loosening of the straitjacket would not only permit a reordering of national priorities. It would also permit the long-range, integrated planning necessary to prevent many domestic crises.

Movement toward world order is *developmental*, rather than revolutionary. Yet its end results of peace, justice and human liberation are fundamentally *radical*, going to both root values and to the root institutions which straitjacket those values. The time frame that we project is reasonable and practical. Few people speak today of immediate solutions to domestic ills. Drug abuse, urban decay, water and air pollution, racial tensions and other problems will not be resolved within a single Republican or Democratic administration. Each is complex and interrelated to other domestic problems as well as to international issues and pressures. Even those who continue to seek solutions within a national framework use similar time frames that extend into the 1980s and 1990s.

What is being asked, then, is not to abandon present problem-solving efforts for some far-distant future utopia. Recommended, rather, is a pragmatism which recognizes that such problem-solving efforts will not bear much fruit without commensurate effort put into structural adaptation at the global level.

12

World Order and Authentic Religion

Religion: from the Latin "religare"; to bind together; to make whole.

Why a chapter entitled "World Order and Authentic Religion"? We have already spoken in the previous chapter of the potential pragmatic role that religious institutions, with their transnational networks and values perspective, can play, along with other global actors, in the development of a just world order. But there is another consideration that merits exploration. That is the actual and potential substantive contribution by persons whose faith fosters commitment and a sense of responsibility to the human community. Further, there is a dimension beyond political and economic considerations which must be considered in a holistic approach to world order.

Our personal experience in meeting with men and women from various faith traditions in programs we have conducted in Africa, Latin America, India, Europe and the U.S. has demonstrated there is a growing interest in the world-order movement. Many are already somewhat aware of the straitjacket imposed on their values concerns and goals by the existent world system. But, too often, there is a lack of awareness of the contributions they can make from their particular experience and insight and of the relevancy of their faith to the development of a more human world order.

While the majority of this chapter will relate itself to the positive contributions to be made by world religions to the development of a viable human future, it must begin by noting that much historical evidence and widely held opinion would seem to contradict this suggestion.

Religion has historically been a cause of divisiveness, hostility and brutal wars among human groups. Religious fanaticism and self-righteousness ("God is on our side") continue to erupt in violence and atrocities. And religious imperialism, utilizing elitist concepts that feed a collective egotism, remains one of the great social evils of our times.

Organized religion has often been a tool of the state, used to manipulate people's loyalties toward unquestioning allegiance. It has also sometimes made itself indistinguishable from the state, wielding political control for its own gains. And one does not need the insights of Marx to know that religion has, indeed, been at times the opiate of the people, drugging human sensitivities with "pie in the sky" concepts that leave individuals impotent against here and now realities of hunger, poverty and oppression.

The word religion also has for many become synonymous with its diverse customs, rituals and external manifestations and aberrations rather than with the internal impetus toward fulfillment and wholeness that is the nerve center of the life impulse and spiritual search.

It is, therefore, not surprising that many persons involved in critical issues of human survival have come to the conclusion that religion, at best, is an irrelevant force and, at worst, is a major obstacle to human progress and social justice.

But while there is ample evidence of human destructiveness perpetrated or justified in the name of religion, there is also much evidence of human spiritual creativity that has energized new and positive thrusts forward in human history. The significance of religion as a historical force for good and for ill in human development is well documented in the work of historians such as Arnold Toynbee. In his explorations of the rise and fall of civilizations, Toynbee ascribes a significant role to religious groups in bridging the time and space between the decline of one civilization and the rise of the next. Religions have also been a motivating force contributing to the rise of "creative minorities" who built new civilizations from the ashes of old ones. Further, his explorations of history led Toynbee to conclude that civilizations which lost their spiritual center were not long sustained.[1]

If we accept Toynbee's conclusions about the historical demise of civilizations without a spiritual center, we are led to certain conclusions about the importance of a holistic approach to the development of a new human order.

Inner growth and transformation and external change in the world system are integral to each other. That is, growth in the *internal* order and growth in the *external* order are inseparable and mutually reinforcing. They are part of one organism. They develop in conformity to each other. The lack of a correlative growth in either the internal or external order is damaging to the development of the whole organism.

The nurturing of a deeper, universal consciousness and the harnessing of spiritual and moral energies in the conception and creation of a just world order are vital aspects of its healthy development.

AUTHENTIC RELIGION

The positive significance of authentic religion in the creative task of developing a more human world order is suggested in the meaning of the word "religion." Derived from the Latin "religare," it means "to bind together," "to make whole," "harmony." In Sanskrit one of the original meanings for "dharma," eternal religion, is the same, "to bind together as one the whole universe."

In both the Western and Eastern meanings of the word, authentic religion is concerned with a vision and celebration of the essential relatedness and oneness of all existence. It points toward a potential and destiny that transcend the immediate evidence of brokenness and incompletion. Authentic religion is developed in the humble awareness of participation in reality and meaning greater than self and beyond measurable physical, social, political or economic relationships. It is a consciousness that carries with it a sense of accountability not just to self but to the greater whole in which one is co-participant. It is with the above meaning of the term religion that we entitled this chapter "World Order and Authentic Religion."

Jung made an important distinction between *authentic religion* and *religious creed*. He suggested that creedal religion or collective belief runs the risk of becoming an oppressive, alienating force if, like a totalitarian state, it is imposed on people as a new absolute and the individual is submerged in the mass authority. When this happens, it is the opposite of authentic religion which, in Jungian terms, is a living and "incontrovertible experience of an intensely personal relationship between man and an extramundane authority."[2]

The religious impulse, which some call the search for God, some ultimate concern, others an awareness of our relatedness to a Ground of All Being, and still others the path of liberation or salvation, is not something which can be superimposed. It is, says Jung, an "instinctive attitude peculiar in man" and will seek its own course. Nor can it be truly separated from the so-called "secular" aspects of our existence without resulting in human alienation and deterioration.

A "SECULAR" ORDER OR A HUMAN ORDER?

"I can only conceive of a just world order as a *secular* world order," advised a noted Gandhian in Delhi. "Unless religions as fashioned in the past are basically modified, they should not have a positive role in a new world order. A just world order should be neutral to religion. That is to say, a World Food Authority should give food to the hungry regardless of their religion or even if they are anti-religion."

Openness toward differences of belief and equality of opportunity are obviously of critical importance in the development of a just world order. A state religion or a Creedal State on a global level would mitigate against all the historic wisdom we should, by now, have gathered. But such openness does not negate the need for an inner moral and spiritual base.

Our Gandhian friend insisted that unless creedal religions are reformed from *within* so that they are no longer a divisive force, but become a unifying force, they should have no part in the development of a new world order. However, he was equally insistent that a *spiritual force is* relevant to world order. For, he reflected, a more human world order will need a values base, a moral base to which the human community subscribes if it is to be effective.

A more human world order will also need the creative power and reinforcement of an interior vision and a commitment to truthful and humble exploration of new ways of perceiving and being in the world. It will require a deeper identification with, and a disciplined capacity to respond creatively to, the needs of others and of the whole earth community. This identification and response must transcend self-centered individualism and the impulse to control or hold the other in bondage or dependency. The growth of an interior consciousness that includes a vision of our shared humanity, the worth of each person and the interrelatedness of all life forms on our one earth, is vital to world order as a creative force in the development of the human community as well as a corrective to abuses of human power.

One effect of contemplation and meditation is that it can deepen consciousness and inner experience of such essential unities. It is also a means of locating ethical direction and creative energy. Out of religious experience have come many of the symbols, images and myths that help communicate and further develop this sense of unity and interrelatedness.

The development of a humanizing world order is *not* a "secular" activity alone. Nor does it involve only exterior activity in the socio-economic-political spheres. To imply such is to impose artificial and meaningless categories. Conserving the value of life, ensuring the means to sustain life, and creating an environment in which human growth can be realized, are deeply human/religious acts. It is irrelevant to make distinctions about initiating such activity in the "secular" or the "religious" spheres. In terms of human survival and development, in terms of growth in wholeness, it is one and the same sphere—the human sphere.

PROPHETIC PRESENCE

We must repeatedly ask ourselves this question: If and when a new world order is born (as it surely must if we would not destroy ourselves), what will be the underlying values and vision that inspire and inform the shaping of its new design?

Surely the survival and security of the human community are fundamental. But underlying and beyond these are many unanswered questions. Who will be the decision-makers? To whom or to what principles will a new world order be ultimately accountable? What code of ethics, if any, will be applied in policy decisions? What will be of central concern: Profit? The continued privilege of the few? Unlimited progress at the expense of the ecosphere and human dignity? Or the common good of the whole earth community? Will individual persons be at the center of concern or only of tangential consequence in the face of expanding technology? These questions and many more that flow from them are of grave moral concern. They are concerns that call for a prophetic presence.

The role of the prophet is to be simultaneously an avant-garde and a conserving force. As avant-garde[3] the prophet calls human groups to an awareness of further potential, to more integral ways of perceiving and being in the world. In this creative task of leading people to a fuller vision of what *is* and what *could be* beyond the immediate surface realities, the prophet makes an important contribution to the shaping of human institutions. The conservative role of the prophet is also important. It keeps before us an awareness of the sacredness and dignity of the human person and takes a firm moral and ethical position against the forces that violate that dignity.

It is the prophetic task to announce that the world was created, not to be destroyed, but to be fulfilled; not to stand still, but to grow toward wholeness. It is part of the prophetic role to identify alternatives and encourage possible directions in that journey toward wholeness. In this regard there is a convergence between the prophetic presence in authentic religion and efforts within the world-order movement to identify the perilous course we are now traveling and explore alternative routes for the human community.

It is part of the prophetic role to call us to task when we lose sight of that whole; to be, as Isaiah, a critic of the established order and institutions when they fail to advance or violate human growth. It is the prophetic task to speak to the inalienable right of all persons to the means to full human development.

It is the prophetic task, while reminding us of our brokenness and vulnerability, to help "bind" and "heal" the wounds and cure the causes of our brokenness; to participate in developing that kind of inner and outer order in which the search for wholeness can be advanced more steadily toward realization.

It is the prophetic role to remind us that our "salvation" or "liberation" is worked out in history—in our time and space, here and now—not by a rejection of history or the world, but in the process of developing and actualizing its full potential. Much as a carpenter enhancing the natural wood grain, the prophet reminds us that this is our time and place to Become who we can be.

CONTRIBUTIONS OF WORLD RELIGIONS

The world's great religious movements can provide significant insight, inspiration and symbolic imagery toward the development of a new world order. An example would be input into the development of a shared ecological ethic as a basis for a global environmental contract.

Who Owns the Earth?

The presumption that man is the most superior presence on earth and therefore has absolute dominion and unlimited rights to determine the uses of the earth's resources has led to grave abuses of the ecosystem. It has nourished a human delusion that somehow one can *earn, buy* and *own* (individually or corporately as groups or nations) sections of this one earth without any limits save the extent of one's economic resources and physical power; and that one then has the right to exercise absolute control over this area and the life forms that inhabit it. It is a presumption which must be seriously questioned as we approach the twenty-first century immersed in deep and serious issues of human survival.

In the cosmological vision of authentic religion the human species is not the master, but rather *part* of the universe. As such, the human person is dependent upon the workings and laws of the natural universe. An ecological ethic has its beginnings in awareness of this dependency.

An Interdependent Whole

A sense of interdependence and relatedness to all

of life was an important aspect of traditional tribal religious vision and is represented intact today in the life and vision of some traditional American Indian, African and aboriginal societies as well as in Eastern mysticism.

Religion in these societies was not apart from life but was seen as integrally related to all one's activities. It was characterized by a keen sense of the world as one and undivided and as informed by a Spiritual Presence immanent in nature and all reality. The human person was perceived as being in dynamic relationship and continuity with all of life, past, present and future. The human community, as comprised by the tribal group, was bound together by a shared understanding of the mutual interdependence of its members.

The social order was developed in conformity to this vision of interdependence and of mutual responsibility for the well-being of the whole. That is, the well-being of the whole depended upon responsible individual and communal activity within the framework of a social order and an environmental order that were integral to each other.

The personification of nature by some tribal groups, as in the poem below by Smohalla, was a way of verbalizing the kinship and identification they felt with their environment and the gratitude for the gifts of nature. The natural environment was a mother upon whom one was dependent. Nature could not be abused or violated without consequently violating one's own best long-range interests.

> You ask me to plow the ground. Shall I take
>   a knife and tear my mother's breast?
>   Then when I die she will not take me
>   to her bosom to rest.

You ask me to dig for stone. Shall I dig under
her skin for her bones? Then when I
die I cannot enter her body to be born
again.
You ask me to cut grass and make hay and
sell it and be rich like white men. But
how dare I cut off my mother's hair?[4]

As the human community moves more deeply and
irreversibly into life as an interdependent, global society, it may be critical to relocate deep in our psyche
this sense of community and integral relatedness to all
life forms that was highly developed in our tribal
parents but which has all but atrophied in modern individualism.

The Middle Way and Ahimsa

Hindu and Buddhist teaching also contributes to
the philosophic base for a global environmental ethic.
Western notions of unlimited growth and consumption,
linked with a dualism that sets humans apart from nature, have been a major cause of such grave ecological
destruction that long-range human survival on the planet is today a serious question. In the Western view,
humans and nature are seen as opponents. Nature is
something to be conquered and subordinated. It is
viewed alternately as a *means* to be used for human
goals, and as an obstacle to the attainment of these
goals.

In the cosmological view of Buddhism, however,
nature is not something apart from human existence.
Rather, human existence is part of nature. One aspect
of the Buddhist journey toward liberation is growth in
awareness of essential harmony with all life forms and

a corresponding ethic of moderation in life styles and consumption habits that is in conformity with that vision of harmony.

Similarly, the Hindu concept of "ahimsa" provides inspiration toward a global environmental ethic. Ahimsa, which means "non-harming," and "respect for life," values the sacred and the divine in all life forms. Other life forms are valued not for how they can be used, but in their *own right*. The human ethic that flows from that is one of respect and active nonviolence in *all*, including environmental, relationships. In accordance with the principle of ahimsa, consumption is limited to that which is essential for sustenance. Ahimsa is an important concept not only in the development of a personal ecological ethic, but also as a philosophic foundation for the development of global structures that reinforce respect for, rather than violation of, the delicate balance and relatedness of all life forms.

A Garden with Limits

The "dominion over nature" quote from Genesis (2:28) has frequently been misused as justification of the Western approach to unlimited growth and expansion. But placing that quote in its greater biblical context provides quite a different perspective on human accountability for the uses of natural resources. In Genesis, the development of the cosmos is the creative activity of an Almighty Power and Intelligence. In the development of the earth within that cosmos, the human species is a late arrival. The earth is not owned by human beings. It is always the Lord's. Man and woman are part of creation, part of nature and subject to the laws governing nature and the universe. The "garden" was there before human life as a given, as an environment in time and space in which humanity could grow in relationship to God and creation. Humans were entrusted with a great responsibility. "The Lord God placed the man in the Garden of Eden as its gardener, to tend and care for it" (Genesis 2:15). But the garden was not to be used wantonly. From the beginning there are limits. The fall of Adam and Eve is a story of the violation of those limits.

Sharing the Harvest

Other biblical references also point to limits and accountability for use of the freely given gift of earth's resources. And throughout the biblical account, there is growing development of an ethic for the uses of what is always God's earth.

There are the seven fat years followed by the seven lean years in Joseph's days in Egypt. They come with the warning that the grain from the fat years is not to be wasted, or to be hoarded individually, but to be collectively conserved against future famine, at which time it is to be shared equally among the people. Hebrew law prescribed that land-holding Israelites were not to harvest all their grain for themselves but were to leave sufficient in the fields for the widows and poor to glean in dignity. And Jesus told the rich to go, sell what they have and give it to the poor if they would seek salvation.

In the biblical account there is developmental growth in conceptualizing the Promised Land, salvation and the Kingdom. They are gradually seen not as physically placed, but as a state of being in relationship to God, each other and the universe as a whole. For the contemporary Christian who perceives Christ as manifest in the poor, the hungry and the oppressed, the law of love imposes limits and accountability for the amount and ways in which the earth's resources are consumed and for the way they are distributed.

The development of a just world order can be viewed as an effort to ensure that the harvest is more equitably distributed.

The above discussion was just a beginning exploration of the contributions of world religions to the development of a world ecological ethic. Other world-order values, e.g., *social justice, war prevention* (nonviolence), *economic well-being, participation in decision making,* etc., also are consistent with and reinforced by authentic religious values. (For reasons of space, these relationships cannot be spelled out here in greater detail. That is a task for another book.) From the religious perspective, world-order values such as these are integrally related to the worth of each person as standing in intimate relatedness to the Ground of All Being.

TRUTH-SEEKING

In false pride, some adherents of creedal religions have fought over who had "the truth." Others, in false humility (related to a sense of infinite smallness in face of a vast cosmos and an omnipotent Absolute) have withdrawn from "this world." The authentic religious impulse is neither self-righteous nor passive. It is actively truth-seeking in both a deeply personal sense and in its mode of participation in the human community.

To be truth-seeking is to be empty and open. It is to trust that persons are called to love, unity, justice, truth (words used to describe God) and that these can be realized if we do not allow self-centered attachments to obstruct the way. To be truth-seeking is to be able to assess our most cherished assumptions and move beyond idolatrous attachment to them, including an excessive attachment to nationalism and ideology.

Thus, Mahatma Gandhi, inspired by his spiritual relationship to a God of Truth, felt his highest goal must be truth-seeking in *all* aspects of his life. And, for Christians, the mystery of Christ's death and resurrection is symbolically related to the need for persons to die to self-centered attachments to the old order and to be reborn in a new order of love, truth and unity.

A truly new and more human world order will be developed to the degree that openness and truth-seeking characterize the efforts of those involved in the formulation and transformation processes.

THE GARDEN AS IT COULD BE

The just world-order movement, like all the world's living faiths, finds motivation in a vision of a preferred future. The process of imaging or conceptualizing that toward which one will move is the beginning point in creative activity. Such creative imaging may be arrived at by rational exploration or by intuitive discovery or both. But it must almost always precede positive movement in new, creative directions.

In the *world-order movement*, concepts of a preferred future are being arrived at by values projections integrated with scientific and socio-economic-political perspectives on the future. In the *world religions* the image of a preferred future and new possibility for the human person was usually arrived at intuitively, by spiritual insight or inspiration. The language to describe one may be clothed in mystical, mythical (in the very positive meaning of that term) and symbolic imagery. The other uses socio-economic terms. But this does not mean that they are not on a path leading in the same direction.

A biblical view of history, for example, begins with a vision of the starting point of the universe. Charged by a tremendous energy of spirit and love the whole cosmos is started in the process of Becoming. Within that cosmos the earth, with all its life forms, is set toward right and harmonious relationship. The story of the garden is a vision of how the earth, in its growth toward completion, in its state of wholeness, is meant to be in the Mind's eye of the Creative Intelligence and Love which set it in developmental motion. Not only how it historically might have been or is now—but what has been promised in the growth potential of the creative process. History is seen as the meantime between creation as first visionary image and its completion in fulfillment of that vision. History is the process of Becoming. It is the story of the actualizing of creative potential (or it is the story of the failure to grow and become). It is the story of human movement, recorded in sweat and tears and joyful discovery, toward fulfillment, wholeness and completion.

In this journey God is not an Intelligence who acts upon history from outside it, but is profoundly present and manifest from within. Scripture does not allow the separation of authentic religion from the concrete development of human history. The direction of human development is seated in the tangible, even when its fulfillment is beyond what is now tangible.

The Kingdom or world order envisioned by Jesus in the New Testament is described in terms of a state of being in which the love of God is related to the love of one's neighbor—a relationship characterized by social justice. It is a state of relationship in which the hungry are fed, the thirsty have drink, the naked are clothed, the sick and imprisoned are attended in love and dignity and the spirit dimension is nurtured along with the physical. It is a state of being where to be fully human is to be fully conscious, alive and living in the reality and unity of God as Love. "That all may be one, as the Father and I are One" (John 17:20).

Christ refused to allow his followers to conceive of this Kingdom, this order of being in relationship, as something to be realized outside of history. When the Pharisees asked when the Kingdom of God would come, Jesus replied, "The Kingdom of God is in the midst of you" (Luke 17:21).

The preferred future envisioned in a just world order shares aspects of this vision of human actualization. It seeks to open history to the possibility of its realization. Today, feeding the hungry and a realization of our relatedness and unity is integrally related to the establishment of a just world order.

SIN AS A REFUSAL TO GROW AND ACT

One way of looking at sin is as a refusal to grow. It is a refusal to take on the activities and tasks of Becoming more fully. It is to make an absolute, a false god, of the present form and way of being, thereby blocking God's creative process in and through us. Sin in this sense is the loss of what could be. It is the loss of holistic relatedness with God and each other. It is the historic tragedy of human potential unrealized.

This can be looked at in the individual, personal sense and also in a communal sense of the species as a whole. That is, the notion of sin carries with it a sense of *individual* and also a sense of *communal* responsibility for human acts or refusal to act. An individual's decisions affect the whole and the activity of the whole affects each of its members.

Teilhard de Chardin, a paleontologist with immense breadth of vision, describes the evolutionary movement of creation toward omega in terms of great pressure points building up within matter; spiritual energy amassing in dynamic interaction and erupting finally in new forms. Thus the development and appearance of new phyla on the tree of evolution have occurred throughout eons in an ever-upward struggle toward higher forms of being. After this great surge of internal activity giving rise to new form, the old phylum is closed off, forever locked in on itself. Those forms that did not advance at the point of critical breakthrough remain forever locked in.[5]

Are we at a similar pressure point of history today? After approximately 2½ million short years of human existence and development are we not, as a species, faced with a critical choice? We are in the midst of a tremendous amassing of spiritual and material energy which can be directed either for creative or destructive purposes. Will we choose to seize the moment to grow in life and love and relatedness to God and each other in the activity of an integral move toward greater wholeness? Or will we refuse to grow, choosing instead to lock ourselves into a form of isolated and self-perpetuating hell?

The world is now on the brink of going toward creation or anti-creation. Historically the role of prophets came to bear in a major way in times such as these. It is important that prophetic voices be clearly raised in today's crisis of growth.

Salvation, growth, human development and actualization are interrelated terms. They all connote movement, activity, life. And that movement is simultaneously away from something and toward something. It is away from incompletion toward wholeness. It is away from fear toward trust. It is away from despair toward hope. It is away from untruthfulness, prejudice, hatred, oppression, injustice and the structures that support these. It is toward truth, love, freedom, justice and the structures that reinforce these. Sin is not outside of history nor is salvation experienced only in the beyond.

In authentic religion there is no avoiding the critical problems of our times, no hiding our heads in spiritual sand. True spirituality is never an escape from the world. It is, rather, an integrating force. It moves toward wholeness and completeness—seeking transformation of institutions and social relationships as well as of self.

HOLISTIC DEVELOPMENT

More than ever before in history, a humanizing future depends on a new integration of moral and spiritual concerns with positive, concrete approaches to crises of human survival and well-being.

New world-order structures in themselves are not enough. There are few illusions in the world-order movement that new structures at the global level will be sufficient in themselves to eliminate existent injustices and hostilities. Ultimately it is not just structures, not just the external coat, that must change and grow. Change and growth must also occur at the fundamental level of each individual human person, in our way of "seeing" and "being" in the world. This is essentially a growth in consciousness, an *inner* transformation.

The development of a just world order is not a matter of *either* interior growth *or* external socio-political change. Nor is it a question of which comes first. Both are integral to a viable world future. Substantial progress in human development will be made to the degree that the inner and outer dimensions of world order proceed as an *organic* activity.

The significance of authentic religion in the development of a new human order lies in its recognition of universal laws which affect the uses of human power. It lies in the affirmation of the importance of each human person and all life forms. And it lies in the call to human consciousness of the unity of all in a greater whole.

Ultimately it is only in a deeper consciousness of our essential relatedness to each other and to the universe of which we are a dependent part, that the development of a new human order takes on full significance. If a new human order is to become more than a mere legal frame, it is essential that we develop this deeper consciousness of our basic unities and a sense of identity with the whole earth community.

13
The Birth of a New Era

> If there is any period one would desire to be
> born in, is it not . . . when the old and the
> new stand side by side, and admit to being
> compared; when the energies of all men are
> searched by fear and by hope; when the his-
> toric glories of the old, can be compensated
> by the rich possibilities of the new era? This
> time, like all times, is a very good one, if we
> but know what to do with it.
>
> Ralph Waldo Emerson

Let us look to the future with common sense. This
is not the End of Time—unless we choose to make it so.
We need not accept the death sentence. We can say no to
dehumanized lives and half existence. These are not inevitable, not the unalterable human condition. We are
not powerless. We are not pitiful creatures without the
capacity to ensure our survival and fulfillment. Everything we need has been given to us.

All of history has been leading to the present moment of decision. Ours is not a time to surrender imagination and courage. It is, above all, a time to affirm
and take bold initiatives toward the emergence of a new
era in the whole earth community.

Much depends upon how we read the signs of the
times: to read them only as signs of decay and death is

to be partially blind. Annihilation is only one among many alternative possibilities. Hunger and poverty for the majority is only one of many alternatives. As are alienation and aborted human development. If these continue as the reality for the earth's children of the future, it will be only because today we lacked imagination to explore the alternatives and the courage to choose life.

We live in a pregnant period of history. The old order of power confrontation and coexistence is dying as a viable order. It has outlived whatever capacity it had to forward life. But while we note its death throes, let us not fail to affirm and celebrate the new consciousness and new life forces that are growing and moving within and among us on this small womb of a planet.

There is today a growing consciousness of the fact that we are unalterably bound together. We share a common dependency on one earth system. We stand together in relationship with one air, water, land and life-support system. We have the same needs, the same potentialities, the same capacities for participating in destruction or for participating in creation. We share a common possibility of annihilation or fulfillment. We no longer have many diverse and isolated histories. Our cultural and national histories have converged in one commonly shared present and future reality.

The Chinese characters for crisis include two concepts: that of imminent decay and that of imminent breakthrough. Both possibilities exist simultaneously.

The crises of our times are not only signs of decay. They are also signs of expectant birth. We live in the Between Times, the time of decision. It is a time of transition from the death of the old civilization to the emergence of the new. We are not sure of what the new will be, but we know and feel the reality of its growing existence within us.

The birth image is apt. The healthy delivery of our shared future is not automatic. Nor will it be without pain. New birth seldom comes without pain. The greater the life reality seeking to be born, the greater the pain that may accompany the birth process.

In the birth process, if the birth passage remains rigid and does not widen, the pain intensifies. The unborn life is in peril and the mother's life is endangered.

This birth image provides insights into the pain being experienced in the human community today. Existing socio-political structures are too rigid and narrow to give healthy delivery to new stages of human growth and development struggling to be born.

But more than human development is at stake. The constriction threatens our very survival.

Our task now is not to fight against our pains and crises, reacting against the symptoms—and in so doing making present structures more rigid than before. It is rather to recognize the positive pregnancy of our times, to work with the birth spasms, giving our energies to a widening of the birth passage, *making ready the way for the birth of a new stage in human development.*

Our labor now is to create the consciousness and structures through which a more just and human order can be born. It is a labor not of tearing down, but of new creation. The great task before us is not one of *rev*olution. It is, rather, what Moltmann calls *pro*volution.

The *re* in revolution focuses on *return*:

> Revolutionary terrorism directed against the old order always turns into the absolutism of the new order which is revengefully directed against its critics and thus against its own future.[1]

The *pro* in provolution focuses on new, forward movement, on the creation of that which has not yet been present in history:

> In provolution the human "dream turned forward" is combined with the new possibility of the future and begins consciously to direct the course of human history.[2]

DISCOVERING SELF

In this great human effort of creating and giving birth to a new, shared future, of *consciously directing history*, we discover our own self and we discover each other.

We discover our self and our own identity to the degree that we become actively involved in creating our own future, in being subjects rather than objects of history. We affirm our personal identity as unique and as human to the degree that we no longer need to conform to external determinants to shape our identity, i.e., we no longer need to define ourselves by national, racial or other external determinants because we have grown beyond these constraining labels on self.

Ultimately, we become actualized as persons not because we seek actualization, but because we act on behalf of and in response to something which is greater than self. In the act of creating a more human future, we discover and become self.

If we would discover self we must discover the other. In recognizing and respecting the identity of the other, we discover and respect our own identity.

Creating the future together makes that discovery of the other, and therefore self, more possible. *The future is mutually shared space and time.* There is no guilt about the future as there is about the past and therefore no need to be defensive about it. The future thus permits us greater psychological freedom and openness to see each other and hear each other. The past is important only insofar as it provides positive meaning and means for building a more humanizing present and future.

Building the future requires our shared participation. We all have a vital stake in how it is developed. Much is to be gained by cooperation. Everything can be lost without it. Working together on the creation of a more just and humanizing future binds us more closely together. It takes us beyond coexistence, the Ik-existence of individual goals and "me first" policies. We become community in the process of formulating a shared future.

Discovering and affirming the other is the opposite of insisting that the other be like me or like "us." It means to recognize and affirm unique differences and diversity while also desiring to see the other realize positive potentialities. It is to recognize and affirm the inalienable right of all persons to full human development. It means getting beyond national or racial or belief systems of identity in order to discover human persons.

A more human future will be created to the extent that it is created not by and for nations, but by and for real men, women and children with names, with needs, with dignity and with aspirations.

That is why it is so important that nation-states not be looked upon as the only, or even the major, actors in the development of a new world order. It is the human person, the human community, which must always be at the center as subjects of a new world order.

In discovering the other in the process of building a more human world order, conflict and differences will be inevitable. Conflict is not something to be avoided for the sake of some false sense of harmony. It is a reality that must be dealt with creatively, not withdrawn from for the sake of one's need for personal peace, nor aggressively pursued for the sake of a sense of personal power.

Out of conflict can come a creative growth in the human community if the respect for and affirmation of the other—whether the other be a person, nation or culture—is preserved as an integral element of conflict resolution. Excessive nationalism and attachment to one's own "we" group, or excessive focus on self-realization for oneself alone, are elements that can prevent this creative growth in the human community.

Seeking self-realization for oneself alone, or for a limited community of like-minded persons, is often undertaken at the expense of others. Apocalyptic withdrawal or the following of an end-of-times scenario in which one prepares oneself to be part of a "saved remnant" can be a form of irresponsible egotism. It can be a failure in awareness of others, a failure in love and a failure in one's responsibility to the human community as a whole.

We must move beyond developing our positive energies and capacities for our personal growth alone and learn to develop and utilize these energies and capacities as gifts for the benefit of the whole earth community.

MISREADING THE SIGNS OF THE TIMES

Rather than seeking inner growth as a foundation, an integrating force for *building the earth*, increasing numbers of people are retreating into meditation and inner consciousness as an escape from a world they judge to be doomed. This limited approach to inwardness is often due to an incomplete reading of the signs of the times. Failing to identify the growth forces that are straining to break free from the restraints of absolute structures, one easily reads today's crises only as evidence of decay and breakdown.

One result of this misreading is an overwhelming sense of powerlessness, a sense that easily leads to an apocalyptic view of history. Focusing on what appears to be imminent catastrophe, history is judged to be closed. Present problems appear too formidable to overcome. The despair and paralysis that follow from such a world view serve to make it a self-fulfilling prophecy.

Another result of such an incomplete analysis is a negative view of human nature—a view which argues that only *heroic* men and women are able to grow toward full human development. This view has been a major factor in preserving the status quo. It has enabled elites to maintain their power and privileges, permitting them to say that human nature cannot be trusted. And it has discouraged creative people from taking the bold initiatives necessary for a more human future.

Part of the pregnancy of our times is the possibility that it holds for vindicating human nature. Historically straitjacketed at the survival and security stages of human development, the positive potentialities of human nature have seldom had a chance to be developed more fully. As a result, human nature has been gravely maligned. What makes our times truly historic is that we are at a point where this straitjacket can finally be removed.

In many ways, we live in a certain *fullness of time*. It is an age in which not only the unmet inalienable rights to food, shelter and other physical needs of two-thirds of the worlds peoples can be achieved. Also within our reach is the fulfillment of the right of every human being to the environment needed to achieve full human development.

AN INTEGRATING FRAMEWORK

A world view that recognizes the crisis-of-growth nature of our times helps us to overcome two factors that contribute to pessimism. One is the lack of a *historical context* for interpreting the signs of the times. The other is a sense of *fragmentation*, a sense of being overwhelmed by a multitude of unconnected and often conflicting issues, crises, programs and strategies. The combination of the two factors often results in alienation and paralysis.

Our experience with people overseas as well as in our North American homeland is that a world-order framework that flows from an identification of the national security straitjacket speaks to these two factors:

1. Identification of the straitjacket of our present world system places our times in a *historical context* of

a social evolution in which humankind is straining to break through to new stages of human development and community. History is not closed: the future remains open and depends upon our imagination and bold initiatives.

2. A world view that identifies the common straitjacket that victimizes leaders and citizens of all nations provides a basis for overcoming a good deal of today's multiple *fragmentation*. It builds upon, adds to and integrates what is valid in other analyses and frameworks.

The result is that previously fragmented events can now be understood and dealt with *in relation to a broader whole*. This broader perspective helps clarify the interrelationships between various issue concerns and has powerful ramifications for problem solving.

This is not reductionism. It is not an effort to reduce a multitude of problems to a single cause. We recognize the complexities and multiple factors impinging on each issue. The National Security State analysis identifies an overriding reason why, despite multiple research and program formulations, there is so little progress in resolving the critical problems of our times. It is an analysis that moves beyond a simplistic "oppressor-oppressed" syndrome. It reveals that "the people" are not alone in their powerlessness. National leaders—despite their great power to wage war and suppress their citizens and expend large sums of money —are powerless to substantially reorder present national priorities. They are confronted by a structural logic for locking out from national agendas those priorities, values and resources that could resolve the growing mountain of unmet domestic needs. And, of course, adding to this internal straitjacket are those global monetary and economic forces that national societies cannot regulate by themselves, forces that are ravaging domestic priorities.

Far from reductionism, we are facing up to the need to throw off this straitjacket—to put aside this coat that got too small—in order that we can move directly to the complexity of the human agenda.

The world security system that is necessary for making real progress on the human agenda will not result in a world that is all milk and honey. Many of the multiple human and societal factors that presently converge around the issues on that agenda would remain. But with the loosening of the straitjacket, national leadership, institutions and resources would be liberated for more effective planning and programing. The difference coming from this liberation would not be between crises and utopia; but, rather, between unsolvable problems and solvable problems.

BENEFITS FOR THE HERE AND NOW

The benefits that would accrue from the evolutionary movement toward a just world order are not located only in the future. Some payoffs from such a movement are *immediate*—payoffs that have strategic meaning on the *local* level:

1. The analysis of the structural straitjacket transcends the *polarization* of diverse issue constituencies who presently find explanations for their powerlessness in demonologies. Blacks and whites, women and men, young and old, "developing" and "developed"—all can rise above their mutual acrimonies to identify a shared victimhood, a shared powerlessness, and to plan a

shared future. Such commonality can modify previous facile judgments; and as polarization is mitigated, coalitions on *local* as well as on national and global issues become more possible.

2. A world-order framework which identifies the straitjacket of our present system provides *hope* for the future. Such hope, in turn, fosters *belief*—in the ability of humankind to resolve its problems and in the reality of a Ground of All Being, present and dynamic in history.

3. Such hope and belief provide a basis for *perserverance*, for the "staying power" needed to successfully deal with the complexities of local issues. They can also provide a basis for *initiative* in seeking new responses and alternatives to local problems as well as to global crises.

4. A world-order frame can prevent a waste of time and resources. It provides a perspective for analyzing each problem in a *macro* frame that identifies all the forces impinging upon it, assuring a more accurate and complete analysis, and therefore more effective problem-solving.

BOLD INITIATIVES

The new life forces that underlie today's Crisis of Growth cannot be brought forth by traditional strategies alone. Some traditional approaches are not commensurate with the crises and opportunities of an interdependent world. It is imperative, therefore, that new and bold initiatives be taken.

One of the conventional beliefs that must be laid to rest is that elites have the understanding and power to lead humankind through the perils of our times. Interdependence has helped to reveal the bankruptcy of this myth. The task of building the earth—at the global as well as at the local level—is the responsibility of us all.

Many of the old text books, formulated for another age, are obsolete. Not only do they fail in concept, i.e., fail to deal with the inalienable right of all people to the means and community necessary for full human development. They also come up short when judged by the criteria of performance in an interdependent world.

A world-order framework provides us with the context for formulating new texts commensurate with the growth crises of our times. It offers a world view and strategies for moving out of the present resignation and despair. Demonstrating that our destiny is still in our hands, a world-order perspective provides a concrete basis for hope—and therefore bold initiatives.

NOTES

Chapter 1: *Crisis of Growth*

1. Donella H. Meadows et al. *The Limits to Growth* (New York: Universe Books, 1972). It should be noted that forecasts such as contained in *The Limits to Growth* have been controverted and that the Club of Rome, which sponsored the study, has since published another report in *Mankind at the Turning Point* (New York: E. P. Dutton, 1974) which modifies the position presented in *The Limits to Growth*.

Chapter 2: *Human Development and the "Security Straitjacket"*

1. For further elaboration, see the following works:

Robert Ardrey, *African Genesis* (New York: Dell, 1961).

_____, *The Territorial Imperative* (New York: Dell, 1966).

_____, *The Social Contract* (New York: Atheneum, 1970).

Lorenz, Konrad, *On Aggression* (New York: Harcourt Brace, 1966).

_____, *Studies in Animal and Human Behavior* (Cambridge: Harvard University Press, 1970).

Morris, Desmond, *The Naked Ape* (New York: McGraw-Hill, 1967).

2. As described by Mimi Palen, *St. Benedict's Today* (March, 1976), p. 1.

3. Irenaeus Eibl-Eibesfeldt, *Love and Hate: The Natural History of Behavior Problems* (New York: Holt, Rinehart and Winston, Inc., 1971).

4. John Nance, *The Gentle Tasaday* (New York: Harcourt Brace, 1975) is a more detailed account of the Tasaday.

Also, see *Cave People of the Philippines*, an NBC Film Documentary.

5. See Eibesfeldt, op. cit.

6. See Alexander Alland, Jr., *The Human Imperative* (New York: Columbia University Press, 1972).

7. See the writings of Abraham H. Maslow, in particular:

> ———, *Toward A Psychology of Being* (Princeton, N.J.: Van Nostrand, 1962; Revised ed., 1968).
>
> ———, *Motivation and Personality* (New York: Harper & Bros., 1954; revised edition, 1970).
>
> ———, *The Farther Reaches of Human Nature* (New York: Viking Press, 1971).

8. Maslow, *Toward A Psychology of Being*, op. cit, pages 3-4, (1962 edition).

9. See Colin M. Turnbull, *The Mountain People* (New York: Simon and Schuster, 1972), a detailed account of the author's observations on the Ik during the several years he lived among them.

10. Turnbull, ibid, p. 294.

11. This incident was described by Turnbull during his presentation at the Pennington Club, Passaic, N.J., Feb. 5, 1975.

12. Turnbull, op. cit., p. 285.

13. Maslow, *Farther Reaches of Human Nature*, op. cit., p. 19.

Chapter 3: *The National Security State*

1. The rise of "mass man" has also been a factor in destroying personal sovereignty. Leo Strauss, Ortega y Gasset and David Riesman, to name a few, have done valuable work on this theme. More has to be done, however, in researching the relationship between "mass society" and the corporate goals and values required by national security imperatives.

2. Members of Congress for Peace through Law presently has about 170 members, although the number varies from year to year, according to elections. The organization has an office in Washington, D.C., which issues periodic newsletters and calls meetings.

Chapter 4: *The Powerlessness of Heads of State*

1. Figures from the U.S. Department of Commerce, *Survey of Current Business.*

2. Figures from the U.S. Department of Commerce, *Survey of Current Business.*

3. *Strengthening the World Monetary System*, a statement by the Research and Policy Committee of the Committee for Economic Development (July, 1973), pp. 19-20.

4. For a more elaborate description of the Soviet elites see Milovan Djilas, *The New Class* (N.Y.: Praeger, 1968). A shortcoming of an otherwise fine book is that it gives inadequate attention to the rubric of national security.

5. Ruth Sivard, *World Military and Social Expenditures, 1976* (WMSE Publications, 1976), p. 6.

6. Ibid.

7. Ibid.

8. 1974 figures. Ibid., (1977 edition) p. 24.

9. Hugh O'Shaughnessy, in an article in the *New York Times*, March 7, 1976.

10. Sivard, op. cit., p. 8.

11. *New York Times*, January 11, 1976.

12. Philip Berryman, "Khaki-ing of Latin America," *New Catholic World*, (Sept./Oct., 1975), p. 217.

13. O'Shaughnessy, op. cit.

14. Sivard, op. cit., p. 7.

15. Ibid., pp. 6-7.

16. For Further description of military governments in Latin America and Africa, see Thomas P. Melady, "Spreading Militarism in Black Africa," *New Catholic World*, op. cit., and Berryman, op. cit.

17. Sivard, op. cit., pp. 26-27.

18. Ibid., p. 5.

19. George Kistiakowsky, as quoted in the *Boston Globe* in an article entitled "Atomic War (by 1999)," (Feb. 15, 1976). This article is an account of the Harvard-M.I.T. Arms Control Seminar.

Chapter 5: *The National Security Big Six*

1. Charles Wilson, *Politics* (March, 1944). See also *Army Ordinance Magazine* (March-April, 1944). For a further discussion of Wilson's rationale see also John M. Swom-

ley, Jr., *The Military Establishment* (Boston: Beacon Press, 1964) pp. 100-101.

2. For further elaboration see Nuel Pharr Davis, *Lawrence and Oppenheimer* (New York: Simon and Schuster, 1968), p. 96 f.

3. Harold Karan Jacobson and Eric Stein, *Diplomats, Scientists and Politicians: the United States and the Nuclear Ban Negotiations* (Ann Arbor: Univ. of Michigan, 1966), p. 497.

4. See Hoover's book by that title: *The Masters of Deceit* (New York: Holt Rinehart & Winston, 1958).

5. President Nixon in a speech given in Kansas City, July 6, 1971.

6. Jonathan D. Aronson, "The Changing Nature of the International Monetary Crisis, 1971-1974: The Role of the Banks." An unpublished paper delivered at the International Studies Association Conference in Washington, D.C., Feb. 19-22, 1975, pp. 25-26.

7. Secretary of State Hughes in August, 1923. (For further elaboration see Herbert Feis, *The Diplomacy of the Dollar 1919-1932* (New York: W. W. Norton & Co., 1966).

8. Bretton Woods is the name commonly given to the United Nations Monetary and Financial Conference held at Bretton Woods, New Hampshire, July 1-22, 1944.

9. See Friedman's testimony at a hearing on "How Well Are Fluctuating Exchange Rates Working?" before the Subcommittee on International Economics of the Joint Economic Committee, June 20, 21, 26 and 27, 1973 (Washington: Government Printing Office, 1973, p. 115).

10. Ricardo Arriazu, ibid., p. 108.

11. Aronson, op. cit., p. 39 (based on a study in Samuel Katz, "The Emerging Exchange-Rate System (Early 1974)," Finance Discussion Paper no. 46 (Washington: Bd. of Governors of the Federal Reserve System, Div. of International Finance, May 23, 1974).

12. Aronson, op. cit., p. 39.

13. *Strengthening the World Monetary System*, a Statement on National Policy by the Research and Policy Committee of the Committee for Economic Development (July, 1973).

14. Ibid., p. 10.

15. Emery Reves, *The Anatomy of Peace* (New York: Harper & Bros., 1944).

16. From President Ford's address in San Francisco, Sept. 21, 1975.

17. Lester Brown, *World Without Borders* (New York: Vintage Books, 1973), pp. 193-4.

18. E. F. Schumacher, *Small Is Beautiful: Economics as if People Mattered* (New York: Harper & Row, 1973).

19. Earl L. Butz, "A Policy of Plenty," *Skeptic* (Issue No. 10, Nov./Dec., 1975), pp. 13-14.

20. Charles E. Lindblom in *Strategies of Decision* (by David Braybrooke and Charles E. Lindblom) (Social Process, 1963), p. 102. Also available in paperback (New York: Free Press).

21. Harold D. Lasswell, "The Political Science of Science: An Inquiry Into the Possible Reconciliation of Mastery and Freedom," in *Toward a Theory of War Prevention*, ed. by Richard Falk and Saul Mendlovitz (New York: World Law Fund—now the Institute for World Order, 1966), p. 287.

Chapter 6: *The Soviet Security State*

1. Emery Reves, op. cit., p. 75.

2. Theodore H. Von Laue, *Why Lenin? Why Stalin? A Reappraisal of the Russian Revolution 1900-1930* (New York: J. B. Lippincott, 1964), p. 126.

3. Ibid., p. 136.

4. Ibid., p. 136-137.

5. Trotsky, 1903. See Von Laue, ibid., p. 108 f. for further elaboration. Trotsky at this point was challenging Lenin's conceptions (so contrary to humanitarian traditions) of what a Russian Democratic Party should be. Later, after 1917, he was to support the way in which the Bolshevik party was evolving.

6. Stalin. See Von Laue, op. cit., p. 211 f.

7. Ibid.

8. Von Laue, p. 212.

9. Alexander Yanov, "Detente and the Soviet Managerial Class," *New York Times* (Aug. 21, 1975).

10. Ibid.

11. Hans J. Morgenthau, "Power and Ideology in International Politics," an essay in *International Politics and Foreign Policy*, ed. by James N. Rosenau (Free Press, 1969).

12. John Adams, as quoted by Morganthau, op. cit., p. 173.

13. "New Class" is the term that Milovan Djilas (see *The New Class,* op. cit.) uses to describe the small group of elites (political, economic and technological) who determine and manage the affairs of the Soviet Union.

Chapter 7: *Liberation for Being*

1. *The Hindu*, April 1, 1954. (Quoted by Cora Bell, "Non-Alignment and the Power Balance," *Survival*, Vol. V, no. 6, Nov.-Dec., 1963.)

2. Proceedings of the First Conference of Heads of State and Government of Non-Aligned Nations (New York: United Nations, 1961).

3. Miller, D. R., *Politics of the Third World* (London: Oxford University Press, 1967).

4. Hugo Assman, "The Christian Contribution to the Liberation of Latin America," (unpublished paper, presented to Iglesia y Sociedad en America Latina, Naña, Peru, July, 1971, trans. Mrs. Paul Abrecht).

5. Ibid.

6. Paulo Friere, *Pedagogy of the Oppressed* (New York: Herder & Herder, 1970) and *Education for Critical Consciousness* (New York: Seabury, 1973).

7. Gustavo Lagos and Horacio Godoy, *Revolution of Being:* A Latin American View of the Future (New York: Free Press, 1977).

8. Gustavo Gutierrez, *A Theology of Liberation* (Maryknoll, N.Y.: Orbis Books, 1973), p. 25.

9. Denis Goulet, *A New Moral Order: Development Ethics and Liberation Theology* (Maryknoll, N.Y.: Orbis Books, 1974).

10. Denis Goulet, " 'Development' . . . or Liberation," background paper for 1971 CICOP Conference. Mimeo.

11. Goulet, ibid.

12. Julius Nyerere, President of Tanzania, outlined his philosophy of Self Reliance in the Arusha Declaration, as one in which Tanzania would try to be as free from external controls as possible while pursuing development objectives that relied on the people and agriculture.

Chapter 8: *Human/Religious Values Are "Subversive"*

1. Jacques Ellul, *Technological Society*, trans. from the

French by John Wilkinson (New York: Random House, 1967).

2. M. Bertrand de Jouvenel, "Some Musings," an essay in *Technology and Human Values,* an Occasional Paper by the Center for the Study of Democratic Institutions, p. 42.

3. John Wilson interpreting Nietzsche in his introduction to *Technology and Human Values*, ibid., p. 2.

4. Arthur Koestler, "Man—One of Evolution's Mistakes?" *New York Times Magazine* (Oct. 19, 1969).

5. David Riesman. See article by Dennis Gabor, "Fighting Existential Nausea," in *Technology and Human Values*, op. cit., p. 13.

6. Colin Turnbull, Op. Ed. page, *New York Times,* Nov. 29, 1972.

7. B. F. Skinner, *Beyond Freedom and Dignity* (New York: Bantam/Vintage, 1971).

8. Robert Heilbroner, *An Inquiry into the Human Prospect* (New York: W. W. Norton & Co., Inc., 1974).

9. Alexander Alland, Jr., *The Human Imperative,* op. cit.

10. Matthew B. Ridgway, "Leadership," Op Ed. page, *New York Times*, Nov. 14, 1972.

11. Arthur Schlesinger, Jr., "The Necessary Amorality of Foreign Affairs," *Harpers Magazine* (August, 1971).

12. E. F. Schumacher, *Small Is Beautiful,* op. cit.

13. H. G. Wells, *The Outline of History*, Vol. II (New York: Doubleday and Co. Garden City Books, rev. ed. 1961), p. 830.

14. Ibid.

15. Rollo May, *Power and Innocence* (W. W. Norton & Co., 1972).

16. Rollo May, "The Innocent Murderers," *Psychology Today* (Dec., 1972), p. 53.

17. Alvin Toffler, *Future Shock* (New York: Bantam, 1970) p. 2 f.

18. Ralph E. Lapp, *The New Priesthood* (New York: Harper & Row, 1965).

Chapter 9: *On Conceiving a New World Order*

1. In the U.S. the W.O.M.P. models are being published by The Free Press (New York) under the following titles: Richard A. Falk, *A Study of Future Worlds* (1975),

Rajni Kothari, *Footsteps Into the Future* (1975), Ali A. Mazrui, *A World Federation of Cultures: An African Perspective* (1975), Saul H. Mendlovitz, Ed., *On the Creation of a Just World Order* (1975), Lagos and Godoy, *Revolution of Being: A Latin American View of the Future* (1977), Johan Galtung, *The True Worlds*.

2. Saul Mendlovitz, Ed., *On the Creation of a Just World Order*, op. cit.

3. Adapted from a preliminary manuscript, "The Revolution of Being," by Gustavo Lagos later published by Free Press as *Revolution of Being*.

4. Elisabeth Mann Borgese, "World Communities," *Center Magazine* (Sept./Oct., 1971, Vol. IV, No. 5).

5. Ibid. (Adapted)

6. Ibid.

7. Frank Tannenbaum, "The Survival of the Fittest," *World Business*, ed. by Courtney C. Brown (New York: Macmillan, 1970), p. 160.

8. Borgese, op. cit.

9. Grenville Clark and Louis Sohn, *World Peace Through World Law* (Cambridge, Massachusetts: Harvard University Press, 1966).

10. Clark & Sohn, ibid., p. xv, the Introduction.

11. *World Constitution and Parliament Association.*

12. *Reshaping the International Order,* A Report to the Club of Rome, Dutton, 1976.

13. *Limits To Growth*, op. cit.

14. Mihajlo Mesarovic and Eduard Pestel, *Mankind at the Turning Point* (New York: E. P. Dutton & Co., 1974).

15. Aurelio Peccei. See article in the *New York Times*, April 12, 1976.

16. As summarized in a special *New York Times* article, April 12, 1976.

17. John R. Bunting, as quoted in the above article.

18. René Dubos, from an address and remarks at Manhattan College, October, 1972.

19. Rajni Kothari, *Footsteps Into the Future*, op. cit., p. 33, p. 159 f. See also his essay, "The Issue of Autonomy," in *On the Creation of a Just World Order*, Saul Mendlovitz, Ed., op. cit., p. 55 f.

20. Ibid.

21. Saul Mendlovitz, quoted by Ian Baldwin, Jr. in "The

World Order Models Project: Toward a Planetary Social Change Movement," submitted June 1972 for publication in *Design for Nonviolent Social Change.* Quote is from preliminary mimeo version.

22. Ian Baldwin, Ibid.

23. John J. Wright, *National Patriotism in Papal Teaching* (Westminster, Maryland: The Newman Press, 1956), p. 195.

24. Ibid.

Chapter 10: *Strategies Toward World Order, Part I: Multi-Issue Coalitions*

1. These stages parallel the time frame outlined by Richard Falk in *A Study of Future Worlds,* (op. cit.), p. 282 f.

2. "Conscientization" is a term and concept developed by Paulo Freire, op. cit. It is more than consciousness raising, for it includes a commitment to positive action.

Chapter 11.: *Strategies Toward World Order, Part II: Network Programing*

1. Richard Falk, *A Study of Future Worlds*, op. cit., p. 289.

2. Ibid.

3. From the ten-year report of the Institute for World Order (1961-1971).

4. C. Douglas Dillon, a summary of the principle points he made in a speech in Wilmington, Delaware, May 3, 1971 (from the ten-year report, ibid.).

Chapter 12: *World Order and Authentic Religion*

1. Arnold Toynbee, *A Study of History*, esp. Vol. VII on Universal Churches (Oxford University Press).

2. Carl Jung, *Undiscovered Self* (New York: Little Brown, 1958), p. 33.

3. For fuller treatment of the prophetic role as an avant-garde, see Harvey Cox, *The Secular City* (N.Y.: Macmillan, 1966).

4. Smohalla (Nez Perce Indians) from the *Biography and History of the Indians of North America,* by Samuel Drake (Boston: O. L. Perkins and Hillard, 1834).

5. See the works of Teilhard de Chardin, particularly *The Phenomenon of Man* (New York: Harper & Row, 1959) and *The Appearance of Man* (Harper & Row, 1965).

Chapter 13: *The Birth of a New Era*

1. Jurgen Moltmann, "Religion, Revolution and the Future," an essay in *The Future of Hope*, ed. by Walter H. Capps (Philadelphia: Fortress Press, 1970), p. 116. The essay was originally prepared for the University of California Symposium on "The Future of Hope," and is also included in Moltmann's book, *Religion, Revolution and the Future* (New York: Charles Scribner's Sons, 1969).

2. Ibid.

Bibliography

Alfaro, Juan. *Theology of Justice in the World*. Vatican City: Pontifical Commission of Justice and Peace, 1973.

Alland, Alexander, Jr., *The Human Imperative*. New York: Columbia University Press, 1972.

Alternatives, A Journal for World Policy. Amsterdam: North-Holland Publishing Co.

Anderson, Marion. "The Empty Pork Barrel: Unemployment and the Pentagon Budget." Lansing, Michigan: Public Interest Research Group in Michigan, 1975.

Ardrey, Robert. *African Genesis*. New York: Dell, 1961.

_____. *The Territorial Imperative*. New York: Dell, 1966.

Arendt, Hannah. *The Origins of Totalitarianism*. Cleveland: World Publishing Company, 1969.

Aronson, Jonathan D. "The Changing Nature of the International Monetary Crisis, 1971-1974: The Role of the Banks." International Studies Association Conference, 1975.

Arrupe, Pedro, S.J. *Witnessing to Justice*. Vatican City: Pontifical Commission Justice and Peace, 1972.

Assman, Hugo. "The Christian Contribution to the Liberation of Latin America." Paper presented at Conferencia de la Iglesia y Sociedad en America Latina, Naña, Peru, July 1971.

Aurobindo, Sri. *The Future Evolution of Man*. Wheaton, Illinois: Theosophical Publishing House, 1974.

_____. *Human Cycle, Ideal of Human Unity*. New York: International Pubuns Service, 1971.

Barnet, Richard J. *Roots of War*. New York: Atheneum, 1972.

Bhagwati, Jagdish, editor. *Economics and World Order: From the 1970's to the 1990's*. New York: Free Press, 1972

Borgese, Elisabeth Mann. *The Drama of the Oceans*. New York: Harry N. Abrams, Inc., 1975.

_____. "World Communities." *Center Magazine*, Center for the Study of Democratic Institutions, (Sept./Oct., 1971).

Borgese, G. A. *Foundations of the World Republic*. Chicago, 1953.

Braybrook, David and Lindblom, Charles E. *Strategies of Decision.* New York: Free Press, 1963.

Brown, Lester. *By Bread Alone.* New York: Praeger, 1974.

_____. *World Without Borders.* New York: Vintage Books, 1973.

Brown, Robert McAfee. *Religion and Violence.* Philadelphia: Westminister, 1973.

Bundy, Robert, editor. *Images of the Future: The Twenty-First Century and Beyond.* Buffalo, New York: Prometheus Books, 1976.

Butts, R. Freeman. *The Education of the West..* New York: McGraw Hill, 1973.

Camara, Dom Helder. *The Desert is Fertile.* Maryknoll, New York: Orbis Books, 1974.

Capps, Walter H., editor. *The Future of Hope.* Philadelphia: Fortress Press, 1971.

Carothers, J. Edward; Mead, Margaret; McCracken, Daniel D.; and Shinn, Roger L., editors. *To Love or to Perish: The Technological Crisis and the Churches.* New York: Friendship Press, 1972.

Chardin, Teilhard de. *The Appearance of Man.* New York: Harper & Row, 1965.

_____. *Building the Earth.* Wilkes-Barre, Pa.: Dimension Books, 1965.

_____. *The Phenomenon of Man.* New York: Harper & Row, 1959.

Clark, Grenville and Sohn, Louis. *Introduction to World Peace Through World Law.* Chicago: World Without War Publications, 1973.

_____. *World Peace Through World Law.* Cambridge, Massachusetts: Harvard University Press, 1966.

Commager, Henry Steele. *Freedom and Order.* New York: George Braziller, 1966.

Commoner, Barry. *The Closing Circle: Nature, Man and Technology.* New York: Knopf, 1972.

A Constitution for the World. (Intro. by Elisabeth Mann Borgese). Santa Barbara, Ca: Center for the Study of Democratic Institutions.

Cordier, Andrew W. and Maxwell, Kenneth, editors. *Paths to World Order.* New York: Columbia University Press, 1967.

Cousins, Norman. *In Place of Folly.* New York: Harpers, 1961.

_____. *Modern Man is Obsolete.* New York: Viking Press, 1945.

Davis, Nuel Pharr. *Lawrence and Oppenheimer*. New York: Simon and Schuster, 1968.

Dawson, Christopher. *The Dynamics of World History*. Editor, John J. Mulloy. New York, 1956.

Deutsch, Karl W. *Nationalism and Social Communications*. New York: John Wiley and Sons, 1954.

_____. *Political Community at the International Level*. Garden City, New York: Shoe String Press, 1954.

Dickinson, Richard D.N. *To Set at Liberty the Oppressed*. Geneva: World Council of Churches, 1975.

Djilas, Milovan. *The New Class*. New York: Praeger, 1968.

Dubos, René. *Beast or Angel?* New York: Scribner's, 1974.

Economic Justice. A special issue of *New Catholic World* (Sept./Oct., 1975).

Eibl-Eibesfeldt, Irenäus. *Love and Hate: The Natural History of Behavior Problems*. New York: Holt, Rinehart and Winston, Inc., 1971.

Elliott, Charles. *Patterns of Poverty in the Third World*. New York: Praeger (published in cooperation with the World Council of Churches), 1975.

Ellul, Jacques, *Technological Society*. (Translated from the French by John Wilkinson.) New York: Random House, 1967.

Erikson, Erik H. *Gandhi's Truth*. New York: W.W. Norton & Co., 1969.

_____. *Identity and the Life Cycle: Selected Papers*. New York: International Universities Press, Inc., 1967.

Falk, Richard. *A Study of Future Worlds*. New York: The Free Press, 1975.

_____. *This Endangered Planet*. New York: Random House, 1971.

Falk, Richard and Mendlovitz, Saul H. *Regional Politics and World Order*. New York: W.H. Freeman & Co., 1973.

_____. *The Strategy of World Order*. New York: Institute for World Order.

_____. *Toward a Theory of War Prevention*. New York: World Law Fund (Institute for World Order), 1966.

Faure, Edgar, et al. *Learning to Be: The World of Education Today and Tomorrow*. Paris: UNESCO, 1972.

Feinberg, Gerald. *The Prometheus Project: Mankind's Search for Long-Range Goals*. New York: Doubleday, 1969.

Freire, Paulo. *Education for Critical Consciousness*. New York: Seabury, 1973.

―――. *Pedagogy of the Oppressed*. New York: Herder & Herder, 1970.

Fromm, Erich. *The Anatomy of Human Destructiveness*. New York: Holt, Rinehart and Winston, 1973.

―――. *Marx's Concept of Man*. New York: Frederick Ungar Publishing Co., 1963.

Galbraith, John Kenneth. *The New Industrial State*. Boston: Houghton Mifflin, 1967.

Galtung, Johan. *The True Worlds*. New York: The Free Press, forthcoming.

Gandhi, Mahatma. *All Men Are Brothers*. Paris: UNESCO, 1969.

―――. *An Autobiography or the Story of My Experiments with Truth*. (Translated from the original in Gujarati by Mahadev Desai.) Ahmedabad: Navajivan, 1927.

Global Justice and Development (Report of the Aspen Interreligious Consultation, June, 1974). Washington, DC: Overseas Development Council, 1974.

Goulet, Denis. *A New Moral Order: Development Ethics and Liberation Theology*. Maryknoll, NY: Orbis Books, 1974.

Gremillion, Joseph. *The Gospel of Peace and Justice: Catholic Social Teaching Since Pope John*. Maryknoll, New York: Orbis Books, 1975.

Guadium et Spes: Pastoral Constitution on the Church in the Modern World (Second Vatican Council, Dec. 7, 1965). English version, *The Documents of Vatican II*. New York: America Press, 1966.

Guerry, Emile. *The Popes and World Government*. Baltimore: Helicon, 1964.

Gutierrez, Gustavo. *A Theology of Liberation*. Maryknoll, NY: Orbis Books, 1973.

Haavelsrud, Magnus, editor. *Education for Peace—Reflection and Action*. London: IPC, Science and Technology Press, Ltd., 1974.

Hayes, Carlton. *Nationalism*. New York: Russell (Atheneum), 1926.

Heilbroner, Robert. *An Inquiry Into the Human Prospect*. New York: W.W Norton & Co., Inc., 1974.

Henderson, George, editor. *Education for Peace: Focus on Mankind* Washington, DC: Association for Supervision and Curriculum Development, 1973.

Hesburgh, Theodore M. *The Humane Imperative: A Challenge for the Year 2000*. Yale University Press, 1974.

Hocking, William Ernest. *The Coming World Civilization*. New York: Harper, 1956.

_____. *Living Religions and a World Faith*. New York: Macmillan Co., 1940.

Hollins, Elizabeth Jay. *Peace is Possible*. New York: Grossman, 1966.

Jack, Homer, editor. *World Religions and World Peace*. Boston: Beacon, 1968.

Jacobson, Harold Karan and Stein, Eric. *Diplomats, Scientists and Politicians: The United States and the Nuclear Ban Negotiations*. Ann Arbor: University of Michigan, 1966.

Jaspers, Karl. *The Future of Mankind*. Chicago: University of Chicago Press, 1961.

John XXIII, *Mater et Magistra: Christianity and Social Progress*. English version, New York: Paulist Press, 1961.

_____. *Pacem in Terris*. English version, New York: America Press, 1963.

Jouvenel, Bertrand de. *Sovereignty: An Inquiry into the Political Good*. Chicago: University of Chicago Press, 1957.

Jung, Carl. *Undiscovered Self*. New York: Little Brown, 1958.

Kahler, Erich. *The Tower and the Abyss*. New York: George Braziller, 1957.

Kahn, Herman and Weiner, Anthony J. *The Year 2000: A Framework for Speculation on the Next Thirty-Three Years*. New York: Macmillan, 1967.

Keohane, Robert O. and Nye, Joseph S., Jr., editors. *Transnational Relations and World Politics*. Cambridge, Mass: Harvard University Press, 1973.

Kohlberg, Lawrence. "Education for Justice: A Modern Statement of the Platonic View." In T. Sizer (editor), *Moral Education*. Harvard University Press, 1970.

————. "Moral Education in the Schools: A Developmental View," *The School Review* (Vol. 75, No. 1), 1966.

Kothari, Rajni. *Footsteps Into the Future.* New York: The Free Press, 1975.

Lagos, Gustavo and Godoy, Horacio H. *Revolution of Being: A Latin American View of the Future.* New York: The Free Press, 1977.

Lakey, George. *Strategy for a Living Revolution.* New York: Freeman & Co., 1973.

Land, Philip, S.J. *An Overview.* Vatican City: Pontifical Commission on Justice and Peace, 1972.

Lapp, Ralph E. *The New Priesthood.* New York: Harper & Row, 1965.

Lasswell, Harold D. *World Politics and Personal Insecurity.* New York: The Free Press, 1965.

Lorenz, Konrad. *On Aggression.* New York: Harcourt Brace, 1966.

Maslow, Abraham H. *The Farther Reaches of Human Nature.* New York: Viking Press, 1973.

————. *Motivation and Personality.* New York: Harper & Bros. 1954, revised edition, 1970.

————. *Toward a Psychology of Being.* Princeton, NJ: Van Norstrand, 1962.

May, Rollo. *Power and Innocence.* New York: W.W. Norton & Co., 1972.

Mazrui, Ali A. *A World Federation of Cultures: An African Perspective.* New York: The Free Press, 1975.

Mazrui, Ali and Patel, Hasu H., editors. *Africa in World Affairs: The Next Thirty Years.* New York: The Third Press, 1973.

Mead, Margaret. *Twentieth Century Faith, Hope and Survival.* New York: Harper & Row, 1972.

————. *World Enough: Rethinking the Future.* Boston: Little, Brown and Company, 1975.

Meadows, Donella; Meadows, Dennis L.; Randers, Jørgen; and Behrens, William W., III. *The Limits to Growth.* Washington: Potomac Associates, 1972.

Melady, Thomas P. "Spreading Militarism in Black Africa", *New Catholic World,* Sept./Oct., 1975.

Melman, Seymour. *Our Depleted Society*. New York: Holt, Rinehart and Winston, Inc., 1965.

———. *Pentagon Capitalism*. New York: McGraw-Hill, 1970.

Melman, Seymour, editor. *The War Economy of the United States: Readings in Military Industry and Economy*. New York: St. Martin's Press, 1971.

Mendlovitz, Saul H. *Legal and Political Problems of World Order*. New York: Institute for World Order, 1962.

Mendlovitz, Saul H., editor. *On the Creation of a Just World Order*. New York: The Free Press, 1975.

Mesarovic, Mihajlo and Pestel, Eduard. *Mankind at the Turning Point*. New York: E.P. Dutton & Co., 1974.

Miller, D.R. *Politics of the Third World*. London: Oxford University Press, 1967.

Miranda, Jose. *Marx and the Bible: A Critique of the Philosophy of Oppression*. Maryknoll, New York: Orbis Books, 1974.

Moltmann, Jürgen. *Religion, Revolution and the Future*. New York: Charles Scribner's Sons, 1969.

Montagu, Ashley, editor. *Man and Aggression*. (Second edition). Oxford University Press, 1973.

Moore, Joseph and Roberta. *War and War Prevention*. Rochelle Park, NJ: Hayden Book Co., 1974.

Morgenthau, Hans J. "Power and Ideology in International Politics." *International Politics and Foreign Policy*, James Rosenau, editor. New York: Free Press, 1969.

Morris, Desmond. *The Naked Ape*. New York: McGraw-Hill, 1967.

Mumford, Lewis. *The Conduct of Life*. New York: Harcourt, 1951.

———. *The Myth of the Machine: Technics and Human Development*. New York: Harcourt, Brace, Jovanovich, Inc., 1967.

———. *The Transformations of Man*. New York: Harper, 1956.

Nance, John. *The Gentle Tasaday*. New York: Harcourt Brace, 1975.

Northrop, F.S.C., editor. *The Taming of the Nations*. New York: Macmillan, 1952.

Nyerere, Julius. "Arusha Declaration." Tanzania, 1966.

———. "Education for Self-Reliance." Tanzania, 1967.

Oates, Joyce Carol. "New Heaven and New Earth." *Saturday Review*, (Nov. 4, 1972).

Ogletree, Thomas W., editor. *Openings for Marxist-Christian Dialogue*. New York: Abingdon Press, 1969.

Orwell, George. *1984*. New York: Harcourt, Brace, Jovanovich, 1949.

Paul VI. *Populorum Progressio: On the Development of Peoples*. Vatican: Polyglot Press, 1967.

Pickus, Robert and Woito, Robert. *To End War*. Berkeley: World Without War Council, 1970.

Radhakrishnan, Sarvepalli. *East and West: Some Reflections*. New York: Harper, 1956.

———— *Religion and Society*. London: Macmillan, 1947.

Reischauer, Edwin O. *Toward the 21st Century: Education for a Changing World*. New York: Alfred A. Knopf, 1973.

Reves, Emery. *The Anatomy of Peace*. New York: Harper & Bros., 1944.

Roy, Maurice Cardinal. *Reflections on the Tenth Anniversary of the Encyclical "Pacem in Terris."* Vatican: Polyglot Press, 1973.

Samartha, S.J. *Living Faiths and Ultimate Goals: Salvation and World Religions*. Maryknoll, New York: Orbis Books, 1974.

Schiffer, Walter. *The Legal Community of Mankind*. New York: Greenwood, 1954.

Schlesinger, Arthur, Jr. "The Necessary Amorality of Foreign Affairs." *Harpers Magazine*, (August, 1971).

Schumacher, E.F. *Small is Beautiful: Economics as if People Mattered*. New York: Harper & Row, 1973.

Simon, Arthur. *Bread for the World*. New York: Paulist Press, 1975.

Simon, Paul and Arthur. *The Politics of World Hunger*. New York: Harpers Magazine Press, 1973.

Singh, Harnam. *Studies in World Order*. Delhi: Kitab Mahal (W.D.) Private Ltd., 1972.

Sivard, Ruth. *World Military and Social Expenditures*. Leesburg, Va.: WMSE Publications, 1976 and 1977 editions.

Solzhenitsyn, Aleksandr I. *The Gulag Archipelago*. New York: Harper & Row, 1974.

Sorokin, Pitirim A. *The Crisis of Our Age*. New York: E.P. Dutton, 1941.

Stapelton, Laurence. *Justice and World Society*. Chapel Hill, N.C.: University of North Carolina Press, 1944.

Strengthening the World Monetary System. (A statement on National Policy by the Research and Policy Committee of the Committee for Economic Development.) New York: Committee for Economic Development, 1973.

Strong, Maurice, editor. *Who Speaks for Earth?* New York: W.W. Norton, 1973.

Subcommittee on International Economics of the Joint Economic Committee, testimony on "How Well are Fluctuating Exchange Rates Working?" Washington DC: Government Printing Office, 1974.

Swomley, John M., Jr. *The Military Establishment.* Boston: Beacon Press, 1964.

Synod of Bishops. *Justice in the World.* Vatican: Polyglot Press, 1971.

Taylor, Edmond. *Richer by Asia.* New York: Time, Inc., 1964.

Taylor, Richard K. *Economics and the Gospel.* Philadelphia: United Church Press, 1973.

Technology and Human Values. Santa Barbara, California: Center for the Study of Democratic Institutions.

Tinbergen, Jan. *Reshaping the International Order.* (Commissioned by the Club of Rome,) Dutton, 1976.

———. *Shaping the World Economy.* New York: The Twentieth Century Fund, 1962.

Toffler, Alvin. *Future Shock.* New York: Bantam, 1970.

Toward the Year 2000: Work in Progress. (Proceedings of the Commission of the Year 2000). Boston: American Academy of Arts and Sciences, 1967.

Toynbee, Arnold J. *Civilization on Trial.* New York: Meridian Books, 1948.

——— *A Study of History,* Vol. I - XII. New York: Oxford University Press, 1934-1961: abridgment of vols. I-X by D.C. Somervell, Oxford University Press, 1947-57.

Turnbull, Colin M. *The Mountain People.* New York: Simon and Schuster, 1972.

United Nations. Conference on the Human Environment, *Report,* Stockholm, June 5-16, 1972 (A/CONF. 48/14; Sales No. 73.11.A.14.), 1972.

United Nations. "Declaration on the Establishment of a New International Economic Order." Resolution adopted by the General Assembly. 3201 (S-VI) (A/9556). New York: United Nations, June, 1974.

United Nations. "United Nations Environment Programme: The COCOYOC Declaration." (A./C.2/292,) November, 1974.

Von Laue, Theodore H. *Why Lenin? Why Stalin? A Reappraisal of The Russian Revolution 1900-1930.* New York: J.B. Lippincott, 1964.

Wagar, W. Warren. *Building the City of Man: Outlines of a World Civilization.* New York: Grossman Publishers, 1971.

———— *The City of Man.* Boston: Houghton Mifflin Co., 1963.

Ward, Barbara. *A New Creation: Reflections on the Environmental Issue.* Vatican City: Pontifical Commission Justice and Peace, 1973.

———— *The Home of Man.* New York: W.W. Norton & Co., Inc. 1976.

Ward, Barbara, and Dubos, René. *Only One Earth: The Care and Maintenance of a Small Planet.* New York: W.W. Norton, 1972.

Wells, H.G. *The Outline of History.* New York: Doubleday and Co. Garden City Books, 1961.

World Constitution and Parliament Association, *A Constitution for the Federation of Earth,* 1977, 1480 Hoyt Street, Suite 31, Lakewood, Colorado.

World Council of Churches. *Christians in the Technical and Social Revolutions of Our Time.* World Conference on Church and Society. Geneva, July 12-26, 1966, The Official Report. Geneva: World Council of Churches, 1967.

World Council of Churches. *To Break the Chains of Oppression: An Ecumenical Studies Process on Domination and Dependence.* Geneva: World Council of Churches, 1975.

World Energy, the Environment & Political Action. New York: The International Insititue for Environmental Affairs, 1973.

Wright, John J. *National Patriotism in Papal Teaching.* Westminister, Maryland: The Newman Press, 1956.

Wright, Quincy, editor. *The World Community.* Chicago: University of Chicago Press, 1948.

Index

383